REACHING FOR THE GOAL

THE LIFE STORY OF
DAVID ADENEY
ORDINARY MAN, EXTRAORDINARY MISSION

BY CAROLYN ARMITAGE

An OMF Book
Harold Shaw Publishers
Wheaton, Illinois

This book has been published by special arrangement with Overseas Missionary Fellowship, U.S. OMF BOOKS is an imprint of Harold Shaw Publishers.

Carolyn Armitage, writer

Fay Goddard, editor

Cover and inside photographs courtesy of David H. Adeney

Cover photo: David and Ruth Adeney leaving for their honeymoon in 1938.

Cover design by David LaPlaca

ISBN 0-87788-712-8

Library of Congress Cataloging-in-Publication Data
Armitage, Carolyn.
    Reaching for the goal : the life story of David Adeney / Carolyn Armitage.
        p.   cm. — (An OMF book)
    ISBN 0-87788-712-8 (pbk.)
    1. Adeney, David H. (David Howard) 2. Missionaries—China—Biography. 3. Missionaries—England—Biography. 4. China Inter-Varsity Evangelical Christian Students Fellowship—History.
5. College students—China—Religious life—History—20th century.
6. China Inland Mission—History—20th century. I. Title. II. Series.
BV3427.A35A76   1993
266'.0092—dc20
    [B]   93-14600
                                                                    CIP

99   98   97   96   95   94   93

10   9   8   7   6   5   4   3   2   1

It is a secret joy to find
The task assigned beyond our powers;
For then, if aught
Of good be wrought,
Clearly the praise is His, not ours!
                                    —*Bishop Frank Houghton*

Contents

A Word from David Adeney

I have greatly appreciated the fellowship and sensitivity of the author, Carolyn Armitage, chosen by OMF to write my biography, and later of the editor, Fay Goddard, who also made a valuable contribution to the book. They were very patient in trying to get me to recall stories of the past!

A biography is quite different from an autobiography. If I had written an autobiography (which I have chosen not to do), there would have been the danger of giving the impression that I had accomplished something special. In reality, many of my contemporaries who are unknown accomplished far more than I did, and their reward will be in heaven. An autobiography could have recorded the faults and failures of which I am very conscious. I could also have written more concerning the vision that God gave for the work, and the amazing privilege of seeing the ministry of the Holy Spirit in the lives of students both in China and in other Asian countries.

On the other hand, a biographer can be much more objective describing virtues and failures as seen by people outside, including some of which I might not be aware. But I must confess that I now find myself in a very difficult position. Even though the book may depict my life "warts and all," the author inevitably interviews many people who will speak only of the successes and leave out the failures. Some of the stories recorded I have completely forgotten! The end result is that the reader is likely to glorify the subject of the biography. How should I react to this? The "self life" tends to rejoice in human praise while protesting that all the glory belongs to the Lord. I fear the danger of being a hypocrite. Without the encouragement of the Holy Spirit speaking through the Scriptures, and the loving support of my wife Ruth, and the fellowship of Asian brothers and sisters, I would have completely failed. I trust that this book will reveal the wonder of God's patience and grace using a very ordinary person, emphasizing the tremendous privilege of serving the Lord Jesus Christ. He alone is worthy of praise.

I myself have been inspired by biographies that have shown how God has used those whose total commitment to the risen Savior has enabled them to experience the joy of having a part in the worldwide ministry of the church. I certainly pray that this book may help young people to see the privilege of lifetime missionary service, by sharing with the Lord Jesus in his work of "bringing many sons [and daughters] to glory" (Heb. 2:10).

1

A Poor Risk?

Tension edged the bustle at the Men's Training Home at the China Inland Mission's London headquarters at Newington Green. Tomorrow the council would meet to decide the acceptance or rejection of candidates. Among the applicants that spring of 1934 was a twenty-two-year-old Cambridge graduate from Bedford, David Howard Adeney.

For ten years this quietly intense young man, tall and lean, had been looking forward to serving in China. Now he was impatient to go. He described his desire as a "tremendous longing. . . . I hope it may be possible to get out in a year's time, this next autumn if the Lord has not come by then," he wrote to Roland Hogben, head of CIM's training school.

David had no doubt that God was leading him to join the China Inland Mission. "I have never thought of any other society as I am so attracted by the principles of the CIM," he wrote on his application papers.

"Everyone expected me soon to be on my way," David recalls.

But everyone, it turned out, did not include the mission doctor.

Three references had mentioned physical frailty on their confidential reports. None was confident of David's stamina. Two mentioned his tendency to push himself too hard. In the doctor's report to the council, the assessment of David's physical suitability for China was not encouraging. In the appropriate blank the examiner had penned three words—"A poor risk." David did not see the other people's comments, but the medical report left him reeling.

"A poor risk!" The words were hardly calculated to build his confidence. Upset and confused, he could only pray—hard—as the day of the council approached.

The day before council, the distressed candidate had one more interview, with a medical missionary from the Solomon Islands, Dr. Northcote Deck. Knowing that this respected pioneer's recommendation would carry considerable weight in the council, David sought the Lord's encouragement in his early morning quiet time. In his Scripture reading for that morning, one verse stood out: "As thy days, so shall thy strength be" (Deuteronomy 33:25, KJV). It was all the assurance he needed.

After breakfast, David walked over to the Mission's offices to meet with Dr. Deck. Most of the long row of offices were occupied. Only one appeared empty, and Dr. Deck took David into that one for the interview. Immediately David spotted a text on the wall. He could hardly stifle a smile as his eyes scanned the words: "As thy days, so shall thy strength be." Surely he had not missed God's way!

"There was, however, an embarrassing moment in the council meeting next day when I failed a Bible question," David relates. "A dear old Scottish general asked me what the main message of the book of Habakkuk was. My mind immediately went blank. I should have answered, of course, 'The just shall live by faith.' "

"Actually," David explains mischievously, "the old general asked the question because he wanted to tell a favorite story about an elderly Scottish lady who was found reading the book of Habakkuk. When asked why she was reading such a difficult book, she replied, 'Before too long I shall be going to heaven, and I want to be prepared—for when I meet the prophet, I'm sure he will ask me, "Have you read my wee bookie?" ' "

The missed question was not to matter, for that day David H. Adeney was accepted as a member of the China Inland Mission. "The council seemed satisfied that the conviction of God's call to China was strong enough for them to accept the 'poor risk,' " David remembers later, approaching eighty. "So I have remained a poor risk for the past fifty-seven years!" A smile framed by uneven rows of wrinkles spreads over his face.

Only God could have known that spring day in 1934 how significant David Adeney's life would be, dedicated to the service of his master. Though he never seemed strong physically and was often unsure of himself, he influenced individual lives, movements, and the church in Asia and beyond. To God, David was no "poor risk." His very weakness was to make him a candidate for God's strength.

About eight years after David's acceptance by the London Council, he met Dr. Northcote Deck again—in America. David had just spoken at an InterVarsity meeting in Detroit, which Dr. Deck had attended. Hearing the students talking to David, he said to him later, "David, they talk to you as if they have known you all of their lives!" He paused a moment, then added, "I have prayed for you every day since you sailed for China."

2

Unusual Family

David Adeney's family was hardly ordinary.

With his father away in Romania for much of David's life, and away himself at boarding school during his teen years, David almost certainly would be judged handicapped by today's Christian counselor.

But David's was a strong family. For generations there had been a devoted Christian or missionary somewhere in their ranks. One ancestor of note, Richard Baxter, a Puritan chaplain to Commonwealth troops during the English Civil War, became one of the outstanding religious leaders of the Cromwellian era. William Adeney, David's great-grandfather, was a man with a passion for preaching. Though he ran a clerical tailor's business on Sackville Street, Piccadilly, he was far more interested in proclaiming the gospel than in making clothes for bishops. Saturday mornings saw him preaching to a mixed crowd of Londoners who, for a penny, would come to listen. When William thought the jostling among the people was becoming too much of a distraction, he unwittingly cut attendance by making sure the men stood separately from the women. On Sundays he walked miles to fulfill preaching engagements and would even have treated the public to open-air readings of Scripture in Hyde Park if he could have obtained the necessary permit.

In David's more immediate family, both his parents and an aunt and uncle served as missionaries—his parents among the Jewish people in Romania, and the uncle and aunt in Egypt.

David's father, J. (for John) Howard Adeney, worked hard to prepare himself for the ministry. As money was scarce, Howard learned early to fend for himself. After school and before going to Cambridge University,

5

he joined the Civil Service to earn a living, passing the required exams by studying at night.

Howard started at a post office in Queen Victoria Street, where the long hours of standing at the counter put such a strain on his legs that they suffered permanent damage. During his first year at St. John's College, Cambridge, lameness often confined him to a sofa and he had to wear boots and iron supports for many years.

With his degree in theology completed, Howard Adeney was ordained to Christ Church, Spitalfields, where he began work among the fourteen thousand Jews of the parish. He already knew he wanted to be a missionary to the Jewish people, and in 1896 he applied to the London Jews Society, later known as the Church Ministry to the Jews. After short placements in Germany and Palestine, he was sent to Bucharest.

In Romania, Howard's first wife died after giving birth to their son Jack. She was a victim of "childbirth fever" and the appallingly low standards of Bucharest midwives. Adding to the pain of losing his wife, Howard had to say good-bye to his baby son, entrusting him to his brother and sister-in-law in England. Howard felt Jack would have a proper home with them, certainly better than anything he could offer the child on his own in Romania.

Florence Wood, a young woman from a privileged family, came out to Romania from England to help in the boarding school Howard founded for Jewish girls. An independent spirit and no stranger to adventure, the young Miss Wood had already traveled around Palestine on a donkey, an unusual feat for a woman at the end of the nineteenth century. Vivacious and devoted to Christ, she caught Howard's attention. In 1910 she and Howard were married in England, in St. Cuthbert's Anglican Church in her hometown of Bedford, north of London.

Howard and Florry worked together in Bucharest until she was about to give birth to their first child. Fearing a repeat of the tragedy that claimed the life of Howard's first wife, they agreed that thirty-five-year-old Florry should go home to Bedford for the baby's birth.

Thus David Howard Adeney was born in England on November 3, 1911. That year the first airplanes were flying a few feet above the ground, and in China, the country that would play such an important part in David's life, Sun Yat-sen had led the challenge against the ruling Manchu Dynasty and had just founded the Republic.

A few months later, back in Romania, Florry watched in horror as blood poisoning threatened to snuff out the life of her tiny first-born son. David survived, but by the time he was a toddler, Florry was anxious at the prospect of bringing up her family where the standards of health and hygiene were so low. She returned again to Britain for the birth of her second child. So it was in Bedford that three-year-old David first looked wonderingly into the face of his little brother Harold.

Before Florry could think through the implications of her worries, World War I intervened, and Howard came back to England to join his wife. Two more boys—Bernard, then Ronald—swelled the little brood to four while their father was at home. Florry had her hands full. Howard found a ministry and a livelihood serving as chaplain to German prisoners of war.

When the war was over, a decision had to be made about Romania. In the short memoir Howard Adeney compiled for his sons, he wrote about what happened: "Your mother felt that it was too much to go out with four children; so she decided to stay at home and bring up the family while I returned to Romania. I am afraid that I did not see why she should not come out as Romania was in Europe. But, as she was not willing, we settled that she should stay in England while I went on with my work and came home in the long holidays to keep touch with you all." From then on—from 1919 to 1939—Howard was away from his family for ten months of the year.

"Did I do right in not staying at home with your mother in 1919?" Howard's final words in the memoir are tinged with sadness. "The Lord only knows."

None of the boys remembers consciously regretting their father's absence while they were growing up. His work meant that he had to be away from them. They accepted that. And they all admired his achievements in Bucharest.

Howard Adeney had founded one school and rebuilt another to provide Christian education to Jewish children. He also established the Anglican church in Bucharest. Richard Wurmbrand, imprisoned for fourteen years in Romania for his Christian faith, testifies warmly to Howard Adeney's influence in Bucharest and in his own life. "He would read the Bible with me, take long walks with me, trying to reply to my hundreds of questions," remembers Wurmbrand. "He formed me."

7

"Thousands of Jewish children came to the schools for instruction," Wurmbrand explained, "because Christian religion was compulsory. Thus Jewish kids got acquainted with Christ. Conversions were rare, but these schools achieved something very precious: they broke down much of the wall of prejudice and misunderstanding between Christianity and Judaism.

"In one of the schools was a great hall for church services. It could seat five hundred. Rarely more than twenty attended. Anybody else would have despaired and given up his work as hopeless. Not so Mr. Adeney. He had a saying: 'Success is not a name for God, but he has the names of loyalty and perseverance.' Mr. Adeney prepared his sermons for these twenty with the same care as he would have done if preaching in a cathedral. He knew the day of harvest would come."

Such was the example from which Howard's four sons learned and which each in his own way sought to emulate. "My father's example had a great impact on my life," wrote David in his later years, "even though he was away most of the year, and it was not until I was quite grown up that I really got to know him. He was very reserved. I don't think any of his sons knew him really well, for he rarely shared any of his own personal experiences. But his upright life, his disciplined times of prayer and Bible reading, his conscientious dedication to the work committed to him made a deep impression upon me.

"My father always kept to his regular Bible reading and prayer and led family prayers. But he did not often speak about his own spiritual experience. Even at the end of his life he spoke little about his personal faith. I remember the Sunday before I left for China he preached on 'Lord, I will follow you wherever you go.' Once he talked to me about the dangers faced by a Christian worker—the temptations relating to pride, sexual desires, and money. At the end of his life he spoke of 'waiting to make the great discovery.'

"My father was a very kind person. The teachers who worked for him in Romania respected his thoughtfulness. He kept careful records and was especially careful in the use of money.

"My mother was very different, both in background and personality. Whereas Daddy came from a poor family, struggled to get enough money for a university education, and lived very frugally all his life, Mother came from a prosperous business family, who were by and large very much involved in the world. Only one sister was a devout Christian.

"Besides being quick-tempered, Mother was outgoing and adventurous, always wanting to explore things. She almost enjoyed trespassing on private property in Switzerland, collecting alpine flowers and smuggling them home in her luggage to plant in her rock garden. She loved travel and took us boys on many holidays to the seaside in England and to places on the Continent."

In Bedford, the family lived at first with Florry's mother in a large, gracious house overlooking the river. This house, where David was born and also where a doctor took out his tonsils on the kitchen table, stood within sight of the Bedford Town Bridge. The old bridge, long since gone, had a prison built on to it. John Bunyan may have been incarcerated there, though he probably wrote *Pilgrim's Progress* in another nearby prison.

During the war years the family lived about ten minutes' walk away, in a small house in Waterloo Road, parallel to the Bedford embankment. This embankment, a broad walk along the river bordered with numerous flower gardens, was judged to be one of the most beautiful in all England.

In 1918 the Adeneys moved around the corner to 71 Bushmead Avenue, across the street from Russell Park. Nestled in a neighborhood of professional people, this three-story brick house became the family base for almost fifty years.

Besides a sitting room and a dining room at the front, the first floor of this house boasted two kitchens, one with a large table as its main feature and a second at the back for cooking. A door from the back kitchen opened into a garden where fruit trees and gooseberry bushes provided makings for tarts and puddings. At the back of the garden was a brick wall; the boys often balanced along its length. And, best of all as far as the boys were concerned, in the wall was a gate that led out onto a large field where children from the whole block of houses met to play.

David remembers when World War I ended, for that was the day he ran away from his nanny while they were out walking. A band in a nearby street was celebrating the Allies' victory, and he had to see. The spanking he was given, rather than the war's end, was probably what helped to make the incident stick in his memory.

Every week during the boys' childhood, one of them would be the honored and somewhat uncomfortable guest for Sunday lunch at

Grandmother's house. Delicious chicken and homemade jelly made up for the need to be on one's best behavior in front of Grandmother and her daughter, Aunt Clara.

"Grandmother always wore 'widow's weeds,'" David's brother Harold remembers, "a long black dress with lace and velvet facing, and a white lace cap like Queen Victoria." The dress held a particular fascination for him because it concealed his grandmother's purse. Occasionally Grandmother produced a generous gift for a visiting grandson from the pocket of her petticoat. David remembers riding with her in her horse-drawn carriage over Bedford's cobbled streets.

The Adeneys were able to live very comfortably because Florry's family, the Woods, were successful sheep farmers in Patagonia, Argentina, where Florry had grown up. David has fond memories of his Uncle Walter, his mother's favorite brother, who brought impressive presents when he came for a visit. On his death, Uncle Walter, a bachelor who used to tease his sister for marrying "that parson fellow," left the family his estate. The money paid for the children's education.

Vibrant and loving, Florry poured her life into her children. While their father usually accompanied them when they traveled during the summer, it was their mother's infectious love for travel and adventure that rubbed off on the boys. Even just going around town was fun, driving with their mother in her Singer. Florry was one of the few women in England to own and drive a motor vehicle at the time. The boys would hold their breath as she tried to get up hills without changing gear, rocking her body in a scooting motion to help the car along. Getting beyond the usual thirty miles an hour was always a cause for triumphant hilarity.

But most significant in the boys' lives was their mother's devotion to God. It permeated everything she did. She longed for each of her sons to discover a living faith for himself. From the time the boys were babies she taught them about God, careful to maintain daily Bible reading and prayer time in their home. Every Sunday she took them to St. Cuthbert's, the Anglican church where she and their father were married.

Even then Florry did not leave exposure to Christian influence to chance. As the boys grew up, she enrolled them in Crusaders, an interdenominational youth organization that met weekly. During school holidays she took them off to the Children's Special Service Missions on east coast beaches, where Christian volunteers drew crowds of children to play games and listen to stories about Jesus. And when they were teenagers, she encouraged their attendance at houseparties CSSM conducted for young people. She gave them their first taste of traveling abroad by taking them to Switzerland for four CSSM winter sports houseparties at which she served as "housemother." Besides savoring the activities arranged for them during these days of fun together at Leukerbad, with its hot springs for winter swimming and its snow-covered slopes for skiing, the boys and other young people imbibed Christian values and understanding.

Florry loved those winter camps in Switzerland. She enjoyed the jokes and hilarity that were a part of them. Old Bishop Taylor Smith, a large man and a very popular speaker among young people, was a good friend. Once one of the camp officers came up behind him at dinner and sprinkled water on his spacious bald head. When the bishop objected, the culprit told him, "It's all right, sir. I was just flooding the skating rink!" As the red-faced bishop tried to muffle his mirth, Florry laughed as heartily as anyone.

These summer and winter holidays are among David's happiest memories. When he was a child the storytelling of Hudson Pope particularly enthralled him. Through vivid stories this celebrated veteran of the beach missions communicated the gospel powerfully to wind-blown youngsters gathered around him in the sand.

David's favorite among Pope's tales was the one about the castle where King Self was resisting the advances of King Jesus and his army. In this story three walls of defense had to come down before Jesus could reach the door of the castle: the wall of ignorance guarded by Captain I Don't Know, the wall of indifference guarded by Captain I Don't Care, and the wall of procrastination guarded by Captain Put It Off. The children hung on Pope's words as he described how King Jesus penetrated each wall, then faced one last barrier: the gatekeeper, Will, who had to decide whether to open the door. Only when he did was the rightful King able to take over from the ruinous King Self. In 1991, on the Sunday after his eightieth birthday, David used Pope's castle story in a sermon for children in a California church.

David does not recall a specific moment of conversion. But his confidence that he was truly a child of God came through listening to Hudson Pope.

During at least four summers while he was attending Monktom Combe School, David went to CSSM-sponsored Varsity and Public School camps at West Runton on the coast. Staffed largely with volunteer help from Oxford and Cambridge students, these camps also offered a mix of holiday fun and Christian teaching. On one occasion David's tent officer, "Neddy" Clarke (R.E.D. Clarke, eventually a brilliant scientist), was alone with David in their tent. "David," he said, "You have been to a Christian school, come from a Christian home, but do you realize the danger, the misery, of being a half-and-half Christian—half following the world and half following Christ?" David never forgot those words. "That was a critical time in my life," he says. "I learned in a deeper way to commit myself to the Lord Jesus, longing that I might be, in the words of Scripture, 'fervent in spirit, serving the Lord.' "

Years earlier, when Ronald was only about three and before David went off to boarding school, the four boys were discussing what they were going to be when they grew up. "I'm going to be a missionary preacher," David announced prophetically. When Harold said he wanted to be a doctor, Bernard piped up with an offer to drive his car and to carry his doctor's bag. Ronald, too little to be quite sure what he wanted to be, later set his heart on becoming a steam-roller driver.

The two older brothers never changed their minds. David became a missionary to China; Harold fulfilled his desire to become a doctor, then took his medical expertise to Rwanda and Burundi as a missionary with the Rwanda Mission. Bernard followed David to China, and Ronald did exactly what he had thought he would never do—follow in the footsteps of his father in serving overseas in ministry to the Jews.

So all four brothers became missionaries. The Adeneys were "world Christians." Florry's desire to bring up her sons to love God was closely tied to a conviction that missionary service was the highest calling. She wanted all of her boys to be missionaries and prayed consistently that God would call them to serve overseas. And by giving hospitality to visiting missionaries, who regaled them all with stories of the mission field, she contributed directly to that end, whether knowingly or not.

All three of David's younger brothers distinguished themselves. Harold, the brother closest to David, married a Scottish lass who was also a medical doctor. The two spent most of their lives in Africa, though for some years Harold served as General Secretary for the Rwanda General

Mission in England. In Africa Harold was involved in the East African revival and was much loved by African Christians. He organized a rescue operation during tribal warfare in which the Hutu were killing the Tutsi. Later in Burundi he watched sadly as the Tutsi slaughtered the Hutu. He tells of his experiences in his book, *By Love Compelled.*

Bernard served in the Anglican district of the China Inland Mission in East Sichwan. But he and Millicent returned to England soon after the birth of their first child, who was in need of surgery. Bernard then served as vicar in several churches, district secretary for the Church Pastoral Aid Society, and was an assistant home director of their father's mission. As he provided a home base for all of the far-flung family, Bernard was a much-loved uncle to his many nephews and nieces as well as father to his own three boys. After Millicent died of cancer, he married Sally, once a missionary in Ethiopia.

Bernard was more athletic than either Harold or David and had a great capacity to enjoy life. He did not take life as seriously as David, and was more relaxed. Because he seemed the strongest of the brothers, his death in 1990 was totally unexpected.

Ronald went to Palestine before the State of Israel was formed, and is still in Israel, retired and living near Haifa. In his early days there he married Laura, a missionary nurse, who nursed the sick and wounded at the Nazareth hospital during the fighting that preceded the founding of Israel. Eventually on Mt. Carmel, about a mile from Elijah's place of sacrifice, Ronald and Laura established "Stella Carmel"—a retreat center for Christian Arabs and Messianic Jews, dedicating the chapel there to the memory of his father, because he had given a lifetime to preaching Christ to Romanian Jews.

Even the four boys' elder half-brother Jack served in chaplaincies in Suez, Basra, and Cyprus. Mediating talks between Britain and Archbishop Makarios, in fact, took place in Jack's Cyprus home.

Some among the next generations have also come along behind. Before her death in 1989, David's own daughter Rosemary spent almost a quarter century in the Philippines with the Nurses Christian Fellowship and Overseas Missionary Fellowship. At the time of writing, his son Michael serves with Intercristo in Seattle, while his wife Miriam teaches in the missions department of Seattle Pacific University and Regent College, Vancouver. Son Bernard and his wife Fran are teaching at Satya Wacana

Christian University in Salatiga, Indonesia, working with a new graduate department on Religion and Society. Grandson Keith lives in Munich, Germany, working with the Studenten Mission Deutchland (IVCF). Harold's son, David, is director of TEAR Fund, and his daughter, Elspeth, serves as a missionary in Africa. A second son also gave some years to Africa, and now a granddaughter has been serving as a short-term missionary in a hospital where her grandfather once served.

An unusual family indeed!

3

Schooldays:
Fine-Tuning a Life

A sober David sat beside his mother as they covered the distance between Bedford and Bath. The twelve-year-old was about to exchange the security of home and the Bedford school near the statue of John Bunyan for the uncertainties of boarding school. It helped a little, perhaps, that his half-brother Jack had attended Monkton Combe ahead of him. But by this time, early in 1924, Jack had gone, already heading for the Anglican ministry and the mission field.

The junior part of Monkton Combe is at the top of Combe Down, overlooking Wiltshire Downs and the Midford Valley. Its broad aqueduct reflects the mood of the sky. The larger senior school takes up most of Monkton Combe Village in the valley. Between the two schools is a steep path, the Drung. Later, when David was at the senior school, he would tramp the Drung regularly because he had some of his meals in a school residence at the top.

On the way to Monkton, on a clear day, Florry and David could get a good view of the Wiltshire White Horse. The huge drawing had been chalked into the hillside hundreds of years before to celebrate, it seems, one of King Alfred's victories over the Danes. On that first day, the sight was a novelty. After that, however, when David's mother would drive him to school at the beginning of each new term, the historic landmark told the returning teenager they were nearing their destination and his heart would correspondingly sink. The journey was always great fun until that moment, having included a stop for tea along the way. David never grew to like being away at school.

Life at the junior school was spartan, according to Maurice Wood, a pupil a few years after David and later Bishop of Norwich. Wood remembers "cold showers and cold water to wash in, beds each made of three broad wooden laths to sleep on, and battered, round-bottomed pewter mugs from which to drink milk and water daily." David welcomed the occasional outing for tea at his Crusader leader's home.

During the course of his five terms at the junior school David earned himself a reputation as a particularly serious Christian. The strongly Christian tradition of the school encouraged this bent, as did his habit of setting aside time to be with God, to pray and to study the Scriptures, a discipline learned from his father. Mischievous classmates once scribbled a cartoon of David on the blackboard, labeling the caricature "St. Adeney".

Admittedly David was not the typical schoolboy, happiest on the cricket pitch or rugger field. He was neither physically strong nor well-coordinated. He had dreaded gym ever since the shameful experience of falling off a wall and being caught by the sergeant major who served as gym instructor at "Inky" (for "Incubator," the nickname for the Bedford Junior School).

David did try his best at games, however, with characteristic dedication to a difficult task. A younger friend at Monkton remembers one occasion when David encouraged a group of small boys in a game of rugger at which he wasn't much better than they were. His best athletic achievement at Monkton was coming in second in the school quarter mile in his final year, and since the winner went on to obtain a Cambridge "blue" for running, he could take satisfaction from his achievement.

In those days masters and prefects at Monkton employed the cane to discipline the boys when it was deemed necessary. In his first year at the senior school, David was beaten more than once for not measuring up to the exacting standards of prefects. With hindsight, David stoically maintains that the regimented routine was good for him. At the time it seemed like hardship.

David's greatest enjoyment came from participating in the lively Christian Union, with its variety of prayer and Bible study meetings. Eventually he joined the committee who ran the CU, not only taking part in CU meetings, but helping to conduct Sunday services in the nearby village of Conkwell.

Going to Conkwell was always an adventure. Unless a master was going with a car and could run them around by road, the boys used to walk. Since the village was on the other side of the valley from Combe Down and half way up a steep incline, the walk was strenuous. In wet weather there was no avoiding the mud.

Villagers met for services in a tiny chapel, built in the same light-colored local stone as the handful of homes which made up the village. These cottages flanked both sides of a single road that was so steep no vehicles could make the grade. The chapel was at the bottom, facing an overgrown wishing well with a protective rail along the near side. Carved into the stone above the chapel door was the date 1876.

Conkwell villagers were patient with the boys' nervous mistakes. The prayer book they used was a very old one, set up in such a way that it was easy to confuse the pages and to read the wrong thing. David once asked those present to confess their sins in the words of the general thanksgiving. On a different occasion another of the boys started reading a prayer for deliverance from the plague. The lad's instinctive reaction, once he realized his error, startled the congregation even more. "As you were!" he ordered, using a term he had learned during military training. Ears and cheeks blushed red.

In his final year at school, David was given responsibility for organizing the Conkwell services. Fellow students soon dubbed him "Bishop of Conkwell." It was the nearest he ever got to fulfilling a phrenologist's prediction at a country fair in his childhood that someday he would become a bishop.

During one term at Monkton Combe Junior School, the much-loved schoolmaster Stanley Houghton sparked in David's heart an interest that would give a clear focus to his life. Soon to head for China with the China Inland Mission, the teacher often talked about China to the boys. Once he lent David the book, *A Thousand Miles of Miracle in China*. Written with frank simplicity by eye-witness Archibald Glover, the book traces the story of mob frenzy, courage, and rescue during China's Boxer Rebellion in 1900. David was deeply moved by the specter of the deaths of hundreds of Chinese Christians and two hundred missionaries and their children.

The testimony of those who died and those who survived gripped him. Fascinated, he read how the band of missionary refugees, about to be sacrificed as scapegoats by villagers made desperate by drought, poured their hearts out to God for rain. They prayed in Chinese so that their captors would know who was responsible if their prayers were answered. And they were. The story pulsed through David's being.

From this time on David could not get away from the implications of China's spiritual need, the reality of millions without a knowledge of Christ. In a new way he saw the cost of missionary life, but that cost also struck him as exhilarating since with God there is no ultimate defeat. David began to wonder whether his Lord might want him to go to China too.

In the following months David had long talks with Stanley Houghton, who told him all he wanted to know about China and the China Inland Mission. Excited by the adolescent's interest and eager to nurture it, Houghton lent him more books about China. One was the biography of the founder of the China Inland Mission, James Hudson Taylor, which David read avidly. He was particularly interested in how God had called Hudson Taylor to China.

Though Hudson Taylor committed his life to Christ when he was seventeen and immediately experienced a great delight in God, David empathized with his deep sense of unworthiness. Taylor felt his life was not totally released into God's service; something still held him back. The Yorkshire youth promised God he would go anywhere and do anything he commanded if God would only help him get beyond his failings. David's eyes moved quickly along the type. "I felt I was in the presence of God," the future founder of the CIM wrote, "entering into covenant with the Almighty. I felt as though I wished to withdraw my promise, but could not. Something seemed to say, 'Your prayer is answered; your conditions are accepted.' And from that time the conviction never left me that I was called to China."

From God's clear call to Hudson Taylor, David took courage that he too would know for sure whether God meant him to go to China. He read on. Taylor gave himself to finding out all he could about China at a time when, among Westerners, little was known of the country. The more

Taylor discovered, the more the numbers of Chinese who had never heard of the gospel of Christ overwhelmed him.

Soberly David took in young Taylor's words: "I have a stronger desire than ever to go to China. That land is ever in my thoughts. Think of it—360 million souls, without God or hope in the world! Think of more than twelve million of our fellow creatures dying every year without any of the consolations of the Gospel. Poor neglected China! Scarcely anyone cares about it."

David began to care very deeply. Stanley Houghton gave him a map of China which visualized its vast population in little black squares. The number of Christians was only a pinpoint of white in the middle of one of the squares, a picture which stayed in David's mind all his life.

About this time David copied into the flyleaf of his Bible a vision for evangelism captured in verse by an anonymous writer:

> The restless millions wait the light
> Whose dawning maketh all things new.
> Christ also waits, but men are slow and few.
> Have we done all we could? Have I? Have you?

David joined China Inland Mission's "Comradeship for China," a group set up for young people, and began receiving the Comradeship magazine, *Young China*. He saved up what he could for the "Missionary Gift Box" for the support of missionaries. He also attended some of the youth rallies the CIM held regularly in different parts of the country. China began to seem less far away, more familiar. He prayed regularly for the Chinese people.

By the time David finished school he was certain that God was calling him to China. His call "wasn't anything spectacular," he told a group of students later. "It wasn't a sudden experience. I didn't hear any voices. But it was a growing conviction that God wanted me to go. . . ."

During one of David's last chapel services at Monkton, he sat wondering how he could get to China—quickly. Could he forget about going to Cambridge University as expected of him? The fire burning within made him impatient to be on his way.

People have long debated whether compulsory daily chapel and a diet of Christian teaching and missionary challenge send youngsters more often into rebellion rather than towards active Christian commitment. Monkton has seen both reactions. In his history of the school, *A Goodly Heritage,* A. F. Lace quotes a former pupil as saying: "The effect, I believe, of a Monkton Combe education has been to make a man in the end do almost without religion." Says another, however: "In these days the religious and evangelical influences under which we lived at Monkton Combe might appear excessive; but to us, and I think to our elders too, they seemed natural at the time. How else should we live, if we believe the Gospel, than all day long in the light of it?"

David pays tribute to his education at Monkton and his debt to Stanley Houghton. At the same time he felt that he would have become a missionary even had he gone to a secular school. God meant it to be. And, even at this point, the influences on his life were far wider than those at Monkton.

In Bedford during the school holidays he was becoming dissatisfied with St. Cuthbert's, the Anglican church the family attended. Both he and his brother Harold were drawn to the active youth group at Russell Park Baptist Church, which conducted open-air services every Sunday evening on the embankment. When David and Harold investigated the possibility of getting involved, they were given a warm welcome by the young people and their pastor. Eventually, Pastor Ferguson was to become a very good friend of the boys' father.

From then on the two brothers, while continuing to attend St. Cuthbert's on Sunday mornings, joined the activities of the young people's fellowship at Russell Park Baptist whenever they could, including the open-air evangelism.

The embankment with its flower gardens was a popular place for a Sunday evening stroll. "Sometimes you had to push your way along," recalls a life-long member of Russell Park, Reg Palmer. On the other side of the river, across a suspension bridge, was another popular area, an attractive park. So, after the evening service teenagers from Russell Park made their way through the crowds and positioned themselves near the well-used bridge.

The young people began their meeting with hymns, accompanied on an old folding organ kept during the week at the Adeneys' home on Bushmead Avenue. Following the music, two or three individuals would tell something of what God meant to them. Listeners sat on benches, stood in clusters, lounged against a railing. David was particularly good at holding people's attention, Reg Palmer remembers. "He was always so pleasant and so simple that people liked to listen to him."

Opportunities to mature as a public speaker began to multiply for David. In addition to school activities, he helped out at the occasional Children's Special Service beach mission. Encouraged by his mentor, Hudson Pope, David was learning to brave the sand pulpit the children built and to give short Bible messages over the sound of lapping waves. These outings led to roles of greater responsibility. Before too long he was leading CSSM houseparties and once a beach mission.

But Bible study, student friends, and association with Russell Park Baptist Church brought tension into David's life on the issue of baptism. Increasingly it made more sense to David for baptism to follow conversion rather than to anticipate it. On a blank page in the loose-leaf Bible his mother gave him he wrote: "As baptism is a type of burial with Christ (Romans 6:3-4), sprinkling could not have been what Christ meant. Just as a few drops of earth will not bury a person, neither will a few drops of water act as a type of burial . . . . " Though he had been baptized as an infant, now he was wondering whether he should go through another ceremony of full immersion.

"It seemed to me my baptism had been quite unknown to me," he explains. "I wanted to have a meaningful one as a believer. The amount of water was not the main question, although it did seem that immersion was much closer to the idea of dying with Christ and being raised again to new life."

David's growing conviction regarding baptism troubled him. If he decided that infant baptism was not valid, he could not ally himself with the Anglican church. This, he knew, would disappoint his father, who was hoping all his sons would go into the Anglican ministry.

When David shared his dilemma with his father, Howard Adeney referred him to his old friend from Cambridge days, Archbishop Harrington Lees, David's godfather. If the Archbishop of Melbourne couldn't sort his son out, Howard thought, no one could.

21

The archbishop's reply to David's inquiry, however, was hardly helpful. "Don't worry about all that," the clergyman suggested. "You'll get over over it just like a child gets over measles. Wait till you have studied Greek." David did not "get over it." He simply became more convinced, whatever the implications, that he should be baptized by immersion.

The opportunity came when David left school. A friend from the Honor Oak Fellowship, an independent church in north London, suggested David come and be baptized there. A baptismal service was being planned for people in the church, and David could join in. So, in a simple service at a church he never visited again, David set his mind at rest. In a short testimony before going into the pool, he declared his allegiance to Christ and his intention to become a missionary to China. To his great surprise, the congregation organized a little additional service for him to show their support. They prayed specifically for his future ministry, laying hands on him, and sent him away with long-treasured words of encouragement.

It was a significant moment. Not only had he been baptized in a manner that expressed his personal identification with Christ, but he had been commissioned to be a missionary in China.

David left his Bedford childhood for Monkton Comb with the flame of missionary desire flickering only faintly within. Boarding school days had fanned the flame and opened the world of ministry to him. Crusaders, CSSM, and Russell Park Baptist shifted his course away from a totally Anglican one. And now this church of a friend had helped focus his thinking. David was convinced that God wanted his life for China. From now on China would be his goal.

4

Significant Interlude

Eight months stretched ahead of David before he would go up to Cambridge. Eager as he was to sail for China, common sense and the advice of his elders convinced him that bypassing important preparation at this point would be counterproductive. So he took Cambridge entrance exams and was accepted at Queens' College. Now he looked for something useful to fill the remaining time, something to equip him for the mission field.

Roland Hogben, in charge of the China Inland Mission training school, wrote to David suggesting three organizations which might be able to offer David some good working experience: the London City Mission, the Open-Air Mission in London, and the Missionary Training Colony near Crystal Palace, just outside London.

"My parents do not like the idea of either the London City Mission or the Open-Air Mission, as they consider that I shall not be old enough for that type of work," David wrote in his reply. "I myself know several people at the LCM and should very much like that work. My mother prefers the Missionary Training Colony, which I think would be most awfully useful if they would take me for the six months. My father feels that it is very important that I should be doing some kind of brain work so that when I go to Cambridge, I shall not find it difficult to start studying again.

"At present, however," he continued, showing considerable spiritual maturity at seventeen, "I feel the only thing to do is to pray about it, trusting that the Lord will open up the right way."

David decided on the Missionary Training Colony, begun by a missionary from the Worldwide Evangelization Crusade with the aim of preparing prospective missionary candidates for the tough realities of their calling. Since evangelistic work in underdeveloped countries was the expected lot of the missionary at that time, the Colony endeavored to give candidates a taste of what their futures might entail. David was willing to give it a try.

But he was not old enough. The minimum age requirement was twenty-one. Unwilling to give up what he saw as the right course, he sat down and put forward his case in a letter to the leader of the Colony, Godfrey Buxton. Something in his plea must have been persuasive, for Captain Buxton added David's name to the thirty or so registered for the upcoming course and sent him a letter of acceptance.

When David arrived at the Colony, he was shocked to find little more than two army huts sitting starkly on a rough piece of land. The building in which he was to sleep was unfinished, and opposite his bed a gaping hole in the wall let in the chill winter winds. Every day he had to be up with the others at 6:00 A.M. to have a cold bath and then go out for a run around the block to prepare for an hour of prayer and Bible study before breakfast.

All thirty would-be missionaries took turns with chores, including the cooking. David jokes about the "burnt offerings" he produced during his week in the kitchen. He did not think it a joking matter at the time since the effort so exhausted him that he collapsed in bed for a few days afterwards. Laying paths, doing the cleaning and washing, darning socks— all were a part of the disciplined routine.

David had disliked the institutional life at Monkton Combe, and now he was being asked to knuckle down to an even stricter program. This time, however, he was fired with a sense of purpose that made it all a worthwhile challenge. He was with people who shared his vision, and felt solidarity with them; he had chosen to come to the Colony, believing that God had sent him, and this too made a difference. David's younger brother Ronald, admiring David's dedication in accepting the rigors of the Colony, remarked, "None of the rest of us did that."

Louis Gaussen, another prospective CIM missionary at the Colony with David, was an Oxford graduate from a similarly comfortable home. He found, like David, that the experience changed his perspective. In addition to doing things that would have been done for them at home, the two young men were also mixing for the first time in everyday life with people from a less privileged background. David was embarrassed by the outspokenness and crude habits of some, but saw the accompanying boldness in evangelism and respected it. Louis likewise recognized that these men were far better at preaching and coping with the routine at the Colony than he and David were. Previous assumptions were being challenged and youthful outlooks broadened.

What impressed David was how closely the teaching program at the Colony matched the teaching Jesus gave his disciples. "Christ chose his disciples in order that they might be with him, and from the beginning the emphasis was upon the spiritual development in the lives of his followers," David wrote several years later. "At the Colony, priority was given to fellowship with God. All the teaching in our lectures was aimed at making us students of the Word of God.

"Christ's followers were constantly reminded that the mark of true discipleship is obedience. At the Colony we were taught to live a disciplined life. Emphasis upon the holiness of God as revealed in the Scriptures called us to be obedient to the leading of the Holy Spirit. Missionaries from overseas warned us of the way young workers often ruin their witness when they are overcome by temptation. The whole purpose of our training was to make us people who would obey God, hate sin, and strive for holiness.

"Christ not only taught his disciples—he sent them out to preach. Likewise every week members of the Colony went out preaching, often speaking at open-air meetings in Hyde Park or Tower Hill, where listeners would frequently heckle and challenge them to answer questions, both serious and ribald. Long talks with inquirers would follow."

In addition, many of the young men taught Sunday school classes for youngsters in tough London slums.

When summer arrived, the trainees faced their most difficult test: the "trek."

Divided into two teams of a dozen each, led by a member of staff, the men piled all their gear for a few weeks on to two carts, one for each team. Six then pulled the assigned cart, two allocated to the front ropes, two to the side ropes, and two to the shaft. The other six in each team walked beside their cart until it was their turn to step in. The idea was to set up open-air meetings in villages along the road, and in the process the teams sometimes walked fifteen miles a day.

At night the men set up a tent if they were not offered hospitality in a church hall or welcomed into private homes. A scout always went on ahead on a bicycle to check out what the opportunities might be. These men made contact with people as they went.

If this was not demanding enough as a foretaste of missionary work, the final week saw the carts and belongings abandoned. The leaders now broke the teams up into pairs and gave them a new mission. Each pair was shown a village on a map and told to go and spend a week there, with nothing but half a crown to live on.

"We experienced a life of faith, being dependent on the Lord for both material necessities and spiritual power," wrote David later in his book, *The Unchanging Commission*. "During those days we learned to practice the principles that had been discussed during the Bible study periods earlier in the year."

Nervously, he and his partner had sat in a ditch munching bread and bananas to prolong the moment before going to their assigned village. When they finally braved entry, they discovered that God had prepared the way. A church prayer meeting was to be held that day, so they decided to go along. They were warmly welcomed, asked if they could conduct a daily meeting there for the whole week, given a roof over their heads and fed in different homes each day. David was jubilant afterwards. "We returned to the team with more money than when we started and a greater appreciation for the grace of God and his power to supply the needs of his servants."

Back in Bedford preparing for university, David took steps to lay the foundations of church support when he went to China. It was not so much financial support that concerned him as much as prayer support and a congregation behind him. He did not feel he could ask St. Cuthbert's in Bedford to be his "sending" church because over the years he had become involved at Russell Park Baptist Church, identifying less and less with the Anglican denomination. It seemed natural to turn to his Baptist friends with his request.

David never became a full Baptist convert in any denominational sense. Once he had started to distance himself from the Anglican church, his Christian allegiance became increasingly interdenominational. Russell Park attracted him because, as he put it, it was "a living church with people active in the service of the Lord Jesus." And this is what he looked for in a church from then on.

All David's brothers became ordained Anglican ministers, fulfilling their father's ambition for them. Howard Adeney believed that ordination opened doors to effective ministry, with the added advantage of financial security. Although he did not oppose David's choice, he encouraged him strongly to reconsider.

David did not move away from his Anglican roots easily. As with everything, he sought God and talked with many people about it. In the end he remained convinced that he should not study for the Anglican ministry. God's call was to China; he wanted to fulfill this without imposing denominational restrictions on his ministry. After all, he reminded himself and others, Hudson Taylor was never ordained.

The pastor at Russell Park, the wise and caring Mr. Ferguson, welcomed David's request to align himself more fully with the church. He well understood the needs David honestly presented to him. Privately Mr. Ferguson undertook to pray for David every day. This he did for all the young people in his charge, although none knew it at the time. Not only that, but he wrote to David weekly after he left for China. The congregation at Russell Park has supported David ever since—for almost sixty years.

For his part, David has given unstinting loyalty to Russell Park all his adult life, keeping them in touch with his activities, taking the trouble to visit them whenever possible, and preaching in the church. Ronald S. Luland, recently retired from the Russell Park pastorate, pays David this tribute: "I doubt if any church has ever had a more loyal or faithful missionary member."

Just before he went up to Cambridge, David took time to attend the weekly prayer meeting of the China Inland Mission at Newington Green, North London. It happened to be the day the new recruits were giving their testimonies prior to departing for China. The hall was packed. Arriving late, David looked anxiously for a seat, but the only ones left were reserved. Someone guided him to a spare seat among the recruits.

As David sat with the new recruits through the meeting, he felt very close to being a CIM missionary himself. The experience excited him. It was as if God had allowed this significant seating arrangement to give him a foretaste of what lay ahead. David went up to Cambridge that autumn of 1930 with his eyes firmly on China.

5

Cambridge

David had hardly unpacked his bags and familiarized himself with scheduled lectures at Cambridge when he joined the university's Christian Union, or CICCU, as it was known (Cambridge Inter-Collegiate Christian Union).

An almost bewildering range of activities was available to Cambridge Christians as members of the CICCU. The daily prayer meeting, fondly known as the DPM, was one. For as many lunch hours as they could manage, students would hurry to Holy Trinity Church in the center of Cambridge, slip through a door in the wall next to the church, and climb breathlessly up a flight of stairs and into Henry Martyn Hall. There they would spend twenty to twenty-five minutes in prayer. Those who led the meeting kept a book of specific prayer requests, updating it regularly as the prayers were answered.

Students also found spiritual stimulation and nourishment at a variety of Bible study, prayer, and mission meetings during the week in the individual colleges. On weekends, those who were interested converged on a large central meeting place for Bible exposition, usually with a well-known speaker. On Sunday evenings they could invite friends to an evangelistic sermon at Holy Trinity Church. Evangelistic missions were also organized regularly in the university, and there was open-air preaching in the summer when brave students went in trepidation to the market square or to the spacious green at the top of the town, Parker's Piece, to speak out in public about their faith. It is no wonder that committed CICCU members often found themselves scrambling for time.

David threw himself into all this activity with unalloyed enthusiasm. His father had been a CICCU member, as had many of the young men who had taught David at the camps and beach missions that had helped shape his life. Thus he came into the organization familiar with all it stood for and positive in his support. His involvement with CICCU was to be central to his life in Cambridge.

The CICCU's emphasis on personal devotion and public witness went back more than fifty years, to its establishment in 1877. At that time the idea of a student-led Christian organization had been "mildly shocking," in the words of Oliver Barclay in his book, *Whatever Happened to the Jesus Lane Lot?*: "It seemed to be taking religion too far and to have the mark of disrespect for ordained leadership and duly-constituted authority." The aim was to emphasize Scripture and the saving grace made available through Christ's death and resurrection in the prevailing climate of skepticism towards the Bible. In the increasingly liberal environment of the university, the CICCU often found itself having to fight to retain its stand.

Belonging to the CICCU when David came up to Cambridge in 1930 still required a willingness to be labeled a zealous extremist. Those who chose a broader view in this "age of enlightenment" joined the Student Christian Movement, aligned with the liberal thinking of the day. David took his stand in the CICCU with firm conviction.

David was so evidently committed and eager to be of service that before he finished his first year, the outgoing president, Norman Anderson, invited him onto the Executive Committee. With three new members each year, this six-member committee served as the CICCU's organizational arm. A larger General Committee pulled together one representative from each college.

If the ordinary student was busy, committee members were doubly so. The six on the Executive Committee carried a variety of responsibilities in turn. David began his duties by helping, at the end of his first year, to plan the activities for the following year. He still keeps on his desk a photo of his first "pre-terminal" weekend meeting, when he and the rest of the committee members met to pray and plan for the next school year.

At the start of any year the older CICCU members focused their attention on new students. In the various colleges they arranged "freshers squashes"—so called because Christian Union members and new students had to squash into a student's room for the occasion. Members would briefly introduce themselves, the CICCU, and the Lord Jesus Christ, and many students committed themselves to Christ at these get-togethers. The opening evangelistic sermon at Holy Trinity had a similar impact.

For both his second and third years, David lived in two spacious college rooms in Friar's Court. In his first year he had lived a little way out of Cambridge, necessitating quite a long cycle ride to get to his lectures. Timekeeping had become an art as a result. Perhaps this was the start of David's habit of packing as much as possible into each day and leaving himself just enough time to get from A to B. A flying gown as he rushed into "Hall" for the formal dinner each evening and breathless arrivals at any given meeting became the norm.

With rooms in the college, it was easier for David to invite friends in for breakfast or lunch. He enjoyed this opportunity to get to know people. "We would perhaps buy cold meat pies or sausage rolls or something like that," he recalls, remembering even more fondly the long conversations over coffee after supper.

Living in the college also made it possible to dash along the red-brick and oak-beamed cloisters of Queens' College to the Erasmus Room to read the daily paper. Erasmus had studied in this room 400 years before, and it was used in David's day as a common sitting room. It was a great satisfaction to Christian students to remember how Erasmus had stirred a revival of Christian commitment among their predecessors. Even today David is thrilled by the potential influence of a man willing to put his intellect and energy at God's disposal.

Almost six decades later David's time at Cambridge remains a highlight in his memory. During those three years he was active and fulfilled, happy to be stretched academically and to be taking responsibility in the CICCU, with the goal of China always ahead of him and drawing closer every day.

David's first job on the Executive Committee was to coordinate CICCU members' help to local churches. In responding to opportunities for willing students to speak at Sunday school or to lead youth events, David had to put the right people in the right places—good practice for a person who would later give a lot of energy to finding people for strategic roles in Christian leadership. Putting students into church ministries also strengthened the CICCU's role of bringing Christian leadership and talent into the church rather than running in competition to it. The Christian Union was not to be an end in itself.

For David a second job succeeded the first very quickly, that of Missionary Secretary. In this capacity he really came into his own.

Every Christian student who was at all involved in the CICCU would have been aware of the missionary tradition at the university. Painted in gilt letters all around the Henry Martyn Hall were the names of graduates who had died as missionaries overseas. Everyone knew also of the famous Cambridge Seven. In the 1880s these students had given up promising careers to volunteer for the then little-known China Inland Mission. Among them were the captain of the university cricket team, Charles T. Studd, and the stroke of the Cambridge rowing team, Stanley P. Smith. The example of these seven, with their burden for China, was a particular inspiration to David. One of the seven, Dixon E. Hoste, had become the General Director of the CIM, and David expected to meet him some day in China.

About the time the Cambridge Seven went to China, the Cambridge Volunteer Missionary Union was established for students committed to going out to the foreign mission field. This group, reviving in membership and activity after the lean war years, became David's main responsibility as missionary secretary. His task was not only to encourage students who were already thinking about going overseas to preach Christ, but to stir missionary concern generally throughout the CICCU. Once started on this course, David never swerved from it; he has preached Christians' responsibility to spread the gospel to earth's farthest corners all his life.

David's responsibilities also included organizing the missionary breakfast at Matthew's Cafe in town. This was a popular and established activity once or twice a term. The breakfast—the price of which was reduced when numbers topped a hundred—provided a forum for visiting missionary speakers such as Norman Grubb or Samuel Zwemer to challenge the students to face the needs of people without Christ. The students seemed to relish the rare opportunity to eat breakfast outside their colleges, indulging in some mild self-satisfaction at having got up early and produced the cost of the restaurant meal. The zest of the occasion concealed a serious intent which always produced new recruits for foreign missions.

Before long David inaugurated a further breakfast meeting for a smaller number, already committed to a missionary calling. This group met each week in one of their college rooms for about an hour to study together and pray.

It was probably through this involvement in the Cambridge Student Volunteer Missionary Movement that David first became familiar with the idea of the "evangelization of the world in this generation," the watchword of the original Student Volunteer Movement in the United States. Adopted by the British movement, this rallying cry was to become ingrained in David's thinking . He referred to it time and again in later years. The urgency of preaching the gospel where Christ was not known had already gripped David; that this unfinished task might be fulfilled in a generation if men and women took up the challenge gave him added fuel. He burned with a passion not only to fulfill his own calling to the mission field, but to urge others to do likewise.

Though David was but one of several CICCU missionary secretaries to stir into flame the embers of missionary concern after World War I, he brought to the role a quality all his own. Basil Atkinson—the assistant librarian in charge of intensely valuable Greek manuscripts in the university library and a greatly-loved advisor—is said to have considered David one of the best missionary secretaries of all. Douglas Johnson, first General Secretary of Inter-Varsity Fellowship of Evangelical Unions and long-standing champion and chronicler of the British evangelical student movement, notes in his book, *Contending for the Faith,* David's "transparent sincerity and almost ascetic devotion to the cause of Christ." Roger Allison, on the Executive Committee with David for a year, remembers his dedication in the service of Christ and his ability to inspire others. "In his speech and in his praying he always seemed to express the urgency of the King's business and his own deep and strong love for God." Another contemporary describes David at Cambridge as an intense activist. This intensity for the cause of Christ is so characteristic of David that, when describing him, friends and colleagues mention it almost before anything else.

Links made among Student Volunteer Movement members persist into these last decades of the twentieth century. David was speaking in a cathedral in Australia in recent years, for instance, when the dean of the cathedral produced his membership card with David's signature on it. And the Cambridge Prayer Fellowship formed in 1934 for 1933-34 graduates is still circulating its annual group letter to sixty individuals. F. F. Bruce, one of the best communicators among evangelical theologians, was among this group. A third of the original Fellowship have served on the mission field.

David claims to regret that he did not give more time and attention to academics when he was at Cambridge, but it is difficult to imagine him doing things differently were he to have his student days again. In *Whatever Happened to the Jesus Lane Lot?* Oliver Barclay observes: "Some CICCU leaders later lamented that they were so involved in the CICCU that they had little time to benefit from the cultural and intellectual riches of student life. But often they made these criticisms from a position of great responsibility in the church or the professions, which suggests that their CICCU involvement had in fact taught them some very important lessons and given them a disciplined use of time which stood them in better stead than the often lazy enjoyment of culture and society that was the attitude of most of their peers. It would have been good to do both; but if there was not time for both, it is not at all clear that they suffered any loss through choosing what they did."

In David's case, more important than any loss he might have suffered through his commitment to CICCU was the value of the experience for what he went on to do.

When David took his first major history exams—part 1 of the honors degree—at the end of his second year, he got through it, he says, because he could waffle. The exam allowed him to choose those questions which required a general response; he knew he would not have done well on those that demanded specific dates and minute detail.

By this time David was pursuing the possibility of studying theology in his final year instead of completing his history degree. Eventually this was agreed upon, and because he wanted time for his Christian commitments he elected to do a "theology special," which was less demanding in terms of time than the honors course.

The change brought him face to face with the rational and liberal methods of biblical criticism prevalent at the time. In the 1930s liberal theologians had such an upper hand that evangelical theological books could hardly be found anywhere. David found himself up against teaching which seemed to specialize in undermining faith in the Bible as the inspired Word of God. This attitude to Scripture, and the fact that the study of theology was little more than an academic exercise for many, so got him down that he could hardly wait to be done with "this wretched theology," as he dubbed it in a letter.

Nonetheless, having to discipline himself to look more closely at the liberal arguments did make David think through his own beliefs more thoroughly. This was important. In the end this process strengthened and clarified his own evangelical viewpoint.

Most important of all, the exposure to liberal theology developed in David a greater appreciation of the fundamental importance of Christ's resurrection. He saw it as the crux of the whole argument between liberals and evangelicals. While many liberal academics might be unsure whether the resurrection really happened, evangelicals see Christianity as nothing but a sham if God did not raise Christ from the dead. Without the resurrection, Christ would not have been who he said he was, the Son of God; his sacrifice would have bought no forgiveness for sin, no reconciliation with God. The very power and love of God would be in doubt. With St. Paul, David shuddered at the thought. If the resurrection did not happen, Paul told the Corinthians, "our preaching is useless and so is your faith. More than that, we are then found to be false witnesses" (1 Corinthians 15:14-15).

This issue of the reality of the resurrection became so important to David that in subsequent preaching he made it a central theme. He once even gently criticized one of his orthodox colleagues for not giving enough attention to the resurrection in a sermon. The man was hurt. He had after all been faithful to biblical truth, but in David's judgment he had not hammered home the crucial point, the resurrection as the key to a life of faith and to the whole existence of the church.

If the study of theology sifted David's thinking and solidified his evangelical convictions, so did the tussle within the CICCU over the matter of the Oxford Groups (which later became known as Moral Rearmament). These groups had first made their appearance in Cambridge in the 1920s, when their instigator, Frank Buchman, had spread his message of moral uprightness and purity of heart. It all seemed very salutary at the time, until it became apparent that Buchman and his devotees gave scant regard to the Bible in their meditative practices. The pattern of emptying one's mind in the morning in order to seek direction and then acting on whatever came into one's head seemed a strange and dangerous way for a person to go about living the Christian life. When the influence of the Oxford Groups was at its height at Cambridge in the

1920s, the CICCU had insisted on retaining a separate identity. But when David was at Cambridge, several people within CICCU who claimed to have been helped by Buchman's approach wanted the evangelicals to take a more tolerant stance towards the movement. They saw no reason why supporters of the Oxford Group should not be included even in CICCU leadership.

The discussion within the Executive Committee was long and involved. Yet the final conclusion was uncompromising. The Oxford Groups did not have the strong biblical basis the CICCU felt was vital. "We felt that if we aligned ourselves with the Oxford Groups," David explains, "we would in the end undermine the strong CICCU stand on biblical doctrine."

Being part of the Christian Union leadership and having to reassess and affirm its basis in such ways heightened the visibility of David's Christian allegiance on campus. His dean respected him as a "CICCU man" and on at least one occasion called David at short notice to come to add an evangelical perspective to a debate round his dinner table. Each time David rehearsed what he believed, his own grasp of it became firmer.

During vacations David plunged into the activities of CSSM houseparties and evangelistic missions, so his shaping and maturing as a Christian was an ongoing process even on the holidays. On a Cambridge mission to a number of different churches throughout Britain, for instance, David was assigned to preach in a high Anglo-Catholic church at a sung Eucharist— hardly an environment he was used to. Having grown up believing that such churches were void of lively spirituality and not at all receptive to the evangelical approach, David was nervous about what was in store. In reality, he was delighted to find not only a warm welcome but a number of people with a deep love for Christ. Instead of feeling distant from the people of this church as he feared, he felt a surprising affinity to many of them. The discovery was an eye-opener. So was the fact that he did not feel constrained by the formal atmosphere when it came to giving his message; he preached with a great sense of freedom and was encouraged by the responsiveness of the congregation.

At the end David was just a bit taken aback when a number of kind people insisted that he should take a strong dose of brandy for his cold. In his own conservative evangelical circles Christians rarely touched alcohol.

Another mission, this time in Bedford, is etched in David's memory both for the encouragement it gave him and for what he considered a painful failure. The encouragement came when a boy with whom David shared the gospel chose to follow Christ. The failure concerned another boy who had shown interest in Christ, but who held back from making a commitment. Although David wrote to him a few times, the two eventually lost touch. Later, when David learned that the boy had committed suicide, he chastised himself bitterly for not obeying God's prompting to continue to write.

This incident no doubt partly underlies David's care in later life to keep in touch with people by letter. He was also following after his father and mother, both assiduous correspondents; the family, though widely scattered, kept close to each other for decades by letter. But his pain at remembering the death of a disappointed boy would never again let him rest when he could find a moment to drop someone a line.

At Cambridge David circulated in an almost exclusively male environment. His close friends were, not surprisingly, members of the then all-male CICCU. Christian women had organized a separate organization in 1919, and not until 1948—long after David was gone—was there a formal amalgamation of this and the CICCU. Women were not admitted as full members of the university, eligible to obtain degrees, until the late forties.

Although David did get to know one of the presidents of the Cambridge Women's Intercollegiate Christian Union quite well, a woman who went on to spend the whole of her life in missionary service, he had few women friends. Florence Adeney was concerned that her son needed some assistance in the matter of relationships with the opposite sex, and on a couple of occasions took one of the Bedford girls with her when visiting David. No relationship blossomed. The woman in question guessed that David was quite unaware of her existence on those visits. David and his fellow students in the CICCU saw little need to be distracted by women. Marriage seemed a matter for the future. For the moment, they agreed, they should give their attention to more important matters.

In his final year David was invited to join the Executive Committee of the national evangelical student movement, the Inter-Varsity Fellowship of Evangelical Unions. The IVFEU aimed to serve and coordinate the growing number of university Christian Unions. In its infancy IVFEU was a missionary enterprise in itself. Not only were the original thirteen affiliated Christian Unions in need of growth in effectiveness, the organization was concerned about those universities that did not yet have an organized evangelical witness.

When recruiting its officers, the IVFEU drew heavily from the pool of experience in established Christian Unions. A number of CICCU graduates had furthered its programs sacrificially. David's case was unusual because he was still an undergraduate when IVFEU recruited his help as Missionary Secretary to further missionary awareness among university Christians unions.

IVFEU's first Missionary Secretary had urged the appointment of missionary representatives in every Christian Union. His successor made sure information flowed to each group from graduates who were already overseas. David took things one step further. "As soon as he was appointed," writes Douglas Johnson in his history of Inter-Varsity, "he began to agitate for a more definite place in the central organization for missionary activities." Chris Maddox, who succeeded David as Missionary Secretary for both the CICCU and the IVFEU, and who was later to be a doctor in the same mission, says, "One of David's dreams had been to extend to the other university Christian Unions the concept of the Cambridge Volunteer Union, whose members pledged themselves to prepare for a missionary calling." He adds, "David bequeathed this dream to me." In the tradition of the Student Volunteer Movement, with its motto "the evangelization of the world in this generation," David wanted to revive a nationwide concern for mission. In one of his first IVFEU meetings he expressed his desire to link up missionary volunteers in the different universities.

The time was ripe. Before the annual IVFEU conference at Eastertime in 1933, David gathered all the missionary secretaries of the various Christian Unions. Together they drew up a proposal to form a special overseas missionary group under the title "The Inter-Varsity Missionary Fellowship." Members were to be those seriously planning to serve overseas, willing to work for mutual support, to pray and to learn, but also to alert others to the importance of overseas mission.

The proposal was accepted.

For students who joined the Fellowship—150 of them by July 1934, a year after David left Cambridge—the level of commitment to overseas mission was extraordinarily high. The "Declaration of Membership" expressed a single-minded purpose: "This declaration is more than a mere expression of willingness or desire to become a foreign missionary. It is a statement of a definite life-purpose formed under the direction of God. The purpose of those who sign this declaration is by God's grace to spend their lives as foreign missionaries. Towards this end they will shape their plans; they will steadily set themselves to prepare for this great work; they will do all in their power to remove the obstacles which may stand in the way of their going; and in due time they will make the necessary arrangements to go out. Only the clear leading of God will prevent their going to the foreign field."

David was about to leave for China a year later when the matter came up as to whether IVMF should adopt a watchword. Generally agreed to be a good idea, the watchword proposed was "Evangelize to a finish, to bring back the King." The suggested wording was based on a combination of Matthew 24:14: "And this gospel of the kingdom will be preached in the whole world as a testimony to all nations, and then the end come," and 2 Samuel 19:10: "So why do you say nothing about bringing the king back?"

These very verses had come together for David while he was on a Mediterranean tour with his mother and brother Harold during the summer immediately after his graduation from Cambridge. On a Sunday morning during their Palestine visit he was having his "quiet time" sitting in a secluded spot on the Mount of Olives. Turning to the passage in 2 Samuel, he read how King David fled from Jerusalem to the Mount of Olives after his son Absalom had turned the hearts of the people against him. The question, "So why do you say nothing about bringing the king back?" was posed when the people hesitated to bring the rightful ruler back after the rebellious Absalom's death. *It is no longer King David for whom Jersualem waits,* thought David, *but King Jesus.* He had a clear view across the Kidron Valley to Jerusalem's Golden Gate, the gate through which the Jews believed the Messiah would come, and then he turned to Psalm 24:7—"Lift up your heads, O you Gates; be lifted up, you ancient doors, that the King of glory may come in." As he pondered these prophetic words and looked across at the the Golden Gate, David felt the certainty of Christ's return as never before. Surely, he thought, Jesus' words in Matthew 24:14 implied that the "gospel of the kingdom" had to be preached in all the world before it could happen! The idea infused him with a renewed sense of urgency. He was impatient to get on with the job.

The proposed watchword for IVMF related so closely for David to the verses that had been part of his experience in Palestine, that each illumined the other. He knew without a doubt where his sights should be: "Evangelize to a finish, to bring back the King."

The Mediterranean trip left David with other significant impressions. Off the coast of Greece he caught sight of a ruin topped by a cross outlined against the sky. *The cross of Christ is the reason for everything I'm doing,* he thought. He felt the same years later when he saw another cross on a ruin in Macao off China's coast, the one that inspired the hymn line, "In the cross of Christ I glory, towering o'er the wrecks of time."

David had been sure that God had called him to serve in China before he went to Cambridge; by the time he left, that certainty was stronger than ever. China had been so much a part of his thinking and conversation that he had inspired at least one other student at Cambridge, Chris Maddox, to take up the challenge of China's millions. And now David was into the last stretch of his preparation to go. All that remained was his missionary training at the China Inland Mission headquarters in London. So sure was he of the outcome of his time at Newington Green that he could almost smell the salt air aboard the ship that would take him to China—at last.

6

The Colony All Over Again

For David the China Inland Mission headquarters at Newington Green in north London was familiar ground. The motto "Have Faith in God" over the main entrance struck the right chord with him as he walked under it to begin a year's candidate training school.

It was 1933, and the Great Depression was still biting. In the U.S., President Franklin Roosevelt, inaugurated in January, had begun his fight to spark economic recovery. In Russia people were starving. Hitler, recently appointed Chancellor in Germany, was whipping up Nazi fervor and had begun transporting Jews to death camps. Communism was gaining ground in China. It was hardly a secure world.

The China Inland Mission was gearing up to spread the knowledge of the gospel further into China's vastness. In China itself, more than two hundred new missionaries were sharpening their language skills to spread the knowledge of the gospel, particularly in inland provinces. David yearned to be among their ranks.

At Newington Green, his ideals had to modify themselves to reality. His last three years had been stimulating and full, but now, with his belongings stashed in the comfortable but somewhat spartan room assigned him at the CIM's men's training home, he felt the reigns tighten. "Lights out at ten" meant lights out at ten; Roland Hogben knocked on doors to make sure.

In many ways it was the Colony all over again. Not as rough around the edges, perhaps, but again he had to learn to live alongside people from different cultural backgrounds in a regimented lifestyle. Gone was the freedom of Cambridge. It was going to be a long year.

The precise and authoritative teaching of Roland Hogben took some getting used to. "Anyone have a Scofield Bible?" Hogben asked early in his classes. "Burn it!" he said as his eyes swept the room. Though hardly meaning his order to be taken literally, he made his point clear: during their time at Newington Green the candidates were to read their Bibles without notes so that they could learn to hear God directly through his Word.

David learned principles for a lifetime from Roland Hogben. The candidates had to discipline themselves to express the subject of any talk or sermon in one word, then in one sentence. Not only did David discover more about preaching, but he learned how to tackle subjects as a teacher. Later he drew on Roland Hogben's example when teaching homiletics.

Before many weeks, David's regard for the head of the training school had grown to one of respect and love. Years later, after his mentor had been killed in an accident in China, David edited a book on prayer Hogben had written. One sentence from that book still shapes David's life: "Prayer is the interruption of human ambition."

To satisfy CIM leaders and council about their Christian standpoint, candidates did not merely sign a prepared doctrinal statement. They had to express their views on essential doctrines in their own words. David's handwritten answers show maturity and clarity. "The Bible is, and not merely contains, God's Word to man," he wrote on the subject of Scripture. "Mistakes in the translations and minor errors in the text as a result of copying do not make any material difference to the revelation as a whole. The Bible contains all that is necessary for salvation and is *absolutely* trustworthy in *every* part." On the atonement: "Christ came to give his life a ransom for many. God saw that natural man was in an utterly hopeless position, bound to pay the penalty of sin, but in his wonderful love and mercy he provided a remedy. The Lord Jesus, who was God manifest in the flesh, took upon himself our nature and bore our sins in his own body on the tree. Because he shed his blood for all, those who put their faith in him are brought into perfect oneness with God and can never be condemned." Any candidate who was vague in his responses faced grilling before the council. Not David.

One particular memory stands out for David from his time at the China Inland Mission training school. During the Keswick Convention he was the only new recruit to participate from the platform among an array of well-known missionary speakers. Waiting to stand up to tell everyone about his call to China as the huge tent filled to capacity, David was a bundle of nerves. Behind him sat his old friend Bishop Taylor Smith, who had inspired David many times through his sermons at Monkton Combe and his teaching on CSSM holidays. The bishop, aware of David's trepidation, pulled a scrap of paper from his pocket and scribbled a message of encouragement: "In quietness (within) and trust (in him) is your strength" (Isaiah 30:15). The note was just what the nervous young man needed. Not only did David take courage from the annotated Bible verse at the time, but he tucked it away in his heart for the future.

The year at the CIM training school was one of fine-tuning. By the time David was ready to leave for China he had set himself a three-fold objective: to *know* Christ, to *please* Christ, and to *preach* Christ. Drawn from the letters of the Apostle Paul, the words became the new recruit's life motto. The first objective, to know Christ, was inspired by what Paul wrote in Philippians 3:10—"I want to know Christ and the power of his resurrection and the fellowship of sharing in his sufferings, becoming like him in his death." The second, to please Christ, was based on 2 Corinthians 5:9—"So we make it our goal to please him, whether we are at home in the body or away from it." And the third was singled out for David's specific encouragement by the CIM Home Director, W. H. Aldis, and written personally on his membership card: "God, who set me apart from birth and called me by his grace, was pleased to reveal his Son in me so that I might preach him," taken from Galatians 1:15-16. No matter how far David went towards achieving these goals in subsequent years, he felt he could always go further. Almost sixty years later they remain goals to strive for.

In the spring of 1934, at the age of twenty-two, the "poor risk" heard the words of welcome into the China Inland Mission. David felt unsure of himself as he looked ahead to China, but very sure of the God who had called him.

7

To China at Last!

It was September 28, 1934. As David opened his eyes that chill Friday morning in his bedroom at home in Bushmead Avenue, he knew that seven years would pass before he would sleep in his own bed again. The length of time was hard to grasp. He would be thirty before he came back to Bedford—that is, if he made it back at all.

Today he would actually sail for China.

A photo still exists of the send-off at Bedford Station. David stands tall near the back, his smile wide with expectation. His mother, attractive in her early fifties, has a brave look on her face. Erect and lean, his father is on leave from Romania. David's younger brother Harold is there too, on vacation from Cambridge. Missing are Bernard and Ronald, already away at Monkton Combe School. Twenty or so from Russell Park Baptist Church, including Pastor Ferguson, cluster around to record their farewell to the church's first missionary for many years. They are proud of David, many of them grateful for his influence in their lives.

In the crowd that day was Ruth Blott. Now Mrs. Ruth McIver, she remembers the impact of David's testimony and ministry in the church and in her own family. Her sister Ranah yielded her life to go to the mission field after hearing David speak on the missionary call. Ranah's twin, Joyce, was converted through one of his sermons. Another sister—there were nine altogether in the Blott family—was the next missionary to go out from Russell Park Baptist, also to China. Here was early evidence of David's gift of touching individual lives in simple, but significant, life-changing ways.

With wheels squealing and steam belching, the train rumbled to a stop, its engine pulling beyond the waiting Bedford Station crowd and its carriages stretching impressively behind. The Russell Park group huddled around to pray for David, afterwards lifting their heads to sing, "God be with you till we meet again." Then strong arms lifted David's several tin-lined boxes on to the train bound for London, from where David and his family would travel to the docks in Southhampton. Soon the travelers and luggage were aboard, and an emotional David was waving from a window. At last he was truly on his way to China.

At the docks loomed the massive P&O liner *Carthage,* loading passengers and cargo. The sight of it caught David in the pit of his stomach. Was it excitement? Anticipation? The finality of the moment? He was ready for China, at least so far as he could imagine. He expected to be a missionary all his life; God had called him. But, inside, the thought of saying good-bye to his mother and father and to Harold was wrenching him inside. Today he was beginning to pay the price of choosing to give his life for China.

Later, with his boxes stashed in the tiny stateroom below, David stood at the railing with other passengers as tugboats pulled the giant ship away from the dock. His eyes were fixed on his mother, her brown hair limp in the salt air, and on his father, stiffly at her side. And dear Harold, the brother he had been closest to—he'd be a medical doctor, probably, by the time they'd see each other again. David smiled to hide the tears and waved. His family did the same. With painful slowness the distance widened. The deep, resonant blast of the ship's horn said farewell to the tugs, and the vibration of huge steam-driven turbines indicated that the liner was heading out under her own power. There was a definite joy in obedience, but David could hardly imagine a harder moment.

A dozen fellow missionaries, together with other passengers kept David company in second class, and the weeks aboard ship were full of fun and interest. He joined in the deck games, enjoyed Bible studies and hymn-singing, marveled at flying fish and dolphins, and watched the changing colors of the sea, in turn gray, blue, and turquoise. Food was good, when rough seas did not destroy appetites.

In groups, the travelers explored the British colonial ports of Gibraltar, Port Said, Suez, Colombo, Penang, Singapore, Hong Kong. As they watched monkeys in botanical gardens, browsed through the shops, and otherwise played the part of tourists, David and his companions gave little thought to the danger of exhibiting pride as part of an "empire on which the sun never set." Ashamed now at the thought of being guilty of imperialistic attitudes, David says, "I was a child of my times."

In Hong Kong David caught his first glimpse, across the New Territories, of the China mainland. On the beach there he also met Donald Gray Barnhouse, well-known evangelical preacher and pastor of Philadelphia's Tenth Presbyterian Church. Years later, David would preach on several occasions in that historic church.

Between Hong Kong and Shanghai, David celebrated his twenty-third birthday. Fellow missionaries aboard ship chose an amusing way to mark the occasion. They had a special breakfast menu printed, featuring "Eggs 1911 Model" and "Fish à la 'Confirmed' Baptist." The eggs and fish, served with a flourish, were raw!

A few days later, more than five weeks after leaving Southhampton, the S. S. *Carthage* slipped up the deep, broad mouth of the Huang Po River. As the ship edged to her moorings in the Shanghai harbor, the new missionaries lined her railings and watched as the water turned ever more murky. In the brown expanse sampans, sailing junks, river steamers, and passenger liners vied for space. From their high perch the missionaries looked down at the variety of craft clustered below, amazed at pajama-clad mothers handling rigging or hanging out washing with babies tied on their backs, the youngsters' heads bobbing like those of rag dolls; at families eating on deck, with even small children managing chopsticks; at fishermen preparing nets and traps. The scene changed by the moment. Only the city in the distance looked gray and sullen.

Eighty-one years earlier the sailing ship *Dumphries* had brought Hudson Taylor to the same port for his first sight of China. He was eventually to set up the China Inland Mission headquarters in the city. The old colonial-style building on Sinza Road was still the hub of the mission, and the new workers' first stop.

At Sinza Road David met Dixon Edward Hoste, one of the Cambridge Seven he had admired. Hoste had succeeded Hudson Taylor as General Director of the China Inland Mission almost thirty years before. "Even in old age," David recalled, "Hoste's bearing was upright, his mind keen. He was a great man of prayer and seemed to have insight into the dangers that lay ahead."

"Beware of national pride," Hoste advised David. "It makes itself known like a man who has been eating garlic."

The words stung David. Had he given himself away in telling Hoste of his activities as Missionary Secretary of the Cambridge Christian Union and the houseparty he had led in Wales just before setting sail for China? Perhaps he was already guilty of exhibiting national pride. True, he had set his sights on serving God in China believing he had a lot to offer. Had he not given up family and any thought of an alternative career to devote himself to the mission field? But what did he have that God had not given? He would take Hoste's warning to heart.

David thought back to an uncomfortable experience he had had on the journey from England. During the ship's stop in Colombo, he had visited a missionary from a very humble home in Bedford. A friend had given David the man's address. With his expectations of simple missionary life, David was shocked to discover the man living in a luxurious bungalow and, while David watched, insisting that his servants pull the huge *punkas* to fan him.

Later, David discovered that this man was not alone in taking a superior attitude towards the people he was supposed to be serving. There was a tendency among some missionaries to expect the Chinese to respect what the foreigners considered their special status. David felt the injustice of this keenly. What barriers it produced! Prompted by Hoste and his own observations, David was determined to live among the local people rather than to isolate himself from them in the walled compounds that traditionally housed foreigners.

From Shanghai the new missionaries traveled by river steamer inland to Anqing, capital of Anhui Province, to begin six months of intensive study. During the three day journey, their eyes took in the kaleidoscope of Chinese life along the banks of the Yangzte River. All the loading and unloading of merchandise at the docks along the way provided an endless variety of bustling activity on this great waterway dividing North and South China.

From the moment they had arrived in China, they had been confronted by an extraordinary combination of smells in the air: the pungency of old vegetables and open sewers, hot fat used constantly in Chinese cooking, a sweet, dusty hint of incense. The odor was impossible to pin down exactly, but was so typical that, once everyone had remarked on it, there was nothing to do but to get used to it. It was just as noticeable on the winds circulating over the river.

At Anqing, in the shadow of a tall, slender pagoda towering high above the city wall, the passengers disembarked via a narrow plank that bounced disconcertingly. Straw-sandalled coolies quickly appropriated their belongings and, balancing them expertly from bamboo poles across their shoulders, scrambled up the riverbank in the direction of the language school.

As the party wound its way through the narrow city streets, many curious faces followed its progress. Peddlers plied their trade at roadsides, shouting hoarsely over the bowed backs of the rickshaw pullers and the blue-gowned crowd going about its business. Open-fronted shops displayed a mesmeric and unfamiliar variety of goods. Wooden signs indicated different businesses with swirls of Chinese characters. Occasional open doors revealed sparsely furnished interiors, stone walls, and usually straw matting covering the floors. David hated the stares and wished he could communicate with the people. But he was in China, and the thrill of it pumped adrenalin into his veins.

With a dozen others from no less than seven different countries, David plowed into language learning with an urgency born of impatience to get on with his job. He was used to talking, to reaching out, to accomplishing things. Being so handicapped with the language was frustrating. It was like being a baby again.

Mr. Yen, the chief language teacher, was an unforgettable character, who infused meaning into the Chinese language without a word of English being spoken. He was a master of sign language and exaggerated gesture. Mr. Yen gave David the Chinese name *Ai De-li*, the Chinese equivalent of the sound of his English name. It meant "receive the truth."

Learning vocabulary was not a problem for David, but he found the complex tones almost impossible. Distinguishing them when listening was bad enough, and reproducing them was another matter altogether. It was a good thing he was learning Mandarin and not Cantonese, he was told; then he would really be in trouble!

Brisk walks in the winter cold and evenings of relaxation together broke the tedium of memorizing vocabulary and practicing unfamiliar sounds. One fun night went sour, David remembers, when one of the English party did a take off of Adolph Hitler, offending a German in the group. In retrospect, the World War was very close.

The language students were just beginning to adjust to their new surroundings and to each other when they received some shattering news. Communist troops had publicly beheaded two colleagues, John and Betty Stam, and had also killed a protesting Chinese Christian. The Stams' bodies had been left where they fell—on a little hill outside the village of Miaoxiou, just a few miles from where they lived in Qingdeh and not far from the language school. A Chinese Christian had provided coffins and tried to sew their severed heads back in place. John and Betty had only just begun their ministry in Qingdeh. Members of the "Two Hundred" recruited after the political riots and unrest of 1927, they were just one step ahead of the current language students.

As details followed, the new recruits were touched by the report of the calmness and trust the Stams showed in facing death by sword. They were awed too at the miracle of the survival of the Stams' baby girl, saved by the brave intervention of a Chinese evangelist. The tragedy shook them to the core and drove them to their knees before God. It became a catalyst to renewed spiritual dedication as each one sought the courage to face up to God's call to the mission field, even if it might be "unto death."

But the murder raised another issue, uncomfortable and unfamiliar, when Western gunboats responded by appearing inland on the Yangtze River. Even though the missionaries had not asked for protection, the presence of Western warships nearby meant they could not avoid the stigma of being associated with imperialist powers. The new workers longed to be identified with the land of their adoption, but they now saw that the Chinese linked them with the imperialist policies that had caused such heartache in China. When the British won the advantage in the iniquitous opium wars, they forged unequal treaties and opened ports for debilitating opium and for wider trade the Chinese did not want, and also gained for themselves the prize of Hong Kong. The treaty ports benefited missionaries as much as anyone else, giving them access into China. Hostility to the invaders was the inevitable result. And since the growing Communist Party was vehemently anti-Christian, attacks such as that against the Stams were bound to happen.

All of this was a staggering realization for the new missionary recruits. When they set sail to fulfill their call from God to minister in China, they had been barely aware of the political turmoil in the country in which they were now guests. The CIM, underestimating the threat of Communism, had not given politics a high priority in its training of missionaries. That was about to change, as it was becoming clear that Mao Zedong was consolidating his strength. Just three months before the *Carthage* docked in Shanghai, Mao and his followers had begun their escape from the encircling Nationalist armies under Chiang Kai-shek and had set out on the historic Long March to Northwest China. That march was still under way. 10,000 men and women would survive the 6,000-mile, 370-day trek.

Meanwhile the new missionaries were forbidden to walk outside the city gates. Until then David had enjoyed walking in the countryside, striding along rice fields and meeting country people.

Another crisis followed almost immediately. Pirates captured the ship carrying CIM children on vacation from Chefoo School. British planes searched coastal waters for the ship in vain, as its captors had disguised the ship with new paint and changed the name on the bow. Though the missionary children were found unharmed after the pirates abandoned ship, such news on top of the Stams' murder could do little but worry everyone at home. David thought anxiously of his mother.

His first months in China were hardly encouraging.

8

Eating Bitterness

W elcome to Henan!" Henry Guinness ran forward to greet David as he emerged from the coal-fueled train onto the platform in Luohe, noisy and busy with milling crowds. "I hope your journey was all right."

David clasped Henry's proffered hand warmly, glad to have reached Luohe after twelve hours on the train and more than a day's travel by river steamer from Anqing. Unable to say much to fellow travelers and awed by the vast unfamiliarity of China, he had felt very much alone.

It was the spring of 1935. The city of Hiangcheng, which was to be David's base for language consolidation and rural church work, was another forty miles by road. Henry Guinness, working in the Hiangcheng area, had cycled the distance to Luohe to accompany David back to the city.

As instructed, David had brought a bicycle with him from Anqing. Besides walking, alternative modes of transport were confined to ox cart, mule, or hand-drawn cart, so a bicycle was a relatively fast way to get around. It was almost indispensable for the rural church worker. Once David's luggage was loaded onto a wooden wheelbarrow to be taken independently to Hiangcheng, the new recruit swung onto his bike with the ease acquired during his Cambridge years when he had gone everywhere by bike. But cycling in China was quite a different matter.

"Stay in the wheelbarrow rut" advised Henry. "It's much easier that way."

Outside the narrow rut worn by the single wheels of heavy barrows the dirt road was hopelessly uneven. "Mules," shouted Henry over his shoulder as he cycled on ahead of David. "They churn up the mud when it's wet."

The two men began their journey about 7:00 A.M., and while the morning remained cool they made good progress. Despite the jolting and shaking, David managed to keep the bike in the wheelbarrow groove, but he was only barely keeping up with the more experienced Henry. Aware that most of the time they were cycling alongside fields of wheat, David saw little else of the country around him as he dared not to take his eyes off the road. Steering was incredibly hard work, the pace unrelenting.

"How about a dip in the river?" Henry's voice broke into David's concentration. "We can cool down a bit."

"That's a very good idea," said David mildly, trying not to betray how relieved he was at the suggestion, for as the sun grew hotter, he had begun to feel dizzy.

"We'll have to push the bikes," Henry said. "It's probably about a third of a mile over there," and he jumped off his bike to lead the way.

The water of the Ru River, flowing towards the Yangtze, was the color of milky tea. The two men waded into it gratefully and soaked their hot, sweaty bodies. When they got out, David was unsteady on his feet, and Henry wondered whether the new recruit could manage the remaining distance to Hiangcheng that day. His concern was well-founded, for as soon as David got back onto his bike, he fainted, slumping, bike and all, to the ground.

"Don't tell anyone," David said miserably to Henry once he had been revived by a basin full of river water. "They'll send me home if they think I'm not strong enough."

Only when the sun began to go down was David fit enough to continue. By then there was no question of trying to get beyond the nearest walled market town. Henry knew better than to stop elsewhere and risk attack from roving bands of brigands, the scourge of rural Henan.

When the two reached the church in the town, David could do nothing except drop exhausted onto the single camp bed kept for missionaries who came to preach at the church and to teach in the surrounding areas. He slept straight away, lying flat and with his arms outstretched. Henry exchanged looks with his Christian friends. *How in the world was this young man going to survive being a missionary?*

By the next day David had recovered. The two men resumed their journey early and completed it without further difficulty. Henry said nothing about what had held them up.

Henan, in the southern part of North China, was the first of nine interior provinces to be visited by a missionary. M. Henry Taylor took two long journeys into Henan in 1875, preaching and distributing Scriptures. When David arrived sixty years later, in 1935, the China Inland Mission had established several mission stations, traditionally comprised of a church, a school, and accommodation for both the missionaries and the Chinese who worked with them. With these stations as their base, workers fanned out in the ongoing task of preaching, starting churches, and teaching new believers.

Henan, roughly 450 miles from north to south and from east to west, was poor and thickly populated. "Extremes of temperature and an unreliable rainfall inescapably endured by the people produced strong men inured to hardship, conservative and anti-foreign in some areas, but intelligent, reliable, friendly and welcoming in other places," summarized A. J. Broomhall in *Hudson Taylor in the Open Century,* describing what early missionaries faced. David met little but friendliness in 1935, though time hadn't changed the harshness of the climate and brigandry increased when prolonged drought created a desperate bid for food. Sometimes drought wasn't the problem, but too much rain. When it poured day after day in the north of Henan, the Yellow River—so notorious as to be called "China's Sorrow"—would burst its banks and flood mile upon mile of land, leaving thousands homeless and without livelihood. The people of Henan "ate bitterness" at such times and instability was the result.

During his early months in Henan David did not venture far from the mission station in Hiangcheng. He divided his time between the grueling task of continuing to learn Chinese, with six language exams looming over the next two or three years, and making tentative efforts to use what he learned to preach to local villagers. Still he struggled with the rising, falling, curving, and flat tones of the language.

He was not alone in his frustration. Ray Frame, another young missionary at Hiangcheng just ahead of David, on reaching a point of utter exasperation in his language study, had thrown one of his books onto the floor and jumped on it, claiming God's promise to Joshua, "I will give you every place where you set your foot!" David knew how Ray felt. He also knew that there had been no miraculous transmission of the contents of the book to this young man's memory. Interestingly, David notes today, in time Ray Frame went on to become not only a language instructor but also one of the most able Chinese speakers in the CIM.

Missionaries to China had to learn a whole new form of communication in addition to the language itself. The villagers thought in pictures rather than in concepts; ideas were lost on them unless illustrated by a story or a situation familiar to them. Largely illiterate, they responded best to simple, but arresting language—story-telling, Chinese proverbs, traditional phrases. These had to form the basis of any preaching if it was to be effective. The common proverb, "If you have no food, ask the old man in the heavens," for instance, provided a natural opening to explain about the true provider. Learning these proverbs and traditions on top of everything else drained David more than he realized.

At this crucial early stage in David's development as a missionary God gave him a precious gift—his language teacher, Wang Yi-Zhai. This man became David's fellow worker and close friend. Later, after David was married, Wang became the evangelist in the church where the Adeneys lived and cycled many hundreds of miles with David over the dusty roads of Henan. "Much of my ability to speak and understand the people," says David, "came from my fellowship with him." Close friendship with national believers, David believes unto this day, is one of the first-term missionary's greatest needs.

Wang Yi-Zhai was not only a good language teacher, but an experienced evangelist. When he and David took preaching trips into the country, David always spoke first so that Wang could subsequently enlighten the puzzled villagers as necessary. Despite the progress the newcomer was making with his Chinese, he still made mistakes. Discovering too late that the word for sin could also mean fate, he was crestfallen to find out that a woman he thought was lamenting her sinfulness was in fact complaining of an unfortunate circumstance in her life. So that was why someone else had been confused when he tried to explain that telling a lie was a sin!

Although David saw the funny side of his blunders, he was humiliated to be so tongue-tied and appear so ignorant in front of the Chinese. He began to feel dispirited, even depressed. He wondered sometimes whether he should have stayed home. At least there he had contributed something useful. His work with Inter-Varsity and at the summer camps now appeared quite significant, certainly more so than anything he had so far managed in China. Would he ever achieve so much again? He began to doubt it.

On top of this bleak sense of uselessness, David was ashamed at the very unspiritual thoughts going through his head. He had expected, once he reached the mission field, to be above thoughts of greed and lust. The Missionary Training Colony and his father had warned him that missionaries had to contend with serious temptations, but the reality was difficult to face. It was sobering to realize that as a missionary he was not a spiritual giant doing wonderful things for the kingdom of God. Not only was he just as ordinary and prone to unholiness as he had ever been, it seemed that he was weaker. David's confidence was completely sapped.

On a mission prayer day David was so low that he could not even pray with his fellow-missionaries. Instead he took himself off for a walk in the hills. He did not know where to turn for help except to the Bible, though at the time he could not summon much hope even in that. In an effort of will he sat down and, with the wind wanting to turn the pages too quickly, read through the Gospel of John. As he immersed himself in Scripture, God's Word poured in its strength as if by transfusion, feeding faith in a sure and indefinable way.

David continued to sit quietly, thinking. Though not yet ready to return to his fellow missionaries, he was deeply thankful for the respite he felt. At that point, he doesn't know why, he remembered a passage: "Faith comes from hearing the message, and the message is heard through the word of Christ" (Romans 10:17), words he had often used when urging others to faith. He shook his head that he had failed to apply such truth to his own life.

Having discovered in such a personal, direct way that God's Word nurtures faith, David never forgot it again. That day in the hills was a milestone, a watershed. From that day forward, in times of difficulty he would turn more readily to Scripture.

Another of David's courses in God's "university of the wilderness" came through David Yang Shaotang, a Chinese teacher and evangelist who spoke at a CIM church leaders conference in Henan in the summer of 1936.

Impressed by the authority and spiritual power of this man's ministry, the young missionary was interested to learn that Pastor Yang ran a training seminar for young evangelists called the *Ling Gong Tuan,* or "Spiritual Work Team," in the neighboring province of Shanxi. Could he join in? he wondered. If anyone could help equip him to be a more effective minister to the Chinese people, surely it was David Yang.

It struck David how similar in concept the Spiritual Work Team was to the Missionary Training Colony in England. Teacher and pupils lived in a simple community life, spending half their time studying the Bible, praying, and learning about Christian ministry, and the other half among the churches, evangelizing and teaching. As David was not the first missionary to be attracted to the *Ling Gong Tuan,* and since anyone was welcome to join in, CIM leaders readily granted him permission to spend a few weeks under David Yang's tutelage.

A graduate of the North China Theological College, David Yang Shaotang had begun his ministry in rural churches in Shanxi, working with a number of CIM missionaries who had been instrumental in starting the churches. At that time the CIM was still implementing a long-standing policy of giving financial support to the churches and their Chinese pastors. "We were living at the end of the missionary era," David Adeney remembers. "Our first superintendent was one of the pioneers. He had traveled thirty years earlier with Hudson Taylor on the CIM founder's last journey in Henan just before he died. In those days the older generation of missionaries were accustomed to the mandarin style of missionary work, employing Chinese workers whom they supervised." That policy had changed in 1928 after the anti-foreign riots of the mid-1920s.

When the China Inland Mission, in a move toward "indigenizing" the churches, began gradually withdrawing financial support for pastors and evangelists (though retaining it for teachers in schools and hospital workers), some of the Chinese Christians felt betrayed and many withdrew their allegiance. For a while, therefore, the number of strong Christian pastors teaching the churches was very small. David Yang started his Spiritual Work Team to rectify this situation.

David Yang's example alone taught David Adeney a great deal. One day, for instance, when the teacher asked David to come to his room to pray with him, he arrived to find his mentor stretched out upon the mud floor of his simple room, crying out to God, confessing his own weakness and sinfulness and asking for cleansing and the filling of the Holy Spirit. As Pastor Yang was already a man whose life was characterized by humility and Christlikeness, David was amazed to see him humbling himself before God in this way. It made an indelible impression on him. "I realized," David says today, "that however greatly a man might be used in the service of the Lord Jesus, he is nevertheless constantly in need of repentance and of waiting upon God."

It was an important lesson for a young missionary striving to do his best for the Master, a lesson that became integrated into his life like a skein of color in a tapestry. He was already sensitive to the personal demands of a life devoted to Christ. Already he was aware of his shortfalls. Now he saw that spiritual strength did not lie in attaining some kind of victory over human weakness and failures. Dependence on God, despite human frailty, and perhaps because of it, was much more important.

David's understanding of this principle deepened as he went through life, and led to an increasing, not decreasing, awareness of his weakness and sinfulness. This was not only because he knew sin was offensive to his Lord, but because he realized the essence of sin—self-sufficiency— got in the way of that dependent relationship which he saw as so vital. Such an awareness led in turn to a greater hunger to draw close to God.

This tension between his own insufficiency and God's great sufficiency was to mark David's life unmistakably. The sense of his own sinfulness— his awareness of human frailty—made him unsure about himself, mistrusting of his deeper motives, abject about his imperfections as God's servant. Conversely, his reliance on God gave him a rocklike strength, an assurance that, no matter how hopeless he felt in himself, God could do all that was needed. Such confidence in God meant that he hung on in situations that others would have given up on. It gave him a tenacity, a determination to see things through to the end no matter how difficult they were or how much heartache they might cause him.

For much of his life David has worked at getting himself out of the picture and letting God in. He has been hard on himself in the process, sometimes hard on others too. But as a result he has seen God at work despite himself. He has never forgotten the picture of David Yang on his face before God.

In training the young men who joined his team, David Yang Shaotang emphasized the importance of the fullness of God. He wanted his pupils to learn how to draw fully on God's resources for effectiveness and power in ministry, and he challenged David specifically to seek for a deeper understanding of the Spirit's work and gifts in his life. As the young Westerner did so, through prayer and studying Scripture—especially the passage in Ephesians 3:19 where Paul talks about being filled with "all the fullness of God"—David became more joyfully aware of God's presence within him. As he put it, "I entered into the joy of the Holy Spirit and came into something of an understanding of his fullness, which I had never known before."

David had prayed for the filling of the Spirit before, at Cambridge. The controversy surrounding the gift of tongues had brought him to his knees to ask God for whatever gift he might need to fulfill his calling. David did not at that time receive the gift of tongues, but did come away with a deep assurance that God had answered his prayer and would go on answering it as he made himself available for service. Now that assurance was confirmed in even fuller measure and with joy. This was the encouragement he needed. He returned to rural church work in Henan with new vigor.

Though David can no longer remember exactly at what point in his early years in China he met the famous evangelist, John Sung, he has never forgotten the experience. Dr. Sung was holding a mission at Xuchang, where the Augustana Lutherans had a large church and school. David stayed with the evangelist in the home of a Lutheran missionary.

"John Sung's unique type of preaching always attracted large crowds," recalls David. "He made good use of pictures and object lessons. I remember his play on Chinese words, *fah tsai* (to produce riches or get rich) and *fah guan tsai* (to end up in a coffin). From a model coffin he drew out all kinds of sins, emphasizing that 'the wages of sin is death.'"

What shocked David was Dr. Sung's reaction if anyone thanked him for his message. The man would not only get angry, but for hours would refuse to speak to the one who had complimented him. The glory belonged to God and not to him.

John Sung could not fail to impress David deeply. Won to Christ while studying for his Ph.D. in Ohio through a family who befriended him, he had turned his back on his field of science and dedicated his life to preaching the gospel throughout China and Southeast Asia. In years to come David would meet people in places as far apart as Northwest China and Singapore whom Dr. Sung had challenged to join evangelistic bands and who as a result spent a lifetime in Christian service.

Visiting "outstations," where there were churches but no resident missionaries, pushed David into situations in which he had no choice but to put his Chinese language into practice. One of his best opportunities was the month he and Henry Guinness spent in Yehsien teaching local Christians and joining them in area evangelism. David stayed with the gatekeeper and Henry lived in another home. Without his Western companion to help him out in conversation with his host family, David learned more Chinese in those weeks than he ever could have done with just his textbooks.

Always seeking to widen his vocabulary, David got into the habit whenever he was in a Chinese home of punctuating his conversation with "What's that?" and pointing to an object for which he didn't know the word. Once in such a situation, to David's amusement, an elderly visitor turned to her friend and remarked, "Just look at this man! He's grown as big as all that, and he still doesn't know what everything is!"

Eventually, without consciously being able to master the individual tones, he began to develop a rhythmic flow of Chinese that included the tones. Increasingly he could make himself understood.

He thoroughly enjoyed working with Henry Guinness. Henry's musical gifts and his trumpet meant that he and David had little difficulty drawing a crowd. This senior worker's enthusiasm and encouragement helped David cope with the very primitive living conditions such as the public toilets, sometimes little more than a pile of stones in a morass of filth.

The object in traveling from village to village and spending extended times in key places was to draw people to Christ and then to encourage new Christians to meet together. David made his first long trip as part of a team to the village of Bukou. "We stayed in the small town, living in a little Chinese house next door to a temple which was also used as a school. We had made a map of the whole area and had as our aim to preach in each of the villages within a ten-mile radius of Bukou. We preached in a different village every day and then came back in the evening to the town and had a meeting on the street. Before leaving we had about sixty people attending a Sunday service in the home of one of the Christians. This is the way the church started in Bukou." Of another preaching mission David wrote, "It is wonderful to see people's willingness to listen to the gospel; it is what makes the country evangelistic work so encouraging."

Though this responsiveness was foundational, it was nothing compared to the spectacular revival and spread of the gospel that would take place decades later, after the missionaries were long gone from Henan and the church had suffered untold persecution. The government described the astonishing spread of the Christian faith in the 1980s as "Christian fever." Why such a contrast? In spite of the "indigenization" of Christian missions in the pre-communist era and the fact that most of the Chinese with whom missionaries worked in those last days were voluntary workers, the large mission stations sent a mixed message. With several missionaries living in foreign-style houses, and with schools, teachers, and sometimes a clinic on the compound, the impression given was of a foreign religion. In these last forty-five years or so, Chinese Christians have been willing to sacrifice their lives for their faith, and this has shown that Christian truth supersedes nationality. Today the church in China is almost free of foreign influence, and the gospel is as Chinese as it is Western.

Today, David points out the continuity between the slow but steady growth missionaries saw in the thirties and forties and the spiritual explosion that took place during the recent revival. Faithful Christians won to Christ in pre-revolution days were the ones who maintained a witness in the midst of the suffering of the Cultural Revolution. And church leaders from those days, after being released from prison following the death of Mao and the arrest of the Gang of Four, trained younger Christians in the late 1970s for the evangelistic teams that have been used by the Holy Spirit to bring about such tremendous recent growth.

In those pre-communist days the missionaries often preached in market squares, where crowds would quickly gather to stare in undisguised curiosity at the foreigners and listen to their storytelling. The preachers often used brightly colored posters to illustrate a variety of aspects of the

Christian faith. David liked to use the poster that showed a man on each side of a cross, one dressed in filthy rags and the other in a beautiful Chinese gown embroidered with the Chinese characters for "fruit of the Spirit." The title of the poster was "The New Man." David used it to explain how, through the cross, people could take off the filthy rags of sin and be clothed in the righteousness of Christ and produce spiritual fruit. As this was very much David's own aspiration, it was no coincidence that he particularly liked this poster.

The further David traveled in Henan, the more the hardships of people's lives wrenched his heart. Famine was almost commonplace. Millet seed and wheat were the basic village fare, cooked in water and sometimes flavored with sweet potatoes or thickened with egg if times were relatively good. Sometimes people were so poor they could offer the missionary visitors only "white tea," plain boiled water. Once David had tea made from potato leaves. Boiled water with egg and honey stirred into it was a rare treat. To keep up their energy during lean times, David and others took tins of condensed milk with them, which they shared with their hosts.

More than one traveling missionary slept on a door lifted off its hinges in a poor household. As fleas and bedbugs did not usually infest doors, David sometimes suggested he'd be pleased with a door rather than straw bedding for sleeping.

Brigands constantly threatened, especially during famine. David saw several villagers with only one ear, victims apparently of unpaid ransoms. Of his own closest call with these notorious bands of thieves, David wrote in a letter edited for *China's Millions* magazine: "The small market town of Xiao Shih-dien was in a state of excitement. People were flocking in from the surrounding countryside, and many of the sidestreets of the town were filled with carts and oxen. The reason for this agitation was the presence of a large band of brigands in the neighborhood. I went up onto the town wall shortly before dark and watched the people streaming into the town, while away in the distance, close to the hills, could be seen the smoke rising from a burning village. That night the brigands occupied places about a mile away, where we had been preaching a few days before. Numbers at our evening meeting were small, as almost every available man was wanted on the wall. But the night passed peacefully, and a day or two later several hundred soldiers arrived, causing the brigands to retire to the hills. We were very conscious those days of the Lord's guidance and protection. When the villages to the east were not safe, we went to the west country. Only once were we unable to get out, and on that day we had quite a good time preaching in the market."

If not famine and roving thieves, flooding was another threat to life and limb. Once traveling on a swollen river to a church for the weekend, David became alarmed by the increasingly fast flow of the current caused by heavy rain upstream. The boatmen were struggling to control the light craft in which he was riding, particularly round the river's bends. There was no choice but to try to land the boat and continue on foot. The first line thrown to waiting hands was whipped away. At the next bend the crew tossed out the line again; this time someone on shore caught it and tied it to a tree before guiding the boat to safety.

With his feet on solid ground, David put his bag on his head and trailed after the others along the flooded road in the direction of the still-distant church. As water was at times as deep as his thighs, he couldn't tell where the road was unless he kept his eyes on the man walking ahead of him. The one time he took his eyes off the leader, he stumbled into a ditch and dropped his bag into the water.

Besides providing a laugh for villagers watching, the incident provided David with an illustration for an article he would later write for *Young China*, CIM's magazine for Comradeship for China youngsters. Stay close to Christ, he urged his readers, to keep to the path and not fall into sin, just as he should have stayed closer to his guide in the floods to avoid falling into the water.

As Henry Guinness worked alongside the young man he had feared might not stand up to the rigors of the missionary life, he was impressed. Under David's apparent physical frailty, Henry discovered a gritty determination. Though David still battled exhaustion, the fainting episode had not been repeated. The new worker had toughened to Henan's terrible roads and the extremes of temperature. He did suffer with stomach problems, but Henry saw a young man determined to ignore those upsets as far as possible, eating whatever food was put in front of him. How could he, David reasoned, do anything else when food was so generously and sacrificially provided?

Henry was blessed with a strong constitution. One chilly November he suggested to David that they go for a swim in the icy river. Henry was used to such exercise himself and enjoyed it. But he was only half serious when he invited David to join him.

David hesitated. "Are you going?" he asked Henry.

"Of course."

"Then I'll come too."

And he did. He hurled himself into the river after Henry, shocked into breathlessness by the bitter cold, but insisting he was enjoying himself and that it was all very good for him.

"It's only cold if you think it is," Henry told the nearly frozen David cheerfully.

Long-limbed and awkward, David tended to be clumsy and was often the object of others' amusement. He was always apologizing for knocking something over or dropping something. Colleagues used to laugh when he was about to cycle off somewhere with his things so loosely tied that they were already threatening to drop off and be lost. Good-natured, David would laugh with them, at the same time protesting that it was difficult to tie all he needed on the narrow rack over the back wheel—luggage, books, and posters.

"David needs someone to look after him," agreed concerned wives and mothers of the missionary community. "He needs a wife!"

9

An Anglo-American Alliance

David was best man at the wedding of fellow worker Gordon Conway in Hankow when he first saw Ruth Temple. It was the summer of 1936. As romantic as the setting was, David was too busy with his responsibilities to do more than notice the young, dimpled American missionary. Ruth clearly remembers noticing him, however, rushing around, often late for meals and apologizing profusely to his hostess each time.

David and Ruth did not meet again until the following summer, this time at the CIM's holiday home at the hill station of Jigongshan. David's mother and brother Bernard were there too. "It was very unusual for anyone's mother to come out to China," Ruth points out, "but this was an unusual mother." Mrs. Adeney, unable to make the journey on foot, had been carried up the mountain in a sedan chair and loved it. Energetic, helpful, and interested in everything, she spent many hours of her days at Jigongshan knitting caps and shawls for all the babies.

Ruth and the vivacious Florry Adeney hit it off from the start. They were united, for one thing, in their concern for David. His paleness and thinness particularly worried his mother. And very soon Ruth was praying with Mrs. Adeney that he would find a wife. "I did not dream I would be the one," she chuckles as she looks back.

While David had not expected to remain a bachelor, neither had he given much thought to meeting a partner. Interest in a young woman he met at Keswick while both were CIM trainees in London had led nowhere, and in China he had simply been too preoccupied with ministry to think about finding a life partner.

Anyway, the China Inland Mission did not allow marriage in the first two years on the field. Its leaders felt that new missionaries needed those first years to build strong foundations for lifetime service. David had no argument with this policy; to him it seemed sensible.

And courtship was difficult in a culture where any public hint of a connection between two unmarried people was greatly offensive. This meant little opportunity for men and women engaged in missionary work to get to know one another.

The holiday station at Jigongshan was one of the few places where everyone mixed freely. Ruth had been asked to help look after the children, and David used to come along and play with them. In this way David and the brown-haired American farmer's daughter got to know one another.

Ruth marveled at David's story—of his growing up with a fun-loving extrovert of a mother in England while his dedicated, workaholic father lived in Romania to preach Christ among Romanian Jews. David was surely like his father, serious, disciplined, not a time waster. His brother Harold, Ruth gathered, was more like their mother, quick-tempered and jolly. Twenty-year-old Bernard was warm and open, obviously in love with life and impressed with China. Around Jigongshan he was the one with the camera. Ronald was the lone teenager now, still in school and unsure where life would take him.

Ruth, David discovered, grew up working hard on a farm in Minnesota and was also, like himself, part of a second family. Both of their fathers' first wives had died in childbirth. An aunt raised Ruth's half-sister just as an uncle had taken in David's half-brother Jack. Founding members of a Baptist church, Ruth's father and mother committed themselves to raising his two boys and their four daughters to love and serve God, as David's parents had done with their four sons. The similarities made interesting conversation. As they talked, David could see that this young woman's love for the Lord was strong and deep.

Though Ruth had committed her life wholeheartedly to God one day when she was twelve and ill in bed, she had not particularly thought of becoming a missionary. She took the missions course at Bible school somewhat reluctantly, in fact. She did read missionary biographies, how-ever—"a dangerous thing to do," she says—and during this time a missionary challenged her with China as the most needy and the most difficult place to be for God. From that moment Ruth recognized her call to China, never doubting God meant her to be there. David admired her response to such a demanding prospect.

Ruth's father was an elder in the church he helped found when the congregation held its farewell for Ruth. "This is the greatest day of my life," he said on the platform, his voice tight with bridled emotion. It was a moment Ruth would never forget. She and her father were very close.

At twenty-two Ruth was the youngest but one in the women's language school in Yangzhou. Though the Mission had considered her mature for her years, she felt very young and vulnerable.

When Ruth described her Victorian senior missionary at Shejizhen, David knew the type: precise and proper, insisting that everything be done right. "Omnipresent" was the nickname the Chinese gave Miss Soderstrom, reflecting her penchant for moving about the compound checking on everything.

Rats were a problem at Shejizhen. When the creatures scrambled over the window sill and into the room, Ruth and her roommate used to take shelter under their mosquito nets. Toughened by farm life, Ruth was usually the braver one, climbing out of bed to open the door and let the rats escape.

Though amused, David found the story raised the level of his approval of this young American woman. Ruth, in fact, was beginning to invade more and more of his thoughts.

David was also impressed by Ruth's zeal and the maturity with which she faced spiritual darkness. She wasn't fascinated by temples and shrines, or the idols they housed. Instead, she felt the weight of idolatry and the powers of evil behind the images, whether of fearsome faces or placid smiles. "I didn't get on with my language as fast as I would have liked," she recalls, "because I had to fast and pray against the powers of darkness." Gods were everywhere—not only in temples, some in a very bad state of repair, but in little shrines in trees, in homes, or on the sides of homes.

Idolatry had such a hold on people's lives! The Chinese spent meager resources to placate the gods and spirits of ancestors with food and flowers and burning incense. As long as the gods were satisfied, the villagers believed they could go about their lives reasonably secure from disaster. But let anyone miss an important ritual, and it was no surprise when misfortune visited. Ruth had never been to a place where she sensed the presence of evil so strongly. Nor had she understood until then how great a barrier idol worship presented to the spread of the gospel.

Even in the church on the mission station the spiritual battle raged. Believers were unsure what was of God and what was left over from their old allegiances. Never had the gift of discernment been needed so badly—among missionaries and Chinese Christians alike. The excitement of miraculous healings and conversions was such that it was not always easy to recognize when the influence of evil crept back in.

An extreme group of Christians, in fact, was setting itself up against the missionaries when Ruth arrived at Shejizhen, claiming special enlightenment from the Holy Spirit. The mix of spiritual wisdom and spiritual waywardness of the group divided the church. The situation sent Ruth to her knees. The oppression of the evil one was so palpable sometimes that all she could do was to hang on to the Lord, pray, and read God's Word.

As David and Ruth shared experiences, they discovered more common ground. In preaching the Good News, both of them had encountered many people so bound by evil spirits that little could be done for them until those spirits were cast out. There was no room in China for arguments that such manifestations of evil do not exist or that deliverance is an over-dramatic, unnecessary ministry!

Ruth was young, but not timid. When she saw evidence of demon control in a life, she would ask the afflicted person if he acknowledged Jesus as Lord. A vehement denial or resistance often signaled the presence of an evil spirit. One person who had been set free through prayer told her that he had not wanted to deny Christ when asked, but could not help himself. Once delivered, that man was free to lead a new life as a follower of Christ, but not before.

David remembers one encounter with a man in the grip of an evil spirit who, though the two had never met, called out David's name in a voice that was nothing like his own. The demon in the man recognized David as a man of God, who had come to minister in the name of Jesus, and the demon was afraid. David and his colleague prayed for the man and saw God deliver him from his bondage.

In time David discovered also a vulnerable side to the pretty young woman from Minnesota. As exciting as it was to see people released and becoming Christians, Ruth found such intense spiritual activity quite overwhelming. She had been homesick since arriving in China, and this draining situation only accentuated her loneliness.

As much as Ruth needed to talk with someone, she felt she could not share her struggles with her senior missionaries when they were up against so much themselves. Writing home to her parents about the turmoil in her heart seemed impossible too; her life as a missionary was so far removed from anything her parents had ever experienced that she felt sure they would not understand. She felt alone, a little lost. David understood.

By Christmastime that hard year Ruth had moved on to the mission station at Wuyang. Many of the Chinese Christians were celebrating the birth of Christ for the first time, and Ruth could see how special it was for them. But she was missing her family painfully.

What would make this lonely Christmas special for me too? she asked herself. *Why, if someone becomes a Christian.* It was the only answer she could think of. *That would certainly make it special.*

Ruth thought no more about her unuttered wish until the party games were starting on Christmas Day. At that point a woman, without prompting, asked her how she could become a Christian. Ruth was astonished. Hesitating only a moment because she had never led anyone to Christ before in Chinese, Ruth carefully explained Jesus' role in dying for sinners, and the need to ask forgiveness for sin and to invite Christ to become Lord in one's life. Fully ready, the woman took her step of faith. Such a simple act! Such a momentous, life-changing result! Both women were thrilled. How graciously God had answered Ruth's unspoken prayer!

From the joy of that Christmas Day, Ruth took new courage for the work to which God had called her. The year she spent in Wuyang was a very happy one. Not only did God bless the Sunday school she started in the church, but she witnessed with joy a large number of people turning their backs on idol worship. "I don't think a Sunday went by without people coming and asking us out to their homes because they wanted to get rid of their idols," she remembers. And after the idols were burned, missionaries and new Christians would invite the neighbors to join in a little service of thanksgiving.

How much of this Ruth told David during that time in the Jigongshan hill station while playing with the children or going for walks as part of a group, neither recalls. Some of the information may have come through his mother. But David remembers being impressed with Ruth's zeal, her capacity for tackling tough jobs without flinching, and her selflessness. All drew him to her.

But what neither knew was that believers at Wuyang were secretly praying that the two of them would get married.

When Ruth's senior colleague had married at the end of the year, Ruth had moved to a new base at Loho. Left in charge of the women's work in Wuyang, she and her Chinese teacher had been going back regularly for one or two weeks at a time. The men's work was conducted in the same way—by none other than David, though he was never in Wuyang at the same time as Ruth, as there was only one mission house. Marriage, the believers thought shrewdly, would mean David and Ruth could live and work together, and the church would have both of them full time.

At first Ruth did not think she was the right woman for David, even protesting to God that the developing relationship was a mistake. She lost three nights' sleep, in fact, debating the issue. God's answer came a Sunday or two later during a sermon on marriage, when the minister unwittingly pointed straight at her and said, "God is preparing you to be a man's wife." For Ruth it was a direct word from God. "The call to marriage and to David," she says, "was as clear as the call to the mission field."

Originally Ruth had given up any prospect of marriage when she pledged herself to missionary service. In order to give herself wholeheartedly to what God was calling her to do, she felt she should let it go. Anyway, with fewer men than women on the mission field, she didn't anticipate being faced with the choice. After one of the CIM directors in Shanghai challenged her to pray for her future husband, however, she did so, careful to leave the matter in God's hands.

Increasingly attracted to Ruth, David was faced with a deepening conviction that God was drawing them together. He too had been advised to pray for his future wife—at a Varsity and Public Schools Camp by Bishop Taylor Smith, the friend who had scribbled down the verse from Isaiah at the Keswick mission meeting.

"But we haven't got any wives in mind," the boys had remonstrated with their teacher on that occasion.

"Ah, but you will have," the Bishop had persisted, and since then David had occasionally remembered to pray for the person who would one day be his life partner. That it might be Ruth Temple now seemed a real possibility.

Florry Adeney approved wholeheartedly, and this encouraged David. It would have been difficult for him to marry someone his mother did not know. The fact was that the two women got on extremely well. "I fell in love with her first," Ruth recalls, smiling.

When someone apparently suggested to Florry that Ruth's being American might be a stumbling block, she made short work on the idea. She would enjoy going to America one day, she said, and anyway, Americans were good cooks. Ruth was quite tickled when she heard about Mrs. Adeney's remarks.

So Ruth was not really surprised when David called in to see her in Loho after accompanying his mother and Bernard as far as Hong Kong on their journey home. Because of the constraints of Chinese culture, David and Ruth's time together had to be carefully orchestrated to keep them from being seen alone together. Ruth's senior missionary organized a room where the two could spend a few precious hours together discreetly, talking and praying about their future.

By Christmas David and Ruth were engaged. Even then, when they next met they had to arrange to go for a walk with friends in order to spend time together. They started out walking separately, each alongside one member of the married couple accompanying them. Only when they were well away from the mission and the possibility of being observed were they free to change places and at last have the chance to talk together. For most of their engagement, they communicated by letter.

After David had proposed to Ruth, however, he began to have doubts. Hardly knowing one another, how could they be sure they were right for each other? They were, after all, from very different backgrounds. David had been sure that God was orchestrating the development of his and Ruth's love for each other, but now everything seemed uncertain. Was it really God's will for them to marry? The responsibility of the step he was about to take suddenly hit him with painful force.

David agonized for days. With engagements in Chinese culture almost as binding as marriages, he felt he could hardly back out now even if he wanted to. That made it all the harder to think through his doubts.

Yet in his heart of hearts David, like Ruth, believed God meant them to be together. It was on this basis that he gradually began to look ahead with confidence. That Ruth was lovingly reassuring when he told her honestly of his struggle helped too. When at one point Ruth tried to give the ring back because of his doubts, his vehement refusal revealed to both of them that he did not want to lose her. And from there the two young people from very different cultures began to build the foundation of their marriage—a foundation of faith in God and commitment to one another.

"Marriage is essentially a covenant between two people and God," David says. "It is as they go forward in obedience that the covenant is translated into the reality of the love and union which is brought about through the working of the Holy Spirit." His convictions have been tested and proved over the years. "One thing we determined from the very beginning," he says, "was that whenever problems arose between us, we would go to the Lord in prayer. This practice of praying together has persisted throughout our married lives, and it is through God's grace that we have been drawn closer and closer to one another. We realize that we need each other's gifts in order to accomplish the work prepared for us by the Lord."

David and Ruth's wedding was a happy occasion. They were married in Hankow, the city on the Yangtze where they first met. Ian Anderson, a fellow missionary David first knew at Monkton Combe, stood with David as best man. Ruth Greening, Ruth's junior missionary, was maid of honor. The mission home host gave Ruth away, and the senior missionary for the area gave the address at the church service that followed the ceremony at the British Consulate.

The bride and groom made a handsome couple—Ruth petite and lovely in her white satin dress, made especially for her, David head and shoulders above most people, his smart suit adding to the distinction of his bearing.

David and Ruth would have loved to have had their families there for the wedding and the small reception afterwards, but with all the missionaries in Hankow joining in the celebrations they felt part of a new family. Whether or not the sun shone on them that last day of March in 1938, David and Ruth were very much aware that God's face was shining on them with promise for their future.

For their honeymoon the two went back to Jigongshan, the hill station where they had first recognized their love for one another. Ruth remembers how much time they spent walking among hills ablaze with azaleas, at last free to be together without constraints.

So the prayer of the young couple's Chinese friends at Wuyang had been answered, if only in part. David and Ruth did not go back there once they were married except for occasional visits, for they had been assigned to a new station in an eastern suburb of Fangcheng, the "square city." Here, in two tiny rooms, one above the other, they began their married life.

Neither David nor Ruth liked the large missionary compounds. Built in a foreign style with foreign money, they seemed to set the missionaries apart from the Chinese people. Thus the newlyweds were delighted to discover they were going to be the first resident missionaries on a small outstation. The church had been established on premises that once belonged to a large Chinese family.

"Outside the front door," recalls David, "was the main street of the suburb. On either side of the road were elevated stone pathways from which you entered the houses. Crossing the threshold of the main door to the church compound, you went through a very large old wooden gate and then past the room belonging to the gatekeeper, who was responsible to check people going in and out. In the front courtyard a Chinese family lived on one side, and on the other was a small room used for meetings and receiving guests. We held our daily prayer meeting there. Immediately ahead was the main building we used for a church, with its red-tiled roof outside and, inside, its high ceiling supported by black-lacquered pillars and beams. The very simple benches and chairs inside were not comfortable. To the left was a passageway with a room over the top which later became my study, and behind this was another courtyard where we sometimes had guests staying. To the right of the church building was our home."

The two small rooms seemed very cramped when David and Ruth first arrived. Their boxes took up most of the downstairs room, and they found it difficult to unpack when the only access to the room above was by ladder.

The two were still unpacking and living in the upstairs room when David, with generous but unthinking warmth, invited two visiting missionaries for lunch, giving Ruth almost no warning. The new bride had to stay behind from the special meeting others were attending to tidy away the contents of a packing case which were strewn over the upstairs floor. Otherwise there would hardly have been room to welcome the visitors. Finding crockery from which they could all eat was another matter. And what could she serve them? Somehow she had everything ready by the time the guests arrived. It was not to be the last time Ruth had to use her ingenuity to provide hospitality for people David invited at short notice.

Gradually the rooms became home. After putting in a steep stairway, David and Ruth covered the rough stone floor downstairs with mats and made it into their dining and living room. The church gave them a beautiful walnut table as a wedding present, and the same village carpenter who had made the table made frames for the seats and backs of easy chairs they had brought with them from Hankow. The kitchen and laundry room, together with an outside toilet, were in another small courtyard.

The mission station did not boast either electricity or running water. The cook or other helpers brought water in buckets dangling from carrying poles, and it had to be carefully boiled. Since the well just outside the compound had been made unusable when a man committed suicide by throwing himself into it, the compound had to rely on the river, anything but clean, for its water supply.

Without ice or refrigeration, keeping food from spoiling when the weather was hot was a problem. David and Ruth improvised with a wire cage which they lowered by pulley into a cool pit in the garden.

Another problem was more difficult to solve. Outside the living room was a small patch of land which for years had been used as a toilet. Beyond it was a peach orchard, but the strong smell from the ground under the window was quite inconsistent, to say the least, with the lovely view of the trees. Breaking people of the habit of using this area as a toilet proved almost impossible. In the end they purchased the land and enclosed it within a wall for a vegetable garden.

When Ruth became pregnant with their first child, she bewildered David by how ill she was. "I was very ignorant of married life," David confesses. Ruth, though not expecting her husband to know about morning sickness or the tiredness that accompanies pregnancy, was hurt when he asked her if she was always as physically weak as this. Preoccupied with the church and evangelistic work and not understanding his wife's needs, David did not encourage Ruth to rest. Only after a visit from their senior missionary was Ruth put to bed to recover her strength.

The birth was a difficult one, keeping David busy running up and down the narrow stairs with basins of boiled water as the mission doctor tended to Ruth. It was the New Year, 1939. Despite a breach birth, Rosemary Joy was born safely, and the new parents were soon proudly inspecting her wee, turned-up nose, well-formed mouth, and tiny, exquisitely perfect hands.

Soon the Chinese had given Rosie a Chinese name—*Mei-ying*—not only a popular girl's name at the time, but a combination of the characters used for America and England, her parents' homelands. Perfect! Besides, her parents noted, the words themselves had significant meaning: *mei*, "beautiful," and *ying*, "brave."

When Ruth took Rosie along on preaching trips, the baby fascinated the villagers, who had never seen a white baby before. Indeed, for many, the arrival of the Adeneys was their first glimpse of foreigners of any age. Their initial reactions were usually long, blank stares—if they were bold enough to emerge at all from the safety of their homes.

But once the villagers got over their early suspicion and shyness, they were unfailingly friendly. Despite strong anti-foreign sentiment in some parts of China, neither David nor Ruth ever experienced animosity among the people of Henan.

The villagers' delight in Rosie was sometimes rather overwhelming. After one or two trips with the baby, Ruth decided that her daughter was more of a distraction than a help in the serious business of preaching the gospel. After this Rosie would stay at home in the care of her Chinese *amah*. Having such help freed Ruth to continue preaching occasionally and to begin teaching at the new primary school on the premises. Rosie and household responsibilities, however, still ate up much of her time. This new lifestyle, with less freedom, took some adjustment.

David was busy preaching and teaching, both in the church and in the villages around Fangcheng, sharing the load with the church pastor. While David and Ruth rarely worked together because men's and women's work were conducted separately, one time they were both invited to help give instruction at a week-long Bible school in a village several miles from Fangcheng. As they were preparing to leave, they heard that smallpox had broken out in the area. Should they go after all? They were not so concerned for themselves, but what about Rosie? Ruth felt that she and Rosie should stay behind. "But the next morning," she testifies, "I awoke very early, and the Lord said, 'Can't you trust me?'" So the whole family went. With people coming from far and wide to see the white baby, both David and Ruth had many opportunities for evangelism as well as for teaching the Christians. When they returned home, their superintendent quickly paid them a visit to vaccinate Rosie. "He did such a thorough job," says Ruth, "that Rosie as a teenager resented the scars!"

As 1940 approached, a very different threat was beginning to make itself felt in Henan—the Japanese invasion.

10

The Planes Are Coming!

For weeks, rumors of approaching Japanese soldiers had kept Fang-cheng on edge. Refugees pouring into the city had been reporting bombings in neighboring towns, and they spread terror with stories of pillaging and rape. The city was so tense that farmers in the market would panic at the sight of a single small Japanese plane.

Government forces had pulled country people from fields and harvests to dig great trenches across the roads to delay the advancing Japanese. The gouged out barriers did little to stop the Japanese, but were a nuisance and frustration to everyone, not the least David as he cycled out to visit churches in outlying areas.

The fear and foreboding David found as he mingled with the people weighed heavily on his mind. It also sharpened the edge of his own dilemma, especially now that he and Ruth had a baby girl. How should he react to the approaching danger? Should he move his little family to a safer place, or should they wait with their Christian brothers and sisters for the invading army?

The answer was not easy. Together David and Ruth talked of God's protection, and they testified to his peace. "But we too were afraid when the Japanese bombers roared overhead," they confessed, telling of scrambling under the walnut table one day with city officials they were entertaining when bombers swooped low. Bombs aside, their being between the motor road and the city meant that they could easily get caught in the middle of the fighting once the Japanese had penetrated the perimeters.

"Of course, we had come to the field ready to lay down our lives," Ruth says, "but we did have a two-year-old, whom we thought, like most parents, was the greatest gift ever given."

Though quite a number of people found shelter in the church compound, many of the Adeneys' friends had fled. Should David and Ruth also take their precious toddler and flee to the country while they could, as the mission advised? What did God want them to do?

Both David and Ruth came up from their knees with the same strong conviction that they should stay.

Well, then, should they hide their things, even bury them in the garden? God's answer was surprising. "I hadn't been reading Genesis," said Ruth, "but the word came to me, 'Regard not your stuff, for the good of the land is yours.' All I could say was, 'Thank you, Lord!' "

The Adeneys did have a simple air-raid shelter dug in the back yard. They were huddled in it one day when a small bomb hit the house next door, even with the huge red cross believers had urged be painted on the church roof.

At the approach of planes the family eventually stopped scrambling for the air-raid shelter, and opted to duck under the walnut table instead. Ruth was pregnant again and was finding the cramped garden shelter increasingly uncomfortable.

Little Rosie did not quickly forget the new routine. In the States a few months later she heard a plane one day and immediately dived under the nearest table, put her arms over her head, and shouted in Chinese the words she had heard so often, "The planes are coming! The planes are coming!"

When an attempt to forestall the advance of the Japanese army by changing the course of the Yellow River succeeded only in submerging whole villages, the stream of refugees heading south swelled noticeably on the road outside the gate. The wide, worried eyes of mothers and children, of husbands and fathers, were haunting. As the dispossessed trudged along, they struggled to hang on to the few belongings they had salvaged. Numb with hopelessness and weariness, hundreds found refreshment and a brief touch of the love of God at the wayside relief station that church members had set up on the road.

The tenacity of faith of one group of Christians who stayed overnight at the church moved David deeply. Having lost their homes and their fields, these people had been able to bring with them only what they could carry. Yet as they left the next morning to continue their long flight toward the new land the government had allotted them, they declared their faith by singing, "Yesterday, today, forever, Jesus is the same. All may change, but Jesus, never! Glory to his name!" Their perseverance in choosing the way of faith proved a foretaste of what was to happen in Henan over the succeeding terrible years, when the communists would try to wipe out Christianity altogether.

When this little band of Christians reached the land on which they were to build new homes, the Adeneys heard later, they set aside one of their number as a pastor and immediately began to erect a little church. Thus in an area previously untouched by the gospel, the uprooted Christians began sowing the seed of the Word of God that would eventually produce an abundant harvest.

Christians in a town thirty or forty miles from Fangcheng showed a similar strength of faith when their town was occupied by Japanese troops just before an Easter conference at which David was supposed to speak. When he heard that both church and many of the surrounding homes had been torched and left in ruins as the soldiers moved on, David expected the conference to be canceled. But, no, the Christians were determined to go ahead, insisting that he come to speak as planned. When David arrived, he found them already building a new church. "We had a very wonderful communion service that Easter Sunday on the foundation of the new church building," he remembers, "with partly built walls rising around us."

During this time Olive Joyce, also of the CIM, was staying with the Adeneys at the Fangcheng mission station. One night, while the city sat half paralyzed with fear at the approach of the Japanese, the Canadian woke up thinking she heard someone on the roof. Was she imagining it? She pulled the bedcovers more closely over her and listened in the dark. There it was again! *Stay calm!* she told herself as her heart pounded in her throat. Silently she put her feet out of bed, grateful for the straw mats that covered the cold stone floor, and tiptoed to the adjoining room.

"Mrs. Ting! Mrs. Ting!" she whispered as loudly as she dared to the sleeping occupant next door. Mrs. Ting, a Chinese Christian who worked at the mission station, was staying the night because she was afraid to be alone in her own house, fearing that the Japanese might arrive at any minute. "Mrs. Ting, do you hear anything?" Olive persisted.

Mrs. Ting stirred, reluctantly leaving sleep behind to appease her foreign friend. "Yes," she said after a moment, suddenly wide awake and afraid. Someone was indeed on the roof!

Olive knew she had to raise the alarm. That meant going across the courtyard and waking the Adeneys. Her padded trousers would be best, she decided, belted so she would look like a man, and a short jacket rather than her gown for the same reason. Cautiously, expecting at any moment to be picked off by a Japanese bullet, she opened the door and peered out into the courtyard. The night was very dark. There could be a whole battalion of Japanese on the roof, as far as she knew. She squeezed her eyes shut for a moment, prayed, and then ran for her life across the open space. How could she bang on the Adeneys' door and not draw attention to herself? No way, she decided, and banged anyway.

"What are you doing out at this time of night?" David's surprise was evident. Hastily Olive explained what had happened. David looked a little doubtful, but lit a lamp and went over to wake the gatekeeper. No sooner had David, Olive, and the gatekeeper started back across the courtyard than a hoarse whisper came from the roof: "Pastor Adeney! Pastor Adeney!"

The trio peered up. Three humped figures were visible above them.

"Pastor Adeney, it is me, your landlord!"

Olive was furious. Didn't the man and his companions know what a fright they had caused?

David was already opening the door to the stairs that led to his little office. Next door to where the women had been sleeping, the room was directly below the dark shadows of the men. "Come down off the roof," he coaxed out of the window. "Come into my office."

The men, it turned out, were trying to escape the draft into the Chinese army. Instead David offered the sheepish intruders a place in Christ's army, explaining Jesus' role as our sin-bearer. *He never misses an opportunity!* Olive marveled as she stole back to bed.

A few days later the Chinese government withdrew its forces from the Fangcheng area to concentrate on protecting the approaches to provinces further west.

During this summer of 1940, Chiang Kai-shek, earlier too preoccupied with the threat of Mao and his followers to be effective against the encroaching armies from the land of the rising sun, was struggling for public support as the Japanese continued to eat away at China. Fangcheng lay open and vulnerable. While some clung to their possessions in town, most of Fangcheng's people had fled, many to a fortified city of refuge on the top of a nearby mountain, used in the past when brigand armies had pillaged the district. A number had crowded into the church compound.

While few people feared that the Japanese would actually occupy Fangcheng—since it was not strategically advantageous nor big enough to warrant bogging down valuable troops to hold it—everyone knew the city would be a target for attack nonetheless. Bands of Japanese soldiers and Korean mercenaries invaded all the towns and villages in their path, searching for whatever valuables and food they might find, and leaving behind them a trail of devastation, death, and dazed victims.

When it was clear that Fangcheng would not get through the weekend unscathed, church members urged David to put up a notice saying that the compound, with its church and mission quarters, was British property. David and Ruth hesitated to hide behind a foreign flag, yet thought of the safety of their own little family, as well as that of all who had taken refuge in the mission premises. Encouraged that the Apostle Paul had taken advantage of his Roman citizenship for protection, David gave in and tacked up on the door a hastily composed sign, "Foreign Property."

That Sunday morning those gathered at station prayers read together Psalm 91. "The Lord, he is my refuge and my fortress". One after another the promises spilled from the readers' lips, each promise standing out sharply as it spoke so perfectly to the situation.

On Saturday the Adeneys' cook and goatherder had disappeared, hiding to escape being conscripted to serve the Japanese. But that Sunday found the two of them back in and joining in prayers. They brought the news that the army had surrounded the city and that Japanese planes were flying low shooting anyone in sight. The group could hear the drone of motors and the rat-a-tat-tat of gunfire in the distance.

Suddenly, all was quiet. An indication that the Japanese army was entering the city, the quiet was as unnerving as the gunfire.

David took his place at the gate, to be there when the Japanese soldiers arrived. Ruth saw that his meals were taken to him as the daylight hours ticked by. At night the men took turns to watch.

With nightfall the invaders pried doors and window frames from homes to build huge bonfires. David and Ruth and the others taking shelter inside the compound could see the glow and hear pigs squealing as they

83

were chased down and killed to be roasted. As the flames roared to the treetops, widespread fire was a real danger. That night, since the Adeneys' two rooms hugged the end of the church and seemed one of the safer places on the compound, all the women on the premises spent the night with Ruth upstairs in the bedroom.

The next morning no one could miss the sound of marching feet, shouts in a strange language, and the rumble of heavy vehicles as the army began its exit past the door of the compound. A great pounding on the door announced the arrival of a retreating Japanese official. The officer wanted David to sign a statement to say the foreigners had not been harmed or robbed. As he and Ruth had lost but one cup and saucer and two eggs by request, they could sign.

"They gave us two cartons of cigarettes," chuckles Ruth, "which I later used as mothball substitutes."

David had to remain at the door most of Monday and the following night as from time to time soldiers would try to get in. Outside was a reign of terror as soldiers raped, pillaged, and destroyed. And as they left, they set fire to the suburb. David and the rest of the already weary men spent the rest of the night putting out fires in adjoining houses.

As Christians straggled back to the sacked city, they were full of stories of deliverance. No one outside the mission compound who had stayed in the city had escaped the Japanese. Every woman, every girl, as far as they could tell, had been raped. Many people died. One godly old elder was cut down by strafing Japanese planes. But of the church people who had fled and those who had taken shelter with the Adeneys, every one was safe.

In the days that followed, David and Ruth had many opportunities to minister to the wounded, using what few antiseptics and medicines they had to bring some relief to the suffering. One old beggar had a terrible hole in his leg. It was crawling with maggots. Because of the awful smell, no one wanted to go near him. But day by day David and Ruth washed his wound, treating it until it was well on its way to healing.

Being on the compound while danger had surrounded it gave David and Ruth an opportunity to identify with their brothers and sisters in Christ and serve in ways never before possible. They were glad they had stayed. To the outside world they were still foreigners. But to the Christians around them they were now truly fellow members of the household of

God. And they had had the opportunity to show something of the love of Christ to the community.

The invaders also unwittingly gave David the opportunity to share Christ with two students. Just before the Japanese came through Fangcheng, a group of high school young people trying to escape the occupation had arrived in the city. They were a part of an ever-growing exodus of students from the east, heading westward and southwestward to attend schools being set up in areas that were still free.

The young people had taken refuge in an abandoned temple, which had been full of wounded soldiers until only a few weeks before, when the Nationalist army had moved on. Christians from Fangcheng had been visiting the sick men and holding services in the makeshift hospital every Sunday. The head of the facility, Dr. Lee, had watched his own son die while stationed in Fangcheng, a loss which generated hours of discussion with David on matters of faith. David shared with him the story of King David's reaction to the loss of a baby son. When the doctor left town, it was with a new confidence in God and a firm friendship with the Adeneys.

David was playing with Rosie in the lower room of their home when two of the high school boys staying at the old temple came to see him. The two lads had been impressed by the faith of a Christian friend. "He was very calm when the Japanese were here and we were in such danger," one of them explained. "He tells us he believes Jesus is the Son of God, and this is why he has peace. We know that Christians have been helping the wounded too; so we are interested to find out more about their faith." Then his voice took on a more defiant tone. "But we have been taught there is a lot of superstition in Christianity, especially the teaching about Jesus rising from the dead, and that it is a tool of the imperialists. We are not interested in hearing about superstition."

David nodded, seeing evidence of suffering in the face of the boy sitting across the room. Later he discovered that when the spokesman was only ten, his father had died from broken health after having been imprisoned by the Kuomintang for his left-wing politics. David responded gently to the boy's challenge with one of his own: "Is it not unscientific to brand something as superstition if you have not studied the evidence?"

The two boys could not deny this and listened as David explained a little about why he believed in Christ. "Come back and study the story of Jesus with me," David invited, "so that you can make up your own minds."

The boys hesitated, saying they might have to move on quickly from Fangcheng—perhaps a polite Chinese way of putting off the whole matter. But as David watched them go, he had an idea he would see them again.

Fighting in the southwest delayed the boys' departure for three weeks. Not only did the two boys seek David out again, but they asked if they could read the story of Jesus with him whenever he was free. By the time the students were packing up to leave a week or so later, they had worked all the way through one of the gospels, discovering that many people Jesus met during his ministry had struggled with similar questions until they got to know him better. Faced at last with the evidence of Jesus' resurrection and with Jesus' promise to reveal himself to them, both boys joined the once-skeptical believers of old and became Christians.

Would David ever see these two new Christians again? The chances were slim. Yet, wonderfully, David says, "a few weeks after they left I had to make a trip to the south to visit some of the country churches. Arriving at the bank of a river where the bridge had been destroyed, I was waiting for the ferry, when, to my amazement, I found a group of students, among them, my two friends. They had been held up because of continued fighting and now had been divided into small groups to work their way through the guerrilla war area and up into the mountains. As the wooden, flat-bottomed ferry could take only a few carts and pedestrians at a time, during the long wait I was able to sit down in a little tea shop and talk with the boys."

"Sometimes our fellow-students have been very worried and depressed about the future," the boys told their rediscovered mentor. "We have been able to tell them about the real source of peace and joy that God has given us."

David was thrilled. His encounter with these high school boys, in fact, refueled his yearning to reach out to China's youth. He had himself benefited so much from Christian teaching and example as he grew up, and he had tasted the exhilaration of fruitful witness among fellow students at both Monkton Combe and Cambridge. Surely it was time for China's youth to hear about God and the redeeming work of Christ.

Actually, when David had first come to China, he had asked the CIM if he could work among students, but the Mission had counseled him to get some experience in church work first. Hudson Taylor's vision had been for work in China's interior, where most people had never heard of Christ, rather than in the cities, where other missions were working. But cities,

David knew, housed the students. Would there ever be an opportunity for him to work among this neglected, important segment of Chinese society? At this stage he did not know. He knew only that he longed for the chance.

As David unloaded his bike from the ferry and waved good-bye to his friends, he wondered fleetingly whether he might manage to travel west sometime to visit the refugee colleges being set up. Not likely, he decided—not soon anyway. He and Ruth would soon be leaving China for furlough.

Ruth gave birth to their second child, a son, prematurely. Harold came eagerly into the world—to all appearances a perfectly formed child. But within a few hours it was apparent that something was wrong—terribly wrong. The baby could not handle his food. Though the CIM doctor who attended the birth suspected a malformation of the intestine, without hospital equipment she could not help the struggling infant. David and Ruth watched sadly as their tiny baby grew weaker and weaker. Harold lived only three days.

"It is hard to describe the mixture of feelings one has at such a time," Ruth says today. "Deep grief flooded over me whenever I was alone. I did want this little one to love and to care for. At the same time I had felt resentful toward David because he so very strongly insisted that the care of the children was solely my responsibility and that I must never let them interfere with his work. He loved children, and it doesn't seem entirely like the David I know now. No doubt his background had something to do with it. His father was away, and his mother had helpers more suited to looking after children than my helpers were."

Both David and Ruth felt unworthy of another child with the tension in their marriage. Perhaps, they thought afterwards, their home in Fangcheng was not ready for baby Harold. David looks back at his ignorance and failure in these early years of married life with deep pain. His own father had put his work ahead of his family; David had seen no reason to resent it. Ruth's attitude left him baffled.

Comforted that the little one they weren't allowed to keep would be perfectly loved in the Savior's presence, David and Ruth looked to the Scriptures for God's word to them. As Ruth read the Lord's response to their seeking—"so that we can comfort those in any trouble with the comfort we ourselves have received from God" (2 Corinthians 1:4)—she wept and worshipped.

"Little Harold weighed four pounds," Ruth remembers. "A year and a half later God gave us a boy who weighed nine pounds and fourteen ounces. Eventually the Lord blessed us with two more sons. We thank him for all three of them."

David and Ruth had come alongside their friends in times of distress; now the love and concern ran the other way. "As the Lord has taken your treasure to heaven," the pastor gently challenged the bereaved parents at Harold's funeral, "may you yourselves be drawn closer to heaven." Later David was able to comfort that same pastor when his wife died in childbirth.

With both of them tired and David's health not very good, David and Ruth needed their furlough when the time came in 1941. Even so, it was hard to leave the church in Fangcheng. The war with the Japanese was still undermining things and huge tracts of the area remained unevangelized.

It was difficult, too, not to be nervous about the journey that lay ahead. With their little girl, they would have to make their way without modern transportation through country where guerrilla armies were active; they would also have to cross Japanese lines. It would be a week before they would catch the train at Zhengzhou for Shanghai.

Prayerfully, the little family set out. David was on his bicycle, Ruth and Rosie on one hand-pulled cart and their belongings on another. Stopping at night at village churches and mission stations, they squeaked and bumped their way eastward, conscious of their vulnerability to bands of armed men. Food was scarce, more so than usual, and at one small church in the hills they ate the chrysalids of silkworm moths gratefully.

As they neared the Japanese lines, they didn't know what to expect. But at the checkpoint the soldiers had eyes only for Rosie. The little girl, with her wispy brown hair and soft olive skin, so charmed the uniformed men that the travelers got through with remarkable ease.

Once safely in Shanghai, the Adeneys boarded a Japanese ship bound for the United States, where Ruth's Minnesota family waited to welcome them. Later, they would go to England and David's family.

As the ship pulled away from its anchorage, David and Ruth watched the land shrink and fade with mixed feelings. They were glad to be going home, yet concerned for those they were leaving behind. Over seven years a deep love for the Chinese people had rooted itself in them both, though David had adapted to the culture more fully and wholeheartedly than Ruth had done. He'd had more opportunity. By working with the villagers, living alongside them and learning their thought patterns and habits, David was becoming more and more at one with them. These years laid a foundation for a lifetime's close identification with the Chinese.

David and Ruth said good-bye to their adopted land sure that they would be back in a year.

But quite a different scenario was about to unfold.

11

Furlough Firelighting

A day out of San Francisco, the *Tatuta Maru* began sailing in wide circles. "There is something wrong with the engines," the captain told everyone.

At first the passengers grumbled with mild impatience. Even Ruth struggled to be patient, so looking forward to seeing her family again and introducing David and Rosie. David was happily talking with Bishop Frank Houghton, General Director of the CIM, who with his wife was also aboard. The Bishop and David shared a passionate interest in Christian work among students and had spent much of their three weeks aboard exchanging ideas.

Then the rumor surfaced that the ship might not dock at all. Passengers with short-wave radios learned that American authorities had frozen Japanese assets in the tightening tensions between the U.S. and Japan. Obviously the captain didn't want to bring the ship to shore only to have it confiscated.

As the sea was very calm, passengers whiled the time away fishing from the deck. Someone even pulled in a shark. But the situation was tense. People wondered whether the ship might turn and steam off for Japan with all passengers aboard.

When word finally spread that passengers were to be unloaded in exchange for the ship's being allowed to return to Japan, everyone celebrated. Christians aboard thanked God. And when, a few months later, Japan attacked the American military base at Pearl Harbor, the passengers saw how close they had come to spending the duration of the ensuing war in a Japanese internment camp. As it turned out, the *Tatuta Maru* was the last Japanese liner to make the journey to the States in the prewar era.

After the devastation of Pearl Harbor and the spread of war to all of the islands and Asian coastlands of the Pacific, the Adeneys had to give up thoughts of returning to China before the conflict was over. More than four years were to go by before David and Ruth saw China again. They had different jobs and different homes for each of these four years and, as God would have it, each sphere of ministry played a part in shaping David's future ministry, as well as preparing both him and Ruth for what awaited them when China again became their home.

When David and Bishop Houghton discussed David's desire to work again among students, neither man knew how soon that opportunity would come. The bishop had been in the States only a few weeks when the pioneer leader of the newly formed U.S. InterVarsity Christian Fellowship, Stacey Woods, approached him looking for help to get this evangelical student movement off the ground. He particularly needed a missions secretary. Could the bishop recommend anyone?

David Adeney, of course! thought the CIM leader. He told Stacey Woods of the Cambridge graduate just home from China and of their conversation on board ship. Very shortly the invitation to the Adeneys was on its way.

David was thrilled at the prospect of the CIM's seconding him to the InterVarsity Christian Fellowship, not least because it was the American counterpart of the movement in England with which he had been so closely associated. This new assignment meant that the family could stay on with Ruth's people in Minnesota, and David could work and travel from there. It also meant the painful deferral of the trip home to Bedford to visit his parents, other family, and friends, including those of Russell Park Baptist Church—but the cause was worth personal sacrifice; it was the kind of task to which he could give his full energies.

When David joined its leadership in November 1941, the InterVarsity Christian Fellowship in the U.S. was just thirteen months old. The U.S. movement, and some of its early staff, came from the Canadian IVCF. That arm of IVCF had been established over ten years previously when British graduate, Howard Guinness, carried the Inter-Varsity vision across to Canada. As General Secretary, Australian Stacey Woods brought to the

U.S. IVCF both his eight years' experience leading the Canadian movement and a firm commitment to foreign missions.

David plowed into his new job with verve. Traveling from university to university in the Midwest, he challenged students to pray for missions and to offer themselves to participate in God's global purposes. He was looking for a missionary secretary for the IVCF chapter at the University of Michigan when a student came with news of the bombing of Pearl Harbor.

Helping to organize a number of missionary conferences, David tirelessly pleaded for the millions who had never heard the name of Christ. With his own commitment obvious, he urged students to put aside self-serving plans in order to answer God's command to go to the ends of the earth to preach the good news and to make disciples. Within two months twenty students had volunteered for front-line missionary service—this in spite of the constraints and uncertainties of a world at war.

David fitted into the American environment amazingly well. He had to endure, of course, the occasional quip about his accent or choice of words. And he did wonder what his friends in England would think when he saw his picture in IVCF's *His* magazine with the caption, "Missionary Secretary Adds Zip to Zeal." But the adjustments were minor compared to those he had worked through in China. And he loved his work with InterVarsity.

Not only did David thrive in a student environment, but he was utterly convinced of the validity of his message: that every Christian, if he or she is to have the mind of Christ, must have a missionary vision, and that every believer should face up to the possibility that missionary work overseas might be God's chosen role for talents given. He felt this so keenly that the fire of his own zeal sparked others alight and quickly spread. "You only had to touch David to feel the fire and catch the fire," said one of his colleagues.

"The fact remains," David wrote in his book, *The Unchanging Commission,* "that a real zeal for world evangelization is to be found in the lives of only a few."

In the mid-twentieth century David's message may have seemed to some as naive or old-fashioned. Who put on a pith helmet these days to pioneer a trail through an African jungle? David did not allow Christian students such a shallow appraisal. Instead, he challenged them to study the Bible with prayerful consideration for the world's needs. No one, he was sure, could come away from an honest look at Scripture believing he or she did not have a responsibility to spread the good news of Christ. The message of the atonement was timelessly and eternally relevant in any society, at any stage.

Yet was it not true that the welcome overseas for missionaries was no longer as warm as it had been? "Obedience, not opportunity, is the keyword to missionary endeavor," David rejoined.

Another misconception David tackled was that the missionary task was entrusted only to the exceptional Christian. Every Christian, David insisted, had a responsibility to be a witness, no matter how ordinary he or she might feel. God's resources were as available to one child of God as to another. "Christians in all walks of life, at home and abroad," he insisted, "should be witnessing and working together as a team in the fellowship of the gospel."

Was it too much to ask students to launch out on a career in missions in which results could neither be guaranteed nor quantified? No. David believed no endeavor undertaken in response to God's commands would be wasted, no matter how many frustrations or apparent failures a person might endure. A far greater waste would be not to go at all, for then no spiritual harvest would be reaped at all.

Even "closed doors" were no excuse to David. Where direct Christian witness was not allowed, as in communist or Muslim countries, he encouraged students to be creative in seeking entrance as a bearer of the light—by taking a secular job in the area of one's profession, if need be.

Here, however, David would inject a caution: because a full-time job in a foreign country demands enormous amounts of energy, it can distract from the primary task of spreading the gospel. Where possible, therefore, he recommended choosing a clear missionary opportunity. He considered taking a secular job a primary option only when other avenues into a country were severely limited.

David was very honest in his appraisal of the demands of overseas work. Going to another land to preach Christ, he felt, should never be undertaken lightly. "The only adequate reason for going overseas is a strong conviction that God has called and is sending forth his witness. Such a conviction alone can help a person survive the discouragements and opposition which a missionary may have to face."

Thus did David give priority to Christ's final command to his disciples: "Go and make disciples of all nations, baptizing them in the name of the Father and of the Son and of the Holy Spirit, and teaching them to obey everything I have commanded you" (Matthew 28:19-20).

Advising student leaders on inviting missionary speakers to the universities, he wrote: "The missionary should call students to consider the need as he has seen it in his own experience, but he should never presume to try to persuade a student that he is the man to meet that need. Only the Spirit of God can reveal to a man his place on the mission field." David called people to think about missions, but in humility recognized that it is God's responsibility to do the calling.

Only the Lord could tabulate the impact of the year that David worked from the Minnesota farm. For much of the year, Ruth was pregnant with John, busy trying to keep Rosie out of mischief and helping with chores. John was born beautifully healthy and in time for Grandpa and Grandma Temple to enjoy his first smiles. Now in his eighties, Mr. Temple had replaced the farm lost in the Depression with a smaller one, and was trying to respond to President Roosevelt's plea for extra effort to produce food for a nation preoccupied with winning a war. By the end of that year, as much as Ruth appreciated being a part of her family again, she was ready for a home of her own.

The Adeneys' next home was to be in Boston. Some of Ruth's ancestors once owned Boston Common, and hearsay has it that the Temple brothers gave the Common to the city.

Stacey Woods had invited David to move to the northeastern United States to continue building up the outreach of InterVarsity there. His focus was to be the Christian fellowship groups at Harvard and the Massachusetts Institute of Technology, and Christian students at Yale and Princeton.

The Bible study at Harvard was soon a particular encouragement for David. Not that the group was large, but its spirit and potential stirred confidence that God was at work. A number would leave their mark for God. In fact, one of the group, Harold Davenport, cannot recall any who did not go on to serve the Lord in some capacity, either at home or abroad. He himself was recruited from Harvard by the government to participate in radar research in Washington, D.C. during World War II, and went on to serve at the Afghanistan Institute of Technology and represent Christ in the Muslim world for twenty-seven years.

Charles Hummel was also among the students David's life touched at Yale. He helped develop IVCF in Japan and was later president of Barrington Bible College. In recent years he has given his energies to Faculty Christian Fellowship in the U.S. At Princeton, missionary leader Christy Wilson was among the young people stirred by what David Adeney said, but more, perhaps, by the man's inner fire. Over that single year in the U.S., the missionary from China touched hundreds of students' lives and in many little ways helped them grow in their commitment to the kingdom of God. Just recently in New England, two members of Boston's Park Street Church, now in their sixties, mentioned to David how much his introducing them to other Christians on campus had meant in their lives as university students.

That year David also organized the IVCF's first New England weekend conference. For Harold Davenport this student conference was a first. He remembers David searching almost vainly through the chorus book to find a hymn of substance. That's when Harold learned to sing, " 'Man of sorrows', what a name for the Son of God who came." "David challenged our shallowness," says Harold. "He taught us not merely to mimic other Christians, to take our standards from them, but to examine ourselves, that we might become Christians of conviction, Christians that command respect."

Charlie Hummel also found an answer to his struggle at that first conference. David got him there by offering to pay his conference fee if Charlie would pay his train fare. Dr. Hummel remembers: "At considerable cost of time I had wholeheartedly tried to 'seek first the kingdom of God,' but the promised academic achievement to keep my scholarship had not been forthcoming. . . . In a small prayer group Saturday evening [at the conference] I poured out my struggle and received, not a specific answer, but an inner assurance that God would keep his promises in his own way and time. That marked a turning point in my prayer life. By the time I graduated six months later, the academics had come out better than

I had expected. In retrospect, David Adeney's example and encouragement was the single most important influence on my Christian life during the years at Yale."

David loved being stretched in this ministry to students. Ruth also enjoyed the months in Boston, being an ordinary wife and mother in an American setting and reaching out to the neighborhood through a child evangelism class. It was during this time that well-known Bible teacher, Edwin J. Orr, turned up at the door. He had just been called into the army as a chaplain and desperately needed a place for his wife and two children to stay. Could the Adeneys take them in? How could the Adeneys say no? Crowded as the small home was, the two families shared quarters for several weeks.

Perhaps the year's greatest blessing for the Adeneys was the family's involvement in Park Street Church. A large Congregational church on the corner of Boston Common, Park Street had for decades given great support to the work of missions. The dynamic minister, Harold Ockenga, became a good friend to the family, and in later years David often participated in the large missions conferences held at the church. Though he was always a bit uncomfortable with the very public way money was raised during missions conferences—with totals loudly relayed to the congregation as the pledges were collected and tallied—since he was much more at home with the China Inland Mission's practice of laying needs before God in prayer rather than soliciting funds publicly, he appreciated the strong evangelical stand and outreach of this great church.

David began to yearn to return to England, though the country was reeling from Hitler's bombs and a short food supply. It had been nine years since he waved good-bye to his parents at Southampton and more than six years since he had seen his mother and Bernard in China. Retired since 1939, his father was now in his mid-seventies, and his mother had suffered a stroke just months after Bernard had gone to China in 1941. Satisfied that the InterVarsity work in the States had gained the momentum it needed to keep moving forward, David gratefully accepted an invitation to become Prayer Secretary on the CIM home staff in Britain.

On the dangerous voyage across the Atlantic, the family received some crushing news: Florry Adeney's health had deteriorated dramatically, leaving her not only paralyzed but unable to speak.

"It was hard seeing my mother unable to communicate," remembers David. "Her mind was clear in every other way, and she desperately wanted to talk, but, besides being able to say most of the Lord's Prayer, she could use only a few single words. She would try to show her meaning with her expressions and actions. She could still sign her name on checks.

"Mother loved to hear me talk about the work," David recalls fondly, "and I was able to take her for walks in her wheelchair on the embankment. She was absolutely devoted to Ruth and Rosie and John, our toddler. We had a job to keep her from spoiling the children; she wanted to give them everything she possibly could."

It was autumn 1943, and England was war-torn. Bedford was relatively quiet—so quiet, in fact, that one of the American soldiers stationed there impishly remarked to David that the town was the only cemetery he had seen with traffic lights! Ruth, not yet known in the community, was once or twice the innocent bystander to a conversation about how nice Bedford had been before the Americans came!

The family stayed a year in the Adeney home on Bushmead Avenue. Again Ruth was managing her family in someone else's home. Wartime also meant contending with shortage and rationing.

David threw himself into his new role as Prayer Secretary with characteristic wholeheartedness. He was again focusing on China, and he loved it. His job was feeding regular information and prayer guidelines to the almost four thousand members of the Prayer Union in Britain, and encouraging the somewhat smaller number of "prayer companions," who supported individual missionaries with regular intercession. No group of people was more important to the China Inland Mission. "The mission was born in prayer," wrote a recent director, "and has always believed that while prayer is not a substitute for devoted, self-sacrificing labor, it is the secret of spiritual prosperity."

Stirring up prayer and making the rounds of missionary prayer circles was a more than profitable way to keep busy while the family waited to return to China. David knew prayer to be a lifeline to fellow workers and Chinese believers in that great land, where Nationalists and communists had formed an uneasy alliance against the invading Japanese.

In the two years since Pearl Harbor, Japanese soldiers had been rounding up "enemy nationals" in occupied China and putting them behind barbed wire. The Japanese had interned more than two hundred missionaries in camps around the Shanghai area. Several more, caught in the Philippines, were languishing behind walls and barbed wire in Manila. And five hundred miles north of Shanghai the would-be conquerors of all Asia had taken over CIM's Chefoo School premises, marching off to concentration camp not only the school's staff, but two hundred children—most of them sons and daughters of CIM missionaries. Even the CIM headquarters was forced to operate with a skeleton staff in emergency facilities in Chongqing when Shanghai headquarters staff were forced into what the Japanese preferred to call "civil assembly centers."

With almost no means of communication with the interned missionaries and children and with believers in occupied China, those who were praying could only imagine what might be going on. But they prayed. Only later did they discover the full story of how God answered their prayers to help Chinese Christians and the interned to survive and triumph, though often ill, underfed, and living in impossibly crowded conditions. It was a significant time to be mobilizing prayer for the Mission. David felt it.

News from free China was more plentiful and also more encouraging. The turmoil of war was apparently bringing an openness to the gospel among the Chinese. The reported hunger for spiritual truth and almost eager willingness to accept the Christian message gave an urgency to prayer for more missionary recruits. World war or no, this was not the time to slacken efforts to pray for laborers to reap a ripening harvest.

A further call went out to prayer partners: for "a very large increase in spiritually and mentally well-equipped Chinese missionaries to their own people," as phrased by the CIM home director in Great Britain. David echoed that call in *China's Millions:* "We believe that there is need for a mighty barrage of prayer which will prepare the way for real advance out in China. Should we not pray especially for reinforcements of Spirit-filled Chinese fellow workers, as well as those who will be prepared when the way opens to go forth from the home countries?"

Actually the Mission was already answering its own prayer request. Leaders had asked themselves what was the most fertile ground for nurturing new Chinese Christians who might eventually become missionaries in their own country. The answer was clear. Young people. Students in particular. Now was the time to take more seriously the responsibility to reach China's youth.

Because the war-time exodus of students from the east had brought huge numbers of young people into the very area where missionaries were now concentrated, the opportunity to contact them was there for the taking. Among the three CIM couples now with their sights on the swelling tide of students in China's West and Northwest were Paul and Maida Contento. Both saw the import of the task ahead: "We . . . pray that many students may be saved and called of God into his vineyard," Paul wrote. "The church of Christ in China is in dire need of pastors, teachers, evangelists, and leaders. It is from this class that they must come."

David followed these developments in China with great interest.

He was also instinctively drawn to the young people in his own country, for they too were potential missionaries. After a year of giving his energies as Prayer Secretary, he gladly took on the responsibilities of Youth Secretary for the CIM, a change which necessitated the fourth move in as many years for his family, this time to London and to an upper flat in the old CIM training school at Newington Green. In the flat below, another missionary couple were amused each evening by David's regular routine of taking his shoes off and dropping each of them with a thud.

Once again in a home of her own, Ruth set about making the flat a welcome one for her family and for the many visitors David could be counted on to invite. With food tightly rationed, she had to become ingenious in making what she had stretch as far as it would go. It was in this corner of London that Michael Adeney was born, in the spring of 1945.

Remembering how much he himself had benefited as a boy by early contact with China through the CIM's Comrades for China program, David did not underestimate what could be achieved among the young supporters of the Mission. While often responding to invitations to speak all over the country, particularly to student gatherings, he worked hard to develop interest and commitment among younger Britons.

As usual, David was inclined to take on too much. Ruth was grateful for the firmness of Fred Mitchell, the CIM's Home Director at the time, who seemed to be one of the few people who could slow her husband down. "He used to take David into his office and tick him off for rushing about so much," Ruth recalls.

The dangers of war were much more real in London. David was returning from meetings in Tunbridge Wells when the notorious buzz bombs made their first appearance. "On the train to Victoria everyone was talking about the rumors of these pilotless planes which the RAF had failed to stop because of their speed," remembers David. "As we approached Victoria, I looked out of the window and saw one of these planes just as the engine cut out and it nose-dived to explode in the middle of London.

"Even more frightening were the rockets which began to come over just before the end of the war. Several of them fell not too far from where we were living, the nearest one coming down just the other side of Newington Green, completely destroying a school, fortunately in the middle of the night. Our windows were shattered by the explosion. The rockets were not only much more powerful than the buzz bombs, but they gave no warning of their approach." Young John, now a toddler, loved them: "Wasn't that a lovely wocket, Mummy?" he would say.

As David heard what was happening in China and compiled news for the younger supporters of the CIM, he became increasingly excited. God was moving wonderfully among the students. Reports told of conversions, baptisms, and thriving evangelical student groups in uprooted schools and universities. Students, hungry in an unprecedented way for the truth, were flocking to English and Bible classes the missionaries offered. And God was, by his Spirit, using both Chinese and Westerners to lead them to a wholehearted allegiance to Christ.

By late 1944 some of the newly formed evangelical Christian groups were meeting together at conferences. While at least two Christian organizations were operating on the Chinese campuses, neither was evangelical. The time was more than ripe for a national organization of evangelical students. One who saw this was Calvin Chao, a pastor and gifted evangelist. CIM missionary Paul Contento encouraged him, and in July 1945 at a summer conference in Chongqing, the war-time capital of China, the China Inter-Varsity Evangelical Christian Students Fellowship was inaugurated, with Pastor Chao as its General Secretary.

One hundred and sixty students represented forty of China's sixty universities at that conference. "Scores of young people told how they had been released from the bondage of sin or how through a new surrender had received again the joy of salvation," David summarized in *Young China*. "Others heard the call of God to go forth as 'ambassadors for Christ.' "

In the same edition of *Young China* was the report of the Japanese surrender and the end of the war. It was the moment the Adeneys had been waiting for. That momentous day they joined the crowds outside of Buckingham Palace to celebrate. But they were celebrating more than the return of peace and plenty; they celebrated because the way would surely soon open back to China.

The China Inter-Varsity, growing fast, needed help. The time was ripe for someone from the Mission to be seconded full-time to contribute to its development, and once again Bishop Houghton thought of David Adeney. From China he cabled David to head for China as soon as possible. With all their energies, the talented Calvin Chao, the Contentos, and the others working with them could not cope with the growth and burgeoning opportunities. David's dream of working among students in China was about to be fulfilled. He would work, the Bishop told him, under the leadership of Calvin Chao, whose preaching God was using to bring large numbers of university students into the kingdom of God. David thrilled at the challenge before him.

But David could not know that in returning to China he would witness one of the most momentous periods in China's history. In a few years, not only would the Nationalist government be overthrown and replaced by a communist regime, but with that change would come the end of the missionary era in that vast and populous land.

12

Back to China—Separately

Shipping was scarce in those months after the war; it could be months before the Mission could secure passage to China. David would have to fly. Ruth and the children could follow later by ship when space was available.

No one pretended that the arrangement was ideal. Yet the urgency for David's help in China seemed to demand the sacrifice. With passage to the U.S. possible within a few weeks, Mission leaders agreed that Ruth and the three youngsters should take the opportunity to visit family in the States.

As excited as David was to be dashing about preparing to leave for China aboard a Sunderland Flying Boat, he found the cost of the step ahead of him as painful as any he had ever faced. Ruth would have to cope with three children without him across two oceans and on the transcontinental trains of America. Weeks of separation stretched ahead. He knew, too, that he was saying good-bye to his mother for the last time. She was not only still unable to speak, except for a few words, but was obviously declining. "She was devoted to me," David remembers with pain and appreciation, "and to Ruth and the children; yet she would never have wanted to hinder us from doing what we believed to be the will of God."

"Just as the day I boarded the *Carthage* in 1934 stands out in my mind," David wrote the year he turned eighty, "so the day I left Bedford at the end of December 1945 remains indelibly engraved in my memory. Even little personal details are still clear. After the strain of kissing my dear mother for the last time, I boarded the train to London with my father, only to discover that the compartment had no access to the toilet. It was an agonizing journey."

In London the morning of January 3, 1946, when David cradled each of the children in turn before leaving the flat for the docks, he knew the whole family was paying a price for his early return to China. Certainly without Ruth's commitment to doing God's will, he could not be going.

Ruth, David's brother Ronald, and his father accompanied David to the London docks where the broad-hulled Flying Boat sat heavily in the waters of the Thames. As David embraced Ruth one last time and grasped in turn the hands of his brother and his father, hesitating momentarily to return the gaze of each, his throat was tight with emotion. Then with a final wave he made his way aboard the Sunderland, threading his hand luggage ahead of him.

As David settled into his seat and was enveloped in the roar of the revving engines, a surge of adrenaline quickened his senses. With almost a boyish delight he relished the idea of flying to China—not only that, but of being the first CIM missionary in history to do so!

The Sunderland lifted ponderously off the Thames and was soon cruising over the English Channel. The craft had been in the air less than two hours, however, when mechanical difficulties forced it to land on a lake in France. Once repairmen had made adjustments, the flying boat lifted smoothly from the lake and hummed confidently toward Switzerland.

When the aircraft was flying low over the Alps, David's gaze picked up a car winding its way along a twisting mountain road below. He could see the town from which the car had started, perhaps an hour or two earlier, and he could also see the town on the other side of the mountain where the car would arrive in a few hours' time. From David's vantagepoint, the whole journey was visible. The driver of the car could see just up to the next curve. *My heavenly Father sees both the beginning and the ending of the journey of my life,* thought David. *I cannot see what lies ahead of me or Ruth during these next months. But down into the valley or over the mountains every curve along the way is known to the God who has called us.* The parable was a great comfort.

The Sunderland Flying Boat spent the next night on the waters of the Nile outside Cairo, its passengers enjoying a night's sleep in a hotel room. For David it was a nostalgic few hours, for when he had visited Cairo over ten years before, he had been with his mother. The two of them had ridden on a camel around the great pyramids. What good days those had been!

The Flying Boat's next stop was a lake at a British air force base not far from the site of the ancient city of Babylon in today's Iraq. From there the lumbering craft crossed the Arabian Sea and the Indian Peninsula to Calcutta. Several days later, on an ordinary plane, David flew the final stretch of his journey, up over the snowcapped Himalayas and on over the less dramatic convolutions of western Sichuan to Chongqing. In this bustling city in eastern Sichuan was the war-time seat of China's Nationalist Government, and here also the makeshift headquarters of the China Inland Mission.

As David made his way to his temporary quarters, he missed Ruth and the children. But not as much as Ruth was missing him! She was packing up the flat at Newington Green, wondering how in the world she and the children would manage the early-spring voyage across the Atlantic and the train trip to the perhaps still-snowy midwest.

David, however, was allowed little time to worry about his family half a world away. He was soon caught up in the work of being a servant in a great movement of God's Spirit in China. Within hours he was bundled off to a winter prayer conference. Students and staff had gathered at a university just outside the city.

The conference was crowded, the atmosphere one of prayer, confession, and delight in God. Students were getting together on their own initiative to pray for each other and for non-Christian friends. Young people were discovering Jesus Christ for the first time. New fellowship groups were taking shape in anticipation of the return to university campuses, and plans were being made for evangelistic missions. What a thrilling introduction for David to what was happening among China's young people! As he bedded down on the gym floor after a full day, he was full of praise.

Even outsiders noticed the difference among the converted students. At one university David visited after the conference, students had confessed to cheating in exams. Some had even repaid the boatman who ferried them across the river for tickets they had obtained fraudulently over the years. In other places as well, almost any onlooker could see the difference God was making in students' lives.

Hundreds of miles along the famous Burma Road to the southwest, in the city of Kunming, was a collection of refugee colleges called the United University of the Southwest—representing too many students to ignore.

So David and another IV staff member clambered aboard a battle-scarred truck one day, bound for Kunming. For the next two or three days the two men hung on for dear life as a succession of overloaded vehicles lurched between precipitous drops and sharply rising peaks. Even as the two men caught their breath and paled at the dangers, it was hard not to revel in the awesome isolation and beauty of the mountains. They had a great time encouraging the Christian students, and came back themselves encouraged.

As exhilarating as developments were in the west, however, there was to be no settling down for the IV staff. Now that the war with Japan was over, the thousands of students who had fled occupied China were preparing to retrace their steps back to the east. The universities were already in the process of relocating. The Inter-Varsity staff would have to follow.

But before the great trek eastward became a reality, China IV decided to hold a series of evangelistic campaigns among students in Chengdu, the capital of Sichuan, several hundred kilometers to the northwest, in the center of the province and at the edge of the great mountains to the west. The home of two great universities—Sichuan and West China—Chengdu had also been a refuge during the war years for five other universities and colleges, among them Christian institutions. Calvin Chao chose Moses Yu, John Chang, and David as his team. When the principal of Cheloo University invited the team to stay in his home, the four men gladly accepted.

The first week, efforts were concentrated on Christian students on campus, some of them converts from the preaching of Andrew Gih a few months previously. Large numbers of students listened as Calvin Chao challenged them to holy living. Many responded with confession of sin. Each morning soon after first light, groups of students gathered at Hart College for prayer, where the emphasis was on the need for the filling of the Holy Spirit. By the earnestness of students' prayers and the personal talks team members had with individuals, it was obvious that many young Christians were indeed claiming the power from on high to enable them to triumph over the temptations with which they were surrounded.

During the second week of the mission, the campus became embroiled in demonstrations protesting the communist threat to China's northeastern provinces. With classes suspended, Christian students took the opportunity to write out notices and stick up posters and lanterns all over campus announcing the series of evangelistic meetings.

"Is There a God?" was the topic for the first meeting. Calvin Chao's thoughtful presentation impressed the students. Still larger numbers came the next evening to hear him speak on "The Christian's Outlook on Life." For the third meeting about eight hundred students packed the hall, some even standing at the doors and windows. While counter-attractions dampened the numbers somewhat for the final meeting, many students heard the answer to "Who is Jesus?"

As the young people followed Moses Yu on his piano accordion in the hall brightened by two dangling pressure lamps, the sound of Christian choruses in both English and Chinese echoed across the campus each night. At about 7:00 Pastor Chao would stand, read a few verses of Scripture, then preach in his strong voice for half an hour, his message "pregnant with spiritual power," as David described it. A meeting afterward for those students interested in learning more provided opportunity to give a clear presentation of the gospel. After being commended to God, each student who responded signed his name and address for follow-up by local Chinese pastors and foreign missionaries stationed in the city. Refreshments and a little informal entertainment at the end helped people get to know one another. Altogether 168 young people took a first step of faith during those four days, and during similar meetings at Sichuan and Yengching Universities over a hundred more joined them in starting the Christian pilgrimage.

In the spring of 1946 David traveled northeastward to the ancient Chinese capital city of Beijing to attend a prayer conference and afterwards to participate in another evangelistic mission. But when he got there, he didn't know where to find the church in which the prayer conference was to be held, nor did he have the addresses of the two or three Christians students he had gotten to know in the west who were now in Beijing. And he had no means of getting about in the city.

Praying for God's solutions, David set off for the nearest bicycle shop to tackle the most urgent of his problems. The shop had few bicycles, and the shopkeeper quoted him an exorbitant price for one of the few bicycles he did have. Then, abruptly, he asked David, "Are you a Christian?"

"Well, yes, I am," David replied.

"I am too," the man told his astonished customer. The shopkeeper was, in fact, a member of the church pastored by the well-known Wang Ming-dao, the very church David was looking for! Not only was the

107

shopkeeper glad to escort David to the church, but the man lent him a bicycle for as long as he might need it.

David still had to find a way to contact his Christian friends. This too was resolved within the day. A Chinese friend from the States, Hong Sit, hearing that David was in Beijing, sought him out and gave him all the information he needed.

Today Hong Sit is a pastor in Texas and president of the Chinese Full Gospel Fellowship International. "While there in Beijing David helped me in a very significant way," he testifies, recalling the impact of David's life on his own. "I had just graduated from the University of Illinois in the U.S. with a major in chemistry. When I met David in Beijing, I was on a tour of duty fighting the Japanese. . . . I remember what a great impression he made on me when we prayed together. It was a chance for rare fellowship, the kind you don't often get in the military. . . .

"He challenged me to pray about resigning from the service and staying on in China to become a missionary with the China Inland Mission. It meant that I would have to give up my passage home, which the army would be obliged to provide me, and to stay on with very little support. . . .

"The decision was difficult because at the same time I was offered a challenging assignment in the army. Every time I prayed about it, the Lord would seem to say, 'Son, go work today in my vineyard.'

"At the end of my week's struggling, I committed my life to serve the Lord and resigned from the service. In January 1947 the army flew me to Shanghai, where I was discharged and began my full-time ministry for the Lord as an associate of the China Inland Mission. Needless to say, it's been over forty years of glorious experience in service for the Lord. I thank God for sending David Adeney along to guide me in the right direction at the right time."

After the prayer conference David threw his energies into the planned student evangelistic mission, the first ever in Beijing. It was his first chance to get to know Wang Ming-dao. As a speaker, the zealous pastor was dynamic. The students listened, deterred neither by Wang's uncompromising message nor by how long he spoke. Before the week was over numbers of these brightest of China's young people became followers of Christ.

David stayed on in Beijing three months before moving on to Nanjing, where the China Inter-Varsity had set up its headquarters. He lived with a

Presbyterian missionary and traveled out from this base to universities around the area, teaching and encouraging the Christians and helping to build up an evangelical witness on the campuses, much as he had done in the States.

In the meantime Ruth continued to struggle without David in the States. Month followed month, and still no passage became available for her and the children to return to China. Besides the weight of caring for the children and managing the letter writing and accountability to supporters and the Mission, she was suffering from a slipped disk. While staying with her sister in South Dakota, she had wrenched her back when picking up a basket of washing. The spinal injury left her in agony. A congenital deformity in her hip discovered by X-ray was assumed responsible for the weakness and pain. Somehow the fact that a disk was out of place as well was overlooked. Ruth found getting the rest doctors prescribed nearly impossible. Having so recently recovered from the surgery she had undergone following Michael's birth, Ruth felt especially exasperated at the new pain that now handicapped her.

When she could, however, Ruth was glad to be able to get out to meetings to speak about China. One evening when staying with her parents, she was on her way out of the door when seven-year-old Rosie asked, in a voice that begged for a negative answer, "Mummy, are you going to become a great big preacher like Daddy?" The child's small hands tugged at Ruth's skirt.

The question pulled Ruth up short. She recognized the youngster's unspoken fear that her mother might also go away for a long time. "No, dear," she said, kneeling down to give Rosie a reassuring hug, "—no, I am not going to become a big preacher like Daddy. I shall stay with you."

Ruth fulfilled that evening's engagement, but after that, when anyone invited her to speak at a meeting, she refused. She realized that if one parent had to be away from the children, the other had to be at home.

Ruth's decision was an important one. The separation now was unusual, but who could tell what others lay ahead? David had already been involved in a great deal of traveling in the work opening up for him, and such demands would be likely to continue. She resolved to accept this sacrifice, believing that God would equip her for making the required choices, however hard they were. It was all part of the calling to marriage she had sensed so clearly and part of her responsibility, she felt, before God.

It was good that Ruth settled matters with God on this issue since it was to be a whole year before she and the children, with tickets in hand and one of Ruth's sisters as escort, were on their way to the West Coast to board the ship for China.

With Michael teething and fussy, Ruth had a terrible Pacific crossing. The baby often cried until both he and his mother were exhausted. A sudden fright had made him terrified of anyone's holding him but Mummy, forcing Ruth at mealtimes, in spite of her back, to carry him down the long corridors and up and down steps on the rolling ship.

David had been living in Nanjing over half a year when word came that his family was on its way. He was at the docks in Shanghai to meet them. With his arms spread wide he gathered them to him. At last they were together! No matter that they had to live for the time being cramped in two rooms in a house shared with other IV staff in Nanjing! The separation was over; they would manage.

And manage they did, for more than a year and a half. Not until Ruth returned from a few weeks in Shanghai for the birth of Bernard in September 1948 was the family to enjoy better housing. By then the new seven-bedroom CIM house was ready. All CIM staff in the city were to share the new accommodation, and eventually the household consisted of the Adeneys, the Henry Guinnesses, and Dr. Pauline Hamilton. But Ruth was to live in the fresh new home just seven weeks before her health, and the deteriorating political situation, would call for evacuation. They were there just long enough for David's brother Bernard and his wife Millicent to spend a happy visit.

The time in Nanjing saw wild inflation and political turmoil, hardly ideal conditions for raising a family. Once, however, caught in the middle of a student riot in the city, Ruth was given a marvelous ministry opportunity. During that terrifying experience, David and Ruth met Mrs. Twineham, advisor to Madame Chiang (Chiang Kai-shek's wife), and Mrs. Twineham invited Ruth to teach Sunday school at the Chiangs' chapel.

As David traveled from one isolated group of Christians to another in and around Nanjing, he was amazed by what he saw of continuing life and growth among the newly-formed groups. "One evening," he wrote, "I arrived late at night at a government medical college outside a city by the side of the great Yangtze River. The students were not expecting me, but as soon as the Christians knew I had arrived, they took me to stay with them in their dormitory. They had returned from the west following the Japanese occupation to find that their buildings were all broken down and furniture practically nonexistent. We stood around the tables for our meals." These Christians were meeting early in the morning in an old Japanese fort, the only place available on the wrecked campus. The next time David visited he found the Christians gathering on a rooftop. Later they built a little chapel off campus, where they could meet even if forbidden later to meet on university grounds.

It was on his second visit to the medical college that David took the time to go to the nearby cemetery, where Hudson Taylor was buried. Says David, "I'll never forget standing by that grave, and being impressed by the simple words on the stone, 'A man in Christ.' "

Listening, talking, teaching, preaching, answering doubts, problem solving, praying, and managing in all kinds of conditions were all a part of David's forays into scattered student enclaves. Humility made him approachable. His touch with God made the approach rewarding. Students appreciated the sense that they were worth his time.

Once a group of students had invited a speaker David felt was unsuitable. Should he say something? He wasn't sure. Interference might only engender resentment and rebellion. So he laid the matter before God and said nothing. A little while later the students came to him; they had made the discovery themselves of the man's unsuitability and were the wiser for it.

One young lady David met during his rounds of the Nanjing universities was a medical student by the name of Charlotte Tan. Ready to specialize, she wondered if David could help her find a residency in the West. He was able to introduce her to Dr. Kiesewetter at Children's Hospital in Philadelphia. Today Dr. Tan is one of the world's foremost specialists in leukemia. In recent years she served on the President's special committee on cancer in Washington, D.C. Today a professor at Cornell Medical School, she is the long-time leader of the New York Chinese Christian Fellowship. For her, David was at the right place at the right time.

111

Accepting the hazards and hard work of those days in post-war China yielded wonderful results. By the late 1940s the China Inter-Varsity had developed into one of the most significant and exciting movements among all the Inter-Varsity groups worldwide. In 1947 the various national groups of IVCF were pulled together under an umbrella organization called the International Fellowship of Evangelical Students. At the inauguration in Boston, Calvin Chao as leader of China Inter-Varsity represented one of the largest of all the national groups.

"Those were tremendous days, the likes of which would never be repeated," writes Leslie Lyall in his book, *God Reigns in China*. Lyall was referring to a summer conference in which he, David, and others took part at an orphanage in the Chungshan Hills, a suburb of Nanjing, in July 1947. "Several hundred students gathered, representing every university in China, the majority of them aflame with their first love for Christ. Others were comparative veterans, having been converted during the war and some having attended the only previous evangelical student conference, in Chongqing in 1945." He adds, "Forty years later the memory lives on."

Preparations had not been easy. Wrote David: "Five or six weeks before the conference we received word that all attempts to find suitable premises in Shanghai had failed. Then a chance remark from a friend caused us to think of Madame Chiang's orphanage and school situated on a hill outside Nanjing, on the edge of the national park and within a few minutes' walk of the beautiful Sun Yat Sen Memorial. Higher up than the city and cooler, situated in large grounds with plenty of room for walks and places for quiet prayer, it was ideal for our purpose, and as the school had not yet been opened, the spacious buildings were all free.

"Permission to use it had to be obtained from Madame Chiang, and our faith was tested as we waited a couple of weeks for her answer. Just a very few weeks before the conference was to start, her gracious consent reached us. But we were still faced with one great problem: we had the use of the buildings, but there was not a stick of furniture; beds, tables, chairs, kitchen utensils. We had to borrow everything in the city and provide transportation to the conference. Five days before the conference we still had only sixty Japanese sleeping mats! Then an American army chaplain came to our rescue and loaned us 247 army cots and the same number of folding chairs. Another answer to prayer was the provision of more than enough rice for the conference at about a third of the price being charged on the street."

During the last few days before the conference, while some took turns on their knees in a room set aside for prayer, workers arranged furniture, put up notices and decorations, set up a public address system, and attended to a hundred and one arrangements needing to be made.

David continued: "students and secretaries began to arrive from distant places several days before the conference started, our own home had to be very elastic, and camp beds began to appear in the living rooms. A special reception center was set up at the railway station, and on the 18th of July army trucks met the main party of over a hundred students that came from Shanghai and neighboring places. Groups from the interior were much smaller, but many of them had wonderful stories to tell of answered prayer for travel, for it is extremely difficult to obtain transportation. One party traveling by boat from Chongqing were stuck in Hankow, and had to spend their traveling allowance for food while waiting for another boat. Then the Lord graciously provided free passages to Nanjing for them. Beijing representatives traveled packed like sardines on a coastal steamer. But the delegate who traveled the furthest (from Lanzhou away in China's Northwest) came through in a day by air. . . .

"Never before had such a large and representative group of evangelical students gathered together in China, and we felt that in this unique conference God was working out his purposes for the church in China.

"The conference prayer—'O my soul, you must strive to advance,' a Chinese translation of Judges 5:21, (RSV)—aptly expressed the attitude of the majority of the students. From the very beginning we were conscious of the power of God in our midst. On the first morning Calvin Chao spoke on the need for repentance. Afterwards the platform was filled with students confessing their sin. Later in the day a large number responded to the call for men and women who would not only believe Christ, but follow him faithfully to the end.

"As we realized the great importance of personal work, all 350 students attending the conference were divided into groups of ten, with an IV staff worker, missionary, or other experienced Christian in charge of each group. An outsider visiting the conference might well have been puzzled by the names that began to appear everywhere. Biblical place names such as Bethel, Bethany, and Elim marked the dormitories, while inside, each group section was marked by a poster containing two Chinese characters representing Grace, Love, Truth, etc., for in Chinese it sounded quite natural to speak of the 'Righteousness Group' or the 'Lovingkindness Group. . . . '

"Perhaps one of the main features of the conference was the small-group prayer meetings which gathered in various places at all times of the day and night. Especially after the evening meetings little clusters of students could be found sitting round on the grass talking over the messages of the day and praying together. It was indeed good to hear some of the leaders speaking of conversions in their groups and of the blessing that had come through personal talks.

"Morning prayer meetings . . . were really in the nature of revival meetings, and from the prayers that followed the addresses, it was very evident that the Holy Spirit was working in many hearts. Pastor Lin Tao-Liang led an hour's Bible study after breakfast, and he was followed during the latter part of the week by old Pastor Chia, with his little white beard and tremendous energy. Preaching from great charts and oft-times breaking into song, he sought to lead the students into the victorious life in Christ.

"One evening just after supper . . . Madame Chiang paid us a special friendly visit. . . . She wanted to speak to the students, she said, not as a high official, but as a fellow Christian. She spoke very fully concerning hers and the Generalissimo's faith. I think she must have been impressed by the spiritual atmosphere and evident keenness of the students, especially the great chorus of amens during the prayer for the country and for the Generalissimo, and the fervor with which the students sang the 'Hallelujah Chorus.' . . . Before leaving, Madame Chiang presented the students with sixty watermelons, which were consumed with great gusto at the picnic the next day in the wooded park surrounding the beautiful pagoda near the Sun Yat Sen Memorial.

"On the last Sunday afternoon visitors were invited from the city, and the students really put on a magnificent program of music. It was a service of praise, with just a short talk in the middle of the musical items.

"Undoubtedly, however, the climax of the conference came in the last evening meeting as we gathered around the Lord's Table. The service was led by Pastor David Yang, who had spoken deeply on 1 Corinthians in these evening meetings all week long, dealing with many of the problems in students' minds and making them realize the wondrous privilege of being members of the church of the living God. How eagerly the students looked forward to his messages!

"It was already late when the communion service ended, but we could not close the conference without giving an opportunity for testimony. So many wanted to speak that testimonies had to be very brief; over eighty, in just a few sentences, spoke of God's goodness to them. What joy! No wonder the songs of praise went on long into the night!"

No one could have guessed how important those days of conference would be, nor how much many of those students would suffer for the name of Christ in the months and years ahead. One of those young people was Chang Yu-Ming, the high school boy Leslie Lyall calls "Henry" in *God Reigns in China*. Still vibrant in witness today, Dr. Yu-ming Chang and his wife Yu Hua, a pharmacologist, are participating in cancer research at Yale University in New Haven, Connecticut, and at Sloan-Kettering Memorial Cancer Center in New York. He is also a lay minister of the gospel. Both Dr. Chang and his wife suffered years of imprisonment and deprivation for their testimony.

Introduced to Christ by a Chinese country preacher and discipled by CIM missionary Edward E. Taylor, the young Chang Yu-Ming found himself at that conference in July 1947 because he just "happened" to meet another CIM member, Maida Contento, at a train station as his middle school was making its way back east. Mrs. Contento not only told him about the conference, but helped him register. Also his school group just "happened" to be in Nanjing waiting for transport that very week. His testimony: "That was the Lord's arrangement for me to be nurtured and rooted in him."

Forty-five years later Dr. Chang still remembers well those days of conference in Nanjing. "It was very hot," he says. "We had just started eating at lunch time early in the conference, when a man stood up in the middle of the dining room with a note in his hand. 'Brothers and sisters,' he said, 'the British Christian student conference sends their greetings to us in the name of Jesus Christ.' Then he read the verse they sent: 1 Corinthians 15:58.

"That was the first time I saw Mr. Adeney face to face," says Dr. Chang. "I came to know him as a caring minister to students and a faithful servant of God. Over the years he was to have a weighty spiritual influence on me."

"Mr. Adeney and Calvin Chao were in charge," Dr. Chang remembers. "Pastor Yang Shao-Tang preached on 1 Corinthians; Pastor Chia Yu-Ming, dean of the Spiritual Life Seminary, on the Seven Generations and the New Heaven and the New Earth (Revelation); and Calvin Chao on Romans. Mr. Chao's message was particularly significant as he related China's political situation and Christian belief, focusing especially on the Christian's need to offer himself as a living sacrifice, ready to be persecuted for the name of Jesus and the glory of God. Bishop Houghton, General Director of the China Inland Mission, in excellent Chinese also urged us young people to ready ourselves to suffer for our Christian faith.

"Before the conference was over I asked Mr. Adeney to write a Bible verse in my souvenir notebook. Later confiscated by the communists, that notebook became the basis for one of the communists' major charges against me for almost my whole life," testifies Dr. Chang without a trace of bitterness. "My crime: treasuring something from the Bible written to me personally by the imperialist and culturally aggressive Adeney." Dr. Chang and his wife were among those rounded up by authorities the night of August 5, 1955, along with their outspoken pastor, Wang Ming-dao. That night the arresting party snatched their fifteen-day-old daughter from her mother's breast, to be nurtured, at God's intervention, by the wife of a lab assistant whom Mrs. Chiang had publicly defended.

Only eternity will reveal how much that summer conference and the earlier conferences meant to the students, and how much those students were to endure for the commitments they made there. For those who took a leadership role, the realization has been humbling.

13

End of an Era

Welcome though it had been, the end of war with Japan simply cleared the way in China for hostilities to resume between the Nationalist government and the communists bent on revolution.

As the civil war gathered momentum, tensions mounted. The war's cloud of death and destruction, and the uncertainty of the outcome, tempered even the IV staff's excitement at working in a climate of almost explosive responsiveness. To supporters back home in 1948 David wrote: "All reports of student work in China need to be considered against the dark background of increasing chaos and suffering throughout large sections of the country. Before setting off on a month's tour of ten universities and colleges in northwest and central China not long ago, we received news that demonstrations among Shanghai students had led to the closing down of all IVF meetings in one of the larger universities. Permission has only recently been obtained to reopen this work."

David continued to tell of disturbing reports of missionary evacuations in several provinces and of persecution of Christians, even martyrdom, in communist areas. "Forces of evil and opposition to the gospel are certainly on the increase." Yet, he went on, "the doors are wide open in a very large portion of this great land for the preaching of the message of salvation. Students everywhere are seeking Christ. I believe that probably more truly converted men and women will be graduating from the universities and colleges this summer than ever before in the history of China." Those students would bear the brunt of the communists' determination to crush allegiance to Christ, and their faithfulness in the face of death and deprivation would lay the groundwork for the explosion of conversions a generation later.

Already in those waning years of the forties Christian students began to feel the pressures of rival factions competing to gain their allegiance. Communist sympathizers accused Christians of being reactionary and holding back the revolution. That was difficult to answer since many of the Christians were as disillusioned as their fellows with the failures and corruption of the Kuomintang and the exhausting and debilitating war.

But how could Christian students take their stand with communists when the bloodthirsty methods of revolution ran so contrary to the commands of Christ? And, more, how could they give their support to a philosophy which disregarded the existence of God? David summarized the dilemma: "We could understand the need to change some of the structures of society and bring justice and righteous government, so that the country people might be delivered from the oppression of landlords, famine, and the sufferings of war and brigandage. But we also knew that the destruction of freedom to worship the living God and the enforced molding of minds into a completely materialistic pattern of thinking was far too high a price to pay."

An associated pressure was the watchfulness of the Kuomintang. The government was already suspicious that the China Inter-Varsity might be hiding communists among its members. Soured relationships with the government, the students knew, would bring orders to disband, severely limiting open witness, their most important function in the uncertain political climate.

David identified the Christians with the early apostles, who were also "living in a society which was disintegrating, undermined by countless intrigues and political struggles." Like the apostles, Christian students had more faith in the transforming power of Christ than the success of any political change. Non-evangelical groups such as the YMCA, persuaded that social rather than spiritual change was China's pressing need, openly opposed this stand and in doing so deepened the evangelicals' isolation.

In the testing some students capitulated. But most stood, many with remarkable resilience. In February 1949 David wrote, trying to put what was happening into perspective: "Many reports have tended to concentrate on the dark side and every kind of rumor has flourished, even that the CIVCF work is closing down. Nothing could be further from the truth.

About thirty CIVCF workers in various parts of this country are finding students whose minds are open and responsive to a message that offers reality, hope, and new life. Inter-Varsity work is to be found in almost eighty colleges. Hundreds of students have indicated their desire to follow Christ; but spiritual results can never be measured in terms of numbers of decisions made at meetings. It is during a time of testing that the real value of the work appears, and if the seed that has been sown is really to bear fruit unto eternal life, there must be the steady building-up work in the college prayer meetings and Bible study groups."

David concentrated on this work of building up from his new base in Shanghai, with its swelling population which faced an increasing threat from the communists. Many considered Shanghai, with its large international community, safer than the capital, Nanjing, where anxiety was at its height. Ruth had obeyed orders and evacuated with the children from Nanjing to Shanghai while David was away visiting campuses. When he got the news, he hurried to Shanghai and met the family at the dockside.

As great numbers of students had also scrambled for the security of Shanghai, Inter-Varsity was already reaching out to them and was considering shifting its headquarters to the city. David had no difficulty at all finding opportunities among the young people, still trying to pursue their dreams. On his motorbike he dodged his way along streets congested with jostling shoppers, pole-juggling carriers, rickshaws, overloaded carts and delapidated trucks. In spite of ominous political stormclouds, it was a heady time for a man seeing so much of what God was doing among the cream of China's people.

Just before the communists marched into Shanghai and Mao declared his victory over Chiang Kai-shek and his Nationalist troops, the beleaguered government arrested several Inter-Varsity students for possessing a mimeograph machine, suspecting them of printing communist propaganda. Vainly protesting that the machines had produced no more subversive materials than fellowship newsletters, the students were held under threat of execution.

In the midst of this crisis, loud pounding on the door late one night brought David hurrying sleepily to answer the summons. It was the secret police! They were looking for an Inter-Varsity co-worker with whom the arrested students had communicated. As the man, whom the police knew by name, lived nearby at the China Inland Mission headquarters, David followed the raiding party to the suspect's room and watched with him as the officers searched for incriminating evidence. Together, in the presence of the police, David and his co-worker knelt by the bed and committed the whole matter to the Lord in prayer. Surprisingly friendly, the officer in charge gave David the name of the police station to which his friend was being taken.

Many of the hundreds praying for the imprisoned students added the staff worker to their prayer list. An S.O.S. went around the world.

Even before the man's arrest, God had prepared the way. During his regular Bible reading a few days before, David's friend had been impressed with the message to the church in Smyrna: "Do not be afraid of what you are about to suffer. I tell you, the devil will put some of you in prison to test you, and you will suffer persecution for ten days" (Revelation 2:10).

Ten days after his arrest the man was freed. Not only had he been given special privileges while in prison, he was spared the ill-treatment and torture sometimes meted out. But, more wonderful, he rejoiced in the great opportunities to witness to those who shared the large cell in which he was kept.

Prayer urgently continued for the Christian students facing execution. On the eve of the battle for Shanghai they walked free.

At just about the same time, in England, Florence Adeney slipped out of the body that no longer served her and walked free in her Savior's presence. But in the crisis and confusion of the civil war in China, David was to wait six weeks for the details of his mother's death.

The communist takeover in May 1949 happened remarkably quickly. Localized in scattered parts of the city, the fighting lasted only a few days. The Adeney's fellow worker, Pauline Hamilton, slept, as perhaps many others did, right through the transfer of government and, as she put it, "awoke the next morning under a new regime!"

That day following the coup, David took advantage of the quiet to ride his motorbike to the IV staff house across the city in an area of some of the fiercest fighting in Shanghai. At that hour a few bodies still lay unclaimed among roadside clutter. As David and IV friends had been in telephone contact during the battle for the city, he knew they were safe, but he wanted to be a part of their rejoicing and their prayerful look to the future.

The soldiers occupying Shanghai behaved in exemplary fashion, and the city seemed to breathe a great sigh of relief that at last the war was over. Those who welcomed the communists as liberators celebrated joyously. Many just celebrated the end of the war. A few stayed out of sight in sober uncertainty.

"In the beginning things were very calm," recalls Dr. Hamilton in her book, *To a Different Drum*, but it was an "eerie kind of calmness." No one knew what communist rule in China would bring. The Christians could only be cautious, despite the declaration of religious freedom that allowed them to continue their activities. After the restrictions and threats preceding the takeover, that freedom almost seemed unbelievable. "We hardly hoped for the liberty we now enjoy," David wrote in one of his regular newsletters.

But the respite was short-lived. Soon the catchy communist slogan, rhyming in Chinese, began to be chanted in the streets: "Don't worship heaven! Don't worship earth! Only worship the efforts of the people!" The remaking of China's people had begun.

David and Ruth watched from their window early in 1950 as the small groups of students gathered each morning to study and talk before classes began. These study groups were part of the communist policy of "thought reform," which took students through a process of looking closely at Mao's theory of the revolution. In the process they were expected to reject old habits and customs and pledge allegiance to the new China. Such indoctrination supplemented the lengthy lectures given with the same objective.

Added to this, the young people were expected to write the stories of their lives and beliefs, criticizing themselves and then subjecting what they said to criticism from their fellows. The new leaders saw personal reform as the route to wholehearted support of the revolution.

Christian students who dared express their beliefs in the study groups were severely chastised for holding to outdated customs and, even worse, for following a religion espoused by the hated imperialists. With purpose, the indoctrination consumed huge chunks of the day, leaving scant time for Christian meetings. Slowly Christian freedom was being strangled.

At those weekly Inter-Varsity fellowships which were still functioning, as David listened to students talking and praying together about what they were going through, he wondered if he and his colleagues were doing enough to help. It was at this point that the literary secretary of the China Inter-Varsity came up with an idea: since the students were obviously grappling with questions from the communists they didn't know how to answer, why not write a booklet that covered the important issues?

When *Questions Concerning the Faith*—written by the Chinese literary secretary who suggested it—came off the press, it met an urgent need. In hindsight, however, the effort seems to have been too little and too late. The scholar Bob Whyte, in his recent account of Christianity in China, *Unfinished Encounter*, observes that by 1949 Christianity had "lost the battle for the minds of the intellectuals." *Questions Concerning the Faith* presented an intellectual defense of the Christian faith and established the strength of Christian claims against those of Marxism. But that little booklet was the only piece of Christian apologetic literature known to have been published under the communist regime. Sadly, as a result, few Christians understood the fundamental challenge of Marxism.

But the little book did have an impact. In the first six months after publication 60,000 copies were sold. Many people came to faith because of it. Even some communists were impressed. One Communist Youth Corps teacher astonished his followers when he declared that the principles contained in *Questions Concerning the Faith* could not easily be dismissed. Christians were treated with respect as a result, and one even received an apology from the local government for its previous attitude towards him. David met one communist group leader who, after reading the book, sought out its author and was converted.

Having a stronger grasp of how their Christian faith related to social and political issues, however, took the students only so far. As David watched their reactions to the endless debates and indoctrination, he saw that "where a high standard of spiritual life existed within the Christian group and where the members were bound in the fellowship of the gospel, they were able to overcome the criticism of their opponents." In his book, *China: Christian Students Face the Revolution*, David talks about the crucial function of regular fellowship meetings. In such meetings as in Shanghai, students "wounded" in the spiritual conflict could find answers, encouragement, and healing. Members who had scattered often wrote letters back. Anyone who was ill or unable to attend knew that he was missed. If he were in special need, he was sure that other members of the "family" were praying for him and that someone would visit him. In a world falling apart the intimacy brought strength.

One Christian brought a recently converted but already shaky brother he had met while sharing a ride in a bicycle rickshaw. The lad had accepted Christ a few weeks before when he had seen his rickshaw puller praying on his knees during a time of great danger. A bomb fell close by, wounding others around them, but sparing the rickshaw puller and the young passenger. As the newcomer listened during the meeting to various students' testimonies, God spoke to him, and before the meeting closed the lad himself was on his feet telling of what the Lord had done for him.

The propaganda of the Communist Youth Party had so influenced another student that he had joined those who had given up attending the fellowship meetings. One day, he happened to pass the Inter-Varsity house as the students were singing hymns. He felt a great longing to go in and see his Christian friends, but feared that, because he had been out of touch with the group for so long, his presence would cause comment. For some time he hesitated. Eventually, however, he slipped into the back of the meeting room. Listening to the Christians talking about the Lord they loved brought him back to the Savior.

One day on his way to a student fellowship meeting with a Chinese IV staff worker hanging on behind, David was maneuvering his motorbike down a busy lane when an elderly lady started across the road a few feet ahead. David aimed the bike to steer clear of her, but suddenly the woman stopped and, in a change of mind, turned to retrace her steps. David slammed on his brakes, his companion flew over his head, and the motorbike slid, almost clearing the woman, but knocking her down and tearing her stockings. No one was more than superficially hurt, but David soon found himself at the police station.

"How can you believe in someone who lived 2,000 years ago?" David's communist captors challenged, after the accident had been investigated and there was time to press their advantage over the foreigner in their charge.

"But that Jesus who lived 2,000 years ago is alive today. He is not dead," David replied quietly. "He —— "

His captors would let him say no more.

David was released and went immediately to the Inter-Varsity house, where a group of engineering students had gathered to pray. David couldn't help noting the contrast between the derision he felt at the police station and the genuine oneness and welcome he felt from the gathered students.

With Calvin Chao now in Hong Kong, believing he could direct the China Inter-Varsity more effectively away from communist restrictions, David carried additional responsibility for the movement, working closely with Chinese colleagues to keep up the student meetings for fellowship and Bible study. But as the months went by, it was becoming more and more clear that his days in China as a missionary were numbered. Communist leaders were emphasizing the building of a new China, including a new Chinese church without the influence of foreigners.

As Easter approached in 1950, David saw with others that China Inter-Varsity could not hold its planned spring retreat on any campus. Students and IV staff gathered instead in a large cemetery. It was a memorable retreat.

By the middle of the year David recognized that his continuing presence would only embarrass and hinder the Inter-Varsity groups. If they were going to survive under communist rule, they would have to stand on their own. Reluctantly, he and Ruth prepared to leave.

The turning point had come with the publication of the *Christian Manifesto* in July 1950, setting out in the clearest terms yet the government's plans for China's church. Prime Minister Zhou En-lai had called together a number of leading Christian pastors, assuring them that they would be allowed to continue preaching as long as they could rally their congregations to government support. He admitted his conviction, however, that in the new climate he expected Christianity eventually to wither and die. Together ministers and communist officials worked out the wording of the *Christian Manifesto*. The group of ministers, including David's friend, a Lutheran pastor who shared the same Chinese surname, promulgated the document. The preface read as follows: "It is our purpose in publishing the following statement to heighten our vigilance against imperialism, to make known the clear political stand of Christians in New China, to hasten the building of a Chinese church whose affairs are managed by the Chinese themselves, and to indicate the responsibilities that should be taken up by Christians throughout the whole country in national reconstruction in New China."

Whereas an earlier document, entitled *Message from Chinese Christians to Mission Boards Abroad,* and issued by an informal group of prominent Christians, had left room for missionaries as long as leadership was firmly in the hands of the Chinese, the *Christian Manifesto* did not. And while the earlier document had acknowledged the troublesome association of the missionaries with imperialism, it appeared to exonerate them from direct involvement. In the new document the antagonism towards imperialistic aggressors fell as heavily on missionaries as on any foreigners, an antagonism fostered by a government anxious to consolidate its control. But the Chinese church felt the heavy hand of this antagonism far more—because of its association with the missionaries. The foreign ambassadors for Christ had no choice but to leave.

As David and Ruth packed, missionaries all around were leaving too, hearts heavy that they had unwittingly contributed to the suspicion the government was feeling toward the church. Everyone was fearful for the future of that church. Yet, had the missionaries been able to see ahead and know how the church was going to develop over the following years when China was cut off from the West, they would have been reassured, indeed astonished.

At this earlier stage Christians were under tremendous pressure, forced to choose their response to the *Christian Manifesto.* Some were cautiously optimistic, seeing the government's determination to implement the "three-self" principles in church government—self-government, self-support, and self-propagation—as at least evidence that the church would be allowed to continue under communism. Of these, many felt that an alliance between church and state was the only way forward. Thus 400,000 Protestant Christians signed the *Christian Manifesto,* pledging their allegiance to the new regime.

Among the signatories, however, were many who opposed the changes but felt they had no choice, and many more who saw no possible compromise between Christianity and atheistic principles of communism. One such pastor described his position to David in the form of a picture. The present situation, he said, was like being on a train. Though the train was running on tracks that could not be changed, he could still witness to his fellow passengers. There were others who refused to have anything to do with the official government body set up to organize the church along the lines laid down in the *Manifesto*. These saw clearly that if the whole church was to come under government control, its ability to evangelize would be compromised. The government-sponsored body was later known as the Three-Self Patriotic Movement and was responsible to the Religious Affairs Bureau of the Chinese Communist Party.

Among those who shunned any association with the government-sponsored church group was Wang Ming-dao and those he inspired with his fiery preaching. That July he was the main speaker at the student summer conference in Tianjin.

At the time David, Ruth, and the children were among the missionaries crowding the Mission center in Tianjin, working to fulfill government requirements to exit the country (such as making lists in triplicate of everything in their luggage and sorting out pictures for inspection). "Mr. Adeney and his family are in Tianjin," the student heading up the conference told Chang Yu-Ming, who had been at the Nanjing conference in 1947 and who was now a medical student. "You go to the CIM and invite him here to be with us."

As David followed by bicycle-driven rickshaw, Chang struggled to lead the way on a bicycle that was constantly losing its drive-chain. The bicycle, the twenty-year-old told David with emotion, was a gift from an uncle whom the communists had killed. David felt sorry for the lad, smeared with black grease by the time the two arrived at the Wesleyan high school. There, students were enjoying Wang Ming-dao's nightly messages entitled "The Seven Great Witnesses of God."

As it was Chang's responsibility to look after the welfare of Wang Ming-dao, he brought David to him at the home of a Wesleyan missionary by the name of Dixon, where Wang was staying. Early on, Wang Ming-dao gave David a copy of his just-published autobiography, *These Fifty Years*. As David, Dixon, and Wang then talked into the night, Chang shuttled continuously between the living room doorway and outside, keeping watch, but overhearing much of what was said.

On the men's minds, for one thing, was the outbreak of the Korean War. The West's involvement was already increasing pressure on Christians in China. Conversation ranged from the prediction of suffering and hardship ahead to the sovereignty of God, from the possibility that all church buildings might be closed to the need for Christians to be faithful to the risen Lord. "I will never join any organization no matter what coat it wears

126

if it is a cover for government control," the pastor of Tabernacle Church said defiantly. "I will never sit on a bench with the so-called social-gospel leaders; they are non-Christian, even anti-Christian. We can be unsuccessful, but we have to be faithful to our Lord and to what we believe—the Bible. If not . . . the foundation has been lost." Wang had defied the Japanese in the past and gotten away with it. In this regime he would not. None of the men could have guessed at that point that the stance of the well-known preacher would cost him much of his life in prison.

The listening Chang Yu-Ming was particularly impressed with David's story of being asked to cheat to save himself tax when providing a motorbike for his brother in Israel. David had refused, and had told the Jewish customs official that he wanted to remain true to his Savior. David hardly remembers the incident or telling it, but Dr. Chang writes: "This strong testimony of David Adeney has been impacting my whole life, even the hard and long years of my communist labor camp experience . . . encouraging me and refreshing me and nurturing me. I told the story to the communist officials, then asked them, 'Was this the way of an evil person?'

" 'No matter of what good character you are, no matter how industrious you are,' they told me, 'no matter how highly you are qualified in science and wisdom, no matter how many people need your medical skillfulness and clinical technique . . . as long as you believe . . . in Jesus Christ as the Son of God, as long as you don't give up your Christian faith, that means you are not a person of atheism, materialism, and evolutionism, but a believer in the Jew Jesus instead of a follower of the Jew Karl Marx.' " And for that Chang Yu-Ming was a prisoner.

David's old mentor, David Yang, took a different route. He was pastoring two churches at the time of the communist takeover. When he was condemned and thrown out of the Nanjing church, he went to his church in Shanghai and received very different treatment from the communists there. He was told that he had been wrongfully accused in Nanjing and that if he would join the Three-Self Movement, he could stay as a pastor in Shanghai. Torn between losing or keeping a ministry through which he felt he could still serve the church, Pastor Yang finally agreed to the conditions imposed upon him, much to the disappointment of some and the bitter criticism of others.

David ached for his old friend, asking himself what he might have done under such pressure. He could not imagine what he might have been led to do in similar circumstances. At one point David Yang phoned to ask David's advice about making a broadcast for the communists in which they wanted him to denounce missionaries. Agonizing over having to do such a thing, Yang wrote and rewrote the script before the program went out.

Although David Yang was allowed to continue preaching for a while, he was finally removed from the pastorate and accused of "leaning too much to one side." He was never imprisoned, but instead was given the job of translating government papers. He died of a heart attack when shoveling snow during the Cultural Revolution in the 1960s.

David and Ruth left China in August 1950, a few months before the official withdrawal of the CIM in 1951. Several Inter-Varsity students had accompanied them to the station in Shanghai, whose farewell gifts and words of gratitude expressed all that the Adeneys had come to mean to them. They were glad the Adeneys had left, however, when shortly afterwards a poster was circulated denouncing David as an imperialist. He had been blacklisted.

David left China deeply shaken by all that he had seen and experienced of the church's struggles. He would not have compromised on the centrality of the gospel or the conviction that evangelism should be above politics, but he worried that if the Christians were out of touch with what was happening around them, how could they be effective witnesses, especially when hit with opposition? What would happen to them now? How would they hold their own?

"There was—and continues to be—no excuse for intellectual laziness," David wrote in *China: Christian Students Face the Revolution.* "A Christian is commanded to be ready at any time to give an answer for the hope that is within him. For this reason it is important that Christians honestly face the criticism that comes from the non-Christian world. Too often we have lived in a ghetto-type existence, out of touch with many of the challenging questions being discussed in student groups around the world."

David was greatly moved by the fortitude of his friends back in China. In one of the last letters he received, a student leader in the China Inter-Varsity, soon to be shut down, wrote: "Recently we have had an immense burden to preach the gospel . . . because, after all, the preaching of the gospel is the duty of every Christian. Even if we can't preach, and if we are not willing to preach, we still must do it, because whatever happens, the gospel must go forth in order that the seed may be scattered. And for this we will gladly die."

Many did die. But because a cloak of silence settled between China and the West, the fate of the Chinese church was unknown for almost twenty years.

John Howard Adeney,
David's father

Florence Mary Wood Adeney,
David's mother

David with Harold as a baby, 1914

David, 18 years old

Ruth, 16 years old

David preaching at a Children's Special Service Mission on the beach, around 1931.

David *(center)* with the executive committee of the Cambridge Inter-Collegiate Christian Union, 1931.

Friends and family gathered to see David off to China, September 1934. David is second row, center, and his mother, pastor, father, and brother Harold are far right.

Aboard the *Carthage* liner sailing for China from Southampton, 1934.

David and Ruth Adeney on their wedding day, Hankow, March 31, 1938.

Henan pastors, 1939. Wang Yi-Zhai *(left)* was David's fellow worker in the Fangcheng church.

Rosemary Joy, born January 1, 1939, in Fangcheng.

Rosie in her Chinese *pao-tzi*, padded gown.

Ruth using the transportation of choice in China.

Farewell picture, Fangcheng, 1941, before leaving for furlough. Olive Joyce, a fellow missionary, is far right, and the Adeney's cook is seated left.

Speaking to IVCF students at Bear Trap Ranch, Colorado.

David and Ruth with John, Michael, Bernard, and Rosemary,
Geneva, Illinois, 1956, prior to leaving for Hong Kong.

Bernard, Harold, Ronald *(standing)*, Jack and David *(seated)* with their father on his 90th birthday, 1959.

A historic picture of the newly-appointed IFES Executive Committee, Nyack, New York, August 1963. David worked with many of these leaders over the years. *Front row, left to right:* Dr. Hans Bürki, Prof. H. Enoch, Dr. D. Martyn Lloyd-Jones (the first president of IFES), Dr. Carl Fr. Wisloff (the first vice president and later president), Dr. Daniel Jonah. *Second row:* Dr. John White, Dr. Oliver Barclay, Mr. C. Stacey Woods (the first IFES General Secretary), Prof. Bodo Volkmann. *Back row:* Mr. P.T. Chandapilla, Mr. Charles Troutman, Mr. Samuel Escobar, Mr. Ephraim Orteza.

With Chua Wee Hian *(left)*, later the General Secretary of IFES, and Bel Magalit, now Principle of the Asian Theological Seminary in Manila. Together these three men covered 25 years serving terms as Associate General Secretary of the IFES for East Asia.

The first group of staff and students at the Discipleship Training Center, Singapore, 1969.

David at an Open House meeting, Singapore. In front is Howard Peskett *(left)*, who succeeded David as dean, and Ernest Chew, chairman of the DTC Board.

Asian delegates to the IFES conference in England, 1983, including three DTC graduates: Otawa *(second row, far right)*, now IFES Regional Director for East Asia, Ellie Lau *(front row, center)*, and Benny Chin *(second row, by David)*, former General Secretary of FES Hong Kong.

The Adeneys celebrate their 50th wedding anniversary with their family, 1988. *Standing:* Fred and Mabel Hubbard (Ruth's sister), David and Ruth, John and Carol, Bernie and Fran, Michael and Miriam, Rosemary. *Kneeling:* Jennifer, Keith, Rina, Peter. (Family members not pictured: Rosemary's husband, Ken Chandler, and children, Mark and Karen; Michael's children, Danny, Joel, and Michael, Jr.)

David and Ruth Adeney, partners for over 55 years.

14

To Count the Most for God

The fire in David Adeney's bones still burned for the kingdom of God. Even before the family left China, at the invitation of Stacey Woods, David was preparing to pour his energies into the work of InterVarsity Christian Fellowship in the U.S. Midwest.

"The true Christian will be motivated, not by selfish ambition," David wrote in *The Unchanging Commission,* "but by a desire to find the place prepared by the Holy Spirit where his life may count the most for God." That was the standard for his own life. "Our only desire," he wrote in a personal letter at the time, "is to fulfill the purpose for which God has called us and to make the greatest possible contribution to the work of the church of the Lord Jesus throughout the world."

David's only hesitation about accepting the leadership of the IVCF team in the U.S. Midwest stemmed from his own misgivings about his qualifications. "I am not a deep thinker or an academic," he explains. The hesitation came more from his tendency to self-doubt than from any ineffectiveness in ministry to young people, who were drawn to him magnetically. They would cluster around him after meetings at which he spoke. "It wasn't that he always had great, polished things to say, either from the platform or in personal conversation," says Dr. Walter Liefeld of Trinity Evangelical Divinity School. "It was the integrity of the man. The students sensed God's presence in him. And because of that they paid attention to what he said. It made a difference in their lives."

When Walter Liefeld first heard of David Adeney in the mid-1940s, he himself was a young person praying about going to China. He was told that as a means of preparation he should choose a missionary in China to pray for. He chose David because he liked what he heard of him. When Liefeld joined IVCF staff in 1951, who should be his supervisor? David Adeney! Dr. Liefeld says today, "David's spiritual influence on my life is probably matched by no one outside of my own family."

After a wait in England for the granting of David's visa and a visit to Ruth's family in Minnesota, David, Ruth, and their four youngsters moved to a small house in Geneva, Illinois, across the street from Stacey and Yvonne Woods. From there David commuted by train to the IVCF office in Chicago, in the beautiful mansion on North Astor, a block away from Lake Shore Drive. It took him little time to be fully absorbed once again in the work of InterVarsity, among students whose horizons had been broadened by their wartime experiences.

For the next five years David spent a lot of time criss-crossing the country, mostly by train, visiting InterVarsity fellowships, speaking at churches and conferences, sometimes accepting the challenge to speak at "Religion and Life" weeks at universities, even Rotary meetings. Often he took a sleeper so that he could travel overnight and be ready for the day's work as soon as he arrived at his destination.

David could not get away from what he had experienced in China, and it spilled over into his ministry. He could not forget the systematic operations of communist students as they set about converting others to their philosophy. How could Christians be any less zealous? he asked audiences. Neither could he forget the cost Chinese Christian students were paying for their faith, and he used illustrations of those hungry, harassed young people to challenge his listeners. Many who were students in the States in those days remember the impact of those stories from China on their lives, leading them to dedicate themselves more purposefully to God.

A jarring scream at 6:00 in the morning stirred a very different memory of China when David was in Boston for a few days, staying with new-found friends Jim and Vera Shaw, advisors of the Harvard IVCF. Jim was a professor in research in a dental school. The scream, from a neighboring house, woke the whole household. A girl, gripped by some terrible fear, was shouting for help in her front yard across the street. Two boys, emerging from another house, ran over to try to restrain her. Her anguished cries struck a chill into the Shaws and David as they took in what was happening. "I am possessed by Satan," the girl screamed.

David spoke urgently to his friends. "I heard that voice in China," he said. "We must go over and pray."

Vera tried to tell him about the family across the street, a widow and three daughters, still fairly new to the area. Italians, they had kept to themselves, perhaps intimidated as Roman Catholics by the staunch Protestants surrounding them. But whatever the reasons, they did not seem to be the sort of people who would welcome an intrusion into their affairs.

But Vera was talking to the air. David had already disappeared down the stairs.

In the few minutes that had elapsed, the girl had gone back into the house. But as David reached the door, she burst out again, still screaming, her face twisted in fear and her lip bleeding where she had bitten it. At the sight of David she became extraordinarily still.

"Who are you?" she asked quite normally.

"I am a servant of the Lord Jesus and used to be a missionary."

To everyone's astonishment, the girl, calm now, invited David into the house. The family, bewildered, raised no objection. As David clearly had some kind of rapport with the young woman, they let him talk and pray with her.

After a while, however, the family began to show impatience, obviously wishing that David would leave. They were embarrassed to be made such a spectacle in the neighborhood. When he tried to give the victim a New Testament, the family insisted that he go.

"The work is not finished," David said unhappily to the Shaws. Indeed it was not, for the girl was eventually admitted to a mental hospital. David never had access to her again.

For a long time afterwards the mother asked after David, whose godly concern she had come to associate with the Catholic priesthood. "How is the dear Father David?" she would ask Vera Shaw. She sent him a card at Christmas, and David reciprocated with messages of encouragement. That was the most he was able to do.

Jim and Vera Shaw's children loved David's visits. Their British friend came to the northeast regularly to visit university campuses and to speak at Park Street Church in Boston. Once when his birthday coincided with his stay with the family, he found two parcels to open in the morning—a different tie from each young friend. David came to breakfast wearing one;

then halfway through the meal he disappeared, reappearing wearing the other. The Shaws were delighted.

Wherever he went, David befriended as many Chinese students as he could, spending time with them, talking, praying, helping in any way possible. In this way he touched hundreds of individuals over the years. An extraordinary number of Chinese students at Trinity Evangelical Divinity School, says Professor Liefeld, have pointed to David as an influence in their lives.

David also squeezed opportunities to get groups of Chinese young people together. In planning the first Chinese conference in the Midwest, he worked with Peter Yuen, who was, years later, to share discipleship training responsibilities with him in Singapore. David arranged one Chinese houseparty in the middle of an InterVarsity conference, when most people would have settled for the demands of the main conference alone. It was typical both of David's capacity for work and of his concern for his Chinese friends. He and Ruth watched many such students go back to China with a mixture of joy and grief—joy that something of Christ's love might go with them and be shared with others, grief that their future in China was so likely to bring hardship.

But beyond the Chinese students were other foreign students, from all over the world. Concerned InterVarsity staff—David prominent among them—knew that if international students of all sorts were to be given a fair hearing of the gospel, they needed special attention, with various programs and events developed to suit their needs and lifestyles. A year after he came back to IVCF from China, David was given the green light to pioneer this work among internationals—this in addition to his responsibilities to train and to support staff on campuses across the Midwest.

David's new role simply gave him and Ruth an official reason to do what they had always made a priority—to befriend international students. They planned houseparties in which a good holiday could be combined with Christian teaching, and looked for opportunities for these students to make friends among Christians—fellow students and also families and individuals—who could give the international visitors the support and care they missed in being so far from their own homes.

"One of the highlights of the year that David was my area director, was the international students' Thanksgiving weekend in Chicago," remembers one of the IVCF staffworkers. "We left from Minneapolis on the evening before Thanksgiving with several carloads of international students and drove all night to Chicago, arriving at Trinity Seminary in the morning. Everyone was farmed out to a family for Thanksgiving dinner. The rest of the weekend was spent sightseeing in the day time and having a gospel meeting in the evening. A very positive work for God was done on these weekends."

At these retreats David always let those students who were not Christians know they were free to speak out, that it was a time to listen to one another. At a houseparty in Washington, D.C., a Muslim student said he would like to speak at the evening meeting on the uniqueness of Jesus Christ. "Of course," remembers David, "he gave the Muslim view of Jesus the prophet and went on to say that Muslims believe nine-tenths of what Christians believe. Trouble was, the one-tenth difference included the main beliefs of our faith. This led to interesting discussion. I believe," David explained, "that it is essential to listen to followers of other religions if we expect them to give serious consideration to the Christian message.

"At another houseparty, this one in the Rockies, a Muslim student came again and again to ask me, 'Why did Christ have to die?' I tried hard to answer, but felt that he left the houseparty still not understanding the heart of the gospel. Some months later, however, I visited his campus and was amazed to find that he was a Christian.

" 'How did you come to believe?' I asked him.

" 'I could not get Christ out of my mind,' he answered.

"He had finally gone to see a pastor, he told me, and eventually came to faith. It was costly for him. Not only did his girlfriend break their engagement, but he suffered great opposition from his family."

On his way to becoming a nuclear physicist, Sid Feng (not his real name) was a student working on his second Ph.D. at the University of Chicago, when David spotted him one day in a science lab and spoke to him in Chinese. The young man had not long before come to know Christ at the University of California at Berkeley. He had been longing for Christian fellowship. David introduced him to the international Bible study group, and there Sid Feng not only grew in his knowledge of Christ but contributed zeal and witness.

Attending that international Bible study was a Japanese student by the name of Miyai-san who, having come from a strong Buddhist background, struggled to accept Christianity. He had told David, "I feel like a man going round and round a house and not able to go in." Sid Feng was the one who helped him through the door into faith. Miyai-san became a vice president for Shell Oil in Japan; his faith in Christ was no secret.

Sid Feng had not quite finished his second Ph.D. when he felt he had to return to China. "I must go back to witness to my family," he insisted. When people remonstrated with him, he quoted Paul in Acts 20:24: "I consider my life worth nothing to me, if only I may finish the race and complete the task the Lord Jesus has given me—the task of testifying to the gospel of God's grace."

"Don't send any books," Sid Feng wrote cryptically from China not long after he returned.

It was the last anyone heard from the young Chinese scientist for twenty-two years.

Then one day a letter appeared in David's mail bearing the return address of the Chinese Academy of Science in Beijing. "These twenty-two years," the letter began, "my Lord has protected me." It was from Dr. Sid Feng. What a joy to know that both Sid Feng and his faith had survived the China holocaust!

Eventually Dr. Feng and David, neither of them young any more, were to meet in an airport in China. Today students pepper the respected nuclear physicist with questions about how he can be both a scientist and a Christian.

Commenting on David's work as IVCF director for the Midwest, a colleague says, "The business of his life was to serve the Lord, and the great interest of his life was then, as now, the Chinese people. Though pleasant and easy to get to know, he was very single-minded and a no-nonsense kind of person. As I recall, he was good as a director, though he tended to push us rather hard. He spent a lot of time with some of the staff who were having problems.

"I always envied his ability to engage students in serious discussion," this former colleague admits. "In the 1950s the small schools in Minnesota and North Dakota were much more remote and 'back woods' than they are now, and the students tended to be very provincial. Consequently David, with his English ways and accent, was quite a novelty. I think he rather enjoyed this and used it to his advantage. Once we were having dinner at a conference, and David asked in his best English accent for 'just a spot of tea.' When I pointed out that he already had one—on his tie—we all laughed, including David."

Sometimes, however, David found himself in the middle of a storm. Stacey Woods, key pioneer of the IVCF work in North America and of the international student movement, was a man who saw things in black and white and who could be hard on other people when he disagreed or disapproved of an action. As good a friend as Stacey was—the Adeneys and Woods lived across the street from each other in Geneva, Illinois—and as much as David truly admired him, he sometimes had to step in as peacemaker. It was a role David would have rather avoided.

After Bill Bright founded Campus Crusade for Christ in 1951 and its influence began to be felt in the universities, Campus Crusade's more structured approach to evangelism cast doubt on the effectiveness of IVCF work. Even David had put too much of himself into IVCF not to feel the negative implications. But concerned that the campus witness should not suffer from disunity and even competition among evangelical Christians, David took time to counsel staffworkers how best to respond to Campus Crusade, taking a positive approach. IVCF should learn from criticism, he told them.

David felt that the arrival of Campus Crusade was an opportunity for InterVarsity to clear out a few cobwebs. To fellow staff members he wrote: "Campus Crusade workers often suggest that IVCF is just a fellowship of Christians enjoying Bible studies together while *they* are militantly pressing forward to reach non-Christians. This is sometimes true, and Christian fellowships need to realize the absolute necessity that every member should be actively seeking to win others for Christ. Within the Christian fellowship there is sometimes a failure to give the instruction and encouragement needed to stimulate active personal evangelism. Staffworkers are sometimes so busy with organized speaking and meetings and travel that they don't have time for personal interviews. While not insisting on a stereotyped approach, staffworkers need to teach by precept and example how to lead students to Christ."

Fresh thinking and reappraisal of objectives was healthy for IVCF groups. In advising his staffworkers, David returned time and again to his passionately held conviction that what mattered above all was spiritual vitality. "We must beware of spiritual mediocrity. We cannot be content with a superficial faith. There is no substitute for deep devotion, experience of the power of the Holy Spirit, and sacrificial service. As staff workers we must not allow ourselves to be pressed by excessive activity into a barren spiritual life. There must be times of very close fellowship with the Lord, including periods of worship in the Spirit and fervent intercession for others."

David's own disciplined use of a daily time before God was the secret of the intensity of the fire that burned in his bones. It was this that kept his focus clear and his life so quietly powerful.

Out of the six years David spent in InterVarsity work in the States after coming out of China, he remembers best the three years he spent as Missionary Secretary, now a much bigger undertaking than when he had vacated it to return to China. He took on this job in 1953. To the multiplying InterVarsity groups had been added Nurses Christian Fellowships in colleges of nursing, and Student Foreign Missions Fellowships on the campuses of Christian colleges. Established as independent bodies, these two entities were now affiliated with IVCF. In 1950, campus groups of all three branches totaled 561.

David's work was cut out for him. His desire to be useful in God's service and his vision for inspiring students to a similar commitment pushed him to work at a furious pace, leaving colleagues gasping with a mixture of bewilderment and admiration.

Not that he missed out on holidays. He loved them. They were opportunities for travel, family togetherness, and for meeting and interacting with different people. But vacations were never excuses to forget the urgency of God's priorities. Michael Griffiths, former General Director of Overseas Missionary Fellowship (China Inland Mission's new name after the pull-out from China), remembers being with David at a Mission holiday home in Japan, when David rushed off to a nearby student holiday camp to give a talk and show a film, though no one was pressing him to do it.

The stories are legion about David's workaholism, usually told with a mixture of affection and exasperation, some perhaps apocryphal—such as the one about his leaving his hospital bed in Shanghai, where he was recovering from having his appendix out, to attend a prayer meeting, jumping out of the window to avoid discovery!

When he was working, David always tried to fit into a day as much as possible. One colleague remembers vainly attempting to ease the punishing schedules David took on. "I would try to schedule a day off, but David would just fill it fuller than other days. So in the end I had to be content with planning a lighter day somewhere in the itinerary. I concluded that getting David to take a day off was impossible."

Ruth bore much of the brunt of David's propensity to cram too much into a day or a week. She had to pick up the pieces when David got overtired, to manage the home and look after the children when he was away, and do a thousand and one practical things that simply would not have occurred to David. She was torn between wanting to support him wholeheartedly in the work she believed he was called by God to do, and longing to put the brakes on for both his sake and her own.

David's health was precarious at the best of times, and he often struggled with physical problems that sapped him of energy. He refused to take much notice of such ailments, however, and simply hung on to the verse that had so encouraged him before he went to China, "As thy days, so shall thy strength be." Friends and colleagues marveled that he seemed to come up with more energy and resources than any of them, no matter how ill or gray he might look.

But Ruth saw his private exhaustion, and often felt she had to step in. If people trespassed on David's time—even though he gave them no reason to suppose they were doing so, and indeed was prepared to talk with them all night if necessary—she was the one to put her foot down. She had never been one to speak other than straight, and sometimes her protests seemed sharp, impatient, even unreasonable. Hers was a difficult role. But friends agree that if it were not for Ruth, David would have burned himself out long ago.

"Both David and Ruth have truly servant's hearts," says a fellow missionary. "David always seemed to be willing to wear the towel and to do the thing that others felt they didn't have time or strength to do. I know that both he and Ruth have sometimes done it to the harm of their own health.

"David and Ruth recognized they were citizens of heaven and lived that way. They weren't out to grab for themselves things of this earth. They are not double-minded. That they are truly citizens of heaven, I think, is what keeps them going. There's no talk about retiring to go fishing or to play golf; they just keep going for Jesus Christ."

In Canada the Pioneer Camps, which combined holiday fun with Christian training, were already popular. Stacey Woods was keen to establish similar camp-based programs for university students in the United States. David was the speaker for the very first camp at Bear Trap Ranch in the Colorado Rockies. About the same time a second site was chosen in an isolated cove on Catalina Island, about thirty miles from Los Angeles Harbor, to be known eventually as Campus by the Sea. One of David's contributions at Bear Trap Ranch was his acting out A. A. Milne's *Winnie the Pooh.* The English accent only enriched the narrative. Campers loved it.

Natural beauty was a key requirement when choosing the camp sites. The more remote the better. The more scenic, whether it be mountains, coast, forest, or a combination of all three, the more aware the students would be of the Creator and the closer he would seem. A third site fitted the bill beautifully—500 acres on the north shore of Lake Huron in Michigan's upper peninsula, donated for the specific purpose of training students to serve Christ. It was here at Cedar Campus that David brought to reality the missionary training program that had been on his mind for some time.

David was as concerned to train students for the foreign mission field as he was to inspire them. Having benefited himself from the Missionary Training Colony and David Yang's Spiritual Work Team, he wanted to put at the heart of the new venture the same combination of practical training and personal study.

The first forty missionary trainees arrived for a month-long program in August 1954. Run separately from the main camp, the Missionary Training Camp was quite spartan by comparison. Up at 6:00 A.M., the missionary recruits took a cold swim, dressed, then spent an hour in quiet prayer and study. Classes for teaching followed breakfast, then a period of personal study. During the evenings, visiting missionary speakers broadened the young people's vision.

Drawing from his own experience in the "university of the wilderness" in Henan, David alerted the young people to the possibility that personal chastening and sifting might well accompany a sincere desire to serve God overseas. "To be an effective messenger of the Cross," he told them, "the missionary has to pass through a stripping process through true identification with the Savior: the flesh has to be crucified. At the same time the personality must be filled with the Holy Spirit."

Again, drawing on the example of the Colony and David Yang's Team, David set the weekends aside for practical evangelistic training. Teams of six or seven campers would take responsibility for an assigned area, to do house-to-house visiting, conduct open-air services, and be involved in church activities. That first year was the hardest, as David and his Missionary Training Camp were unknown, and churches were suspicious. Later the missionary teams were more than welcomed.

Dolores Henry Wilson, part of the Overseas Missionary Fellowship since 1957, was one of the early missionary trainees at Cedar Campus. "It was great," she says, "especially the street meetings on weekends." But what impressed her the most was that when David met her in Thailand years later, he not only remembered her name, but that she had been one of his Cedar Campus recruits.

David planned his program carefully. Knowing, for instance, that a mix of nationalities would help the students appreciate the delicacy of cross-cultural communication, David encouraged international students to attend Missionary Training Camp. One of these was Dr. Sid Feng, the physicist. To culturally naive Westerners David longed to pass on lessons he himself had learned over the years, particularly in the areas of national pride. He wanted the young people to see the importance in cross-cultural ministry of sensitive cooperation rather than domination.

For three summers David worked with Keith Hunt, director of Cedar Campus, in shaping and directing these missionary training sessions. The whole Adeney family, in fact, enjoyed being a part of the experience. In a simple walk from one building to another, Rosie remembers, she would see porcupine in the undergrowth, deer peeping through the trees, and beavers building dams in the nearby streams. Her brother John would go hunting Winnie-the-Pooh's "heffalump" in the woods. Rosie also went out with one of the Missionary Training Camp teams to help in a local church.

"We thought we had got missionary experience because we learned how to milk cows by hand!"

Jim Nyquist, later to play a key role in InterVarsity Press, worked with David during these years and became a lifelong friend. "My first impressions were that David was a man utterly dedicated to the Lord, that he cared greatly for people, and that he was a man of prayer and faith.

"Once in Chicago when I went to welcome David back from a meeting in Indianapolis, he had several people with him and was taking care of their suitcases. But in the distractions he left some of the bags in the middle of the street, and it took several phone calls to find them. That was characteristic of the way in which he handled the world around him—at sixes and sevens, always apologetic, always thoughtful of other people, never quite able to get things to go as they should."

At one conference repeated announcements were made for a missing suitcase. Not until David and his roommate were leaving did they discover that the suitcase sitting in the middle of their room, which each assumed was the other's, was the missing one!

David was absent-minded only inasmuch as he was easily distracted, not because he failed to harness his concentration. Because he would focus so hard on something else—or more likely, someone else—he would forget things of relatively slight importance such as luggage, papers, his hat. His first secretary, May Koksma, got used to hearing that David had left Ruth's carefully packed lunch at a train station, and to receiving parcels at the office with items of clothing left behind. "I suppose that's my hat again," David would say ruefully whenever she put another square packet on his desk.

Prayer also sometimes distracted him from the more mundane realities. On one occasion he was praying with Stacey and Yvonne Woods on the station platform before setting out on a trip to Canada. Ruth and the children were already seated on the train, waiting for David to join them. Suddenly the train started to pull away, but David did not notice it until it was almost too late to clamber on board.

Losing or forgetting tickets for a journey was another frequent problem of David's, slightly more awkward than leaving his hat behind. Forgetting his passport posed even greater difficulties.

But somehow David always managed to get himself out of such scrapes. On one occasion he even persuaded the airline personnel to hold the plane while he retrieved his passport from wherever he had left it.

More often than not, David made his appointments by the skin of his teeth. He was a man who hated to waste a moment of time, and would be on the phone or scribbling a note or praying with someone rather than be idle while waiting to set off on a journey. But it was sometimes hard for those who were transporting him from place to place, especially if they had to race back to retrieve lost tickets or luggage. Though it happened often, few seemed to begrudge the fact. People loved and admired David, so they suffered the inconveniences willingly or with a laugh, brushing aside his apologies.

In administration, however, people's patience would sometimes be sorely tried. Says Jim Nyquist, "Whenever I arrived at Cedar Campus, someone would be tearing their hair out because David had made good arrangements but had not communicated to the right people at the right time. We learned to provide administrative back-up for him. But he gave vision and leadership, which were key ingredients for the camp. For the most part I couldn't get angry with him. Administration was simply his weakness. His overall leadership was fine; I inherited his job and his staff, and it was a strong team."

Once, remembers Jim, "David was one of the judges for the summer regatta—swimming, sailing, waterfront competitions—that kind of thing. David made himself a hat out of flowers and cavorted around like a kid, enjoying the day tremendously and bringing delight to everyone." It was the sort of thing his mother would have done in the days she took a lively part in the CSSM houseparties.

David was an incredible recruiter. He was always on the lookout for people who might be challenged to make a commitment to full-time Christian service. He combined a genuine interest in the individual with the urgency he felt for pressing forward with the affairs of the kingdom of God. One of his early Canadian recruits was the dining room hostess at Campus in the Woods in Ontario. He urged her to consider joining the American staff as preparation for the day when she thought she might go to China as a missionary. "Pray about it," he counseled. She did, and the

151

result was that Ruth Bell not only joined the staff of the American IVCF, but later married Jim Nyquist.

The same year that David put together the first Missionary Training Camp, he organized the Fourth International Student Missionary Convention at the University of Illinois at Urbana, held every three years between Christmas and New Year's. Though still in its infancy, the convention had already demonstrated its significance. Of almost six hundred students who attended the first conference in Toronto in 1946, probably half went abroad as missionaries. By the third convention, attendance had jumped to fifteen hundred, so David and his planning committees felt they had to expect at least that many. In the end, two thousand made the rafters ring with their singing and listened intently to outstanding speakers.

David and his crew worked a whole year on organizing the event. It was a massive task—not least the mobilizing of prayer for spiritual preparation.

"Changing World; Changeless Christ" was the theme chosen. During the course of arranging speakers, David was impressed with the response of William Nagenda of Africa, who was a great friend of his brother Harold. Nagenda wrote: "You know, David, how we long to get deeper with the Christians all over the world so that their walk with the Lord may mean a continuous revival. I really wouldn't think of traveling to America simply to create a missionary interest for Africa, because I believe this to be a secondary cause." David, his colleagues, and other speakers agreed. They would place primary emphasis on the spiritual qualifications needed for being a missionary. Wrote David, "Guidance for life's service depends essentially upon the closeness of our fellowship with the Lord Jesus."

The messages during those days at the convention were powerful and varied. "A. W. Tozer gave powerful messages on biblical characters—Abraham, Elijah, and others," record Keith and Gladys Hunt in IVP's 1992 publication, *For Christ and the University.* "William Nagenda spoke from his background of God's work in the revivals in Rwanda. Samuel Moffat and Arthur Glasser helped students interpret what they were experiencing in a world now dominated by communism and change. Alan Redpath of Moody Church gave students new insights into a favorite topic: how to know the will of God. Paul White from Australia, a master storyteller, demonstrated practical helps for going on with God. Two hundred missionaries from seventy mission boards came.

Paul Beckwith and Homer Hammontree led the music...." Many students went back to their campuses with a new commitment to Jesus Christ and world evangelism.

David loved these years with IVCF, though they were not without frustration. He believed that the campus fellowships, the camps, and the Urbana conventions were bringing glory to God through changed lives and young people's fresh commitment to doing his will. The testimonies to IVCF's effectiveness are many. Billy Graham has written: "Virtually every place I go in the world I meet men and women who first received their call to missionary service through Urbana or who have been influenced by InterVarsity in other ways." From a mission board David received this word: "As we listened to candidates' testimonies, several of us were struck by the frequency with which IVCF was mentioned as an influence in conversion, spiritual growth, or in the call to the mission field." It was the kind of encouragement anyone who has given his full energies to a ministry needs to hear.

But David continued to think globally. As his son Michael said, "He saw the big picture." The world was his workplace. Thus when in 1956 Stacey Woods decided the time was ripe to invite David to become the first International Fellowship of Evangelical Students (IFES) Associate General Secretary for the Far East, to be based in Hong Kong. David was ready and eager to accept. He still had Asia in his blood.

The Adeneys' move from the States back to Asia was not unanticipated. The idea was already taking shape five years before when Stacey Woods first invited David back to IVCF after the Adeneys' withdrawal from China. As General Secretary of the International Fellowship of Evangelical Students, Stacey was looking for help in developing Christian student groups around the world, particularly in Southeast Asia, where an evangelical student witness was nearly nonexistent. He involved David in plans for this as soon as the Adeneys were back in the States. He even sent the returned missionary to Japan in 1951 to appoint two recent graduates from seminary as staffworkers for the KGK *(Kirishutosha Gakusei Kai)*, pioneered by a Japanese student, Reiji Oyama, just after World War II. The KGK was drawn into the fellowship of IFES by Shintaro Hasegawa, Charlie Hummel, and Irene Webster-Smith, a missionary in Japan since 1916.

David's new responsibility would again be a pioneering one—to challenge Christian students in a dozen different countries to take their stand as witnesses for Christ through the formation of national campus fellowships.

The International Fellowship of Evangelical Students had grown out of a small conference of evangelical student leaders in Oslo in September 1934. It was a time of new vision, new hope. "It is as if I see the glow of morning, the dawn of a new day over the old unhappy world after a long, dark night," Ole Hallesby said in his opening address to the conference. As a professor of theology and a key evangelical leader in Norway, he was only too aware that Bible-believing Christianity had been largely eclipsed in the universities by prevailing liberal thinking. Now he dared to hope things might be changing. A new work of God was evident. "The Bible talks much of the 'hour of God,'" he said in what was to become a widely quoted address. "In God's hour something always happens. . . . When movements so alike suddenly and spontaneously spring up in so many countries at the same time, then we must see that God wishes to do something. It is God's hour." By the end of the conference, the vision for an evangelical student witness on every campus of the world had taken shape. Twelve years later, after the war, the vision became reality when the International Fellowship of Evangelical Students (IFES) was formed.

"Without wishing to be pious or presumptuous," writes Stacey Woods in his autobiography, *Some Ways of God*, "in those glorious beginning days all of us felt we were under the direction of the Holy Spirit. We loved students, longed for their spiritual well-being and that witness in the universities should be worldwide, but always with the sense that we were behind the living God, following him, entering through doors he opened."

David and Ruth were caught up in a similar excitement as they prepared to go to Hong Kong, again to be among the Chinese. Surely it was God's hour for students of Asia!

Just one thing clouded the Adeney's joy. Rosie, about to finish high school and to begin training as a nurse, was going to stay in the States. She would live in Illinois with some good friends of the family, the Charles Smiths. As Rosie was a companion to her now and a help in so many ways, Ruth especially found it wrenching to leave their eldest child and only daughter behind.

"Christ also suffered, leaving us an example," God reminded Ruth for both challenge and comfort. Still it was hard. Family separations, Ruth felt, were among the hardest sacrifices a missionary had to make, bearable only "for Jesus' sake."

It would be two years before Rosie could visit Hong Kong and another two before the family were reunited again for a short while in the States. By then Rosie was applying to the OMF herself, sensing God's call to Thailand, and had met the man she was to marry, Arthur Lumm, who was also preparing for missionary service in Thailand.

Rosie would always remain close to her parents. Though they would be separated by great distances in the years ahead, they would keep in touch through frequent letters and the occasional phone call.

John, Michael, and eight-year-old Bernie were glad that in returning to Asia they were going to Hong Kong, where they would go to school locally and live at home as they had been doing in the States. John was especially pleased. At thirteen he did not relish the idea of going back to boarding school after his experience at Chefoo, the CIM school in China. He had never settled down there, perhaps because he was tall for his age and a lot had been expected of him. As soon as he heard about the new job in Hong Kong, he told his parents, "Mummy and Daddy, you can go anywhere you want to in the world as long as you take me with you." They were glad to be able to reassure him.

In accepting his new role, David needed no convincing of the critical importance of establishing an evangelical witness on the campuses of Asia. But facing the task of building up campus witness in many different countries made him aware again of his own insufficiency. At this point he could never have guessed at the key role he would play in creating a pool of intelligent, trained, and committed Asian Christians for witness and leadership in Asia and around the world. He and Ruth were simply stepping out in obedience, counting on God's sufficiency.

15

Catalyst in Hong Kong

One of the fastest-developing countries in the world, Hong Kong was changing by the moment when the Adeneys arrived in 1956. In those days, the famous Star Ferry, which shuttled back and forth between the mainland and Hong Kong island, still docked at wooden piers, and the airport runway precariously crossed a main road. Neighborhoods that reflected old China, with shopfronts at street level and a floor or two of crowded living space above, hung on bravely in the shadow of multiplying high rises. When the Adeneys left twelve years later, gleaming ferries were docking at steel and concrete piers, the runways of a large, modern airport stretched from Kowloon out into Hong Kong Harbor, and old China was becoming harder to find among the skyscrapers in which people increasingly lived and worked.

David saw another side of Hong Kong, a side which didn't change so rapidly. "It is hard to describe the artificial, worldly, insecure society which is Hong Kong," he wrote soon after the family's arrival in the British colony. "Great wealth and abject poverty are to be seen on every side. Very high rents enable landlords to make vast sums of money, and everywhere new building projects are to be seen as multistoried apartment houses constructed with very cheap labor dot the landscape. In the evenings especially, one is forcibly reminded of the refugee problem by the sight of numbers of people sleeping on the streets, rolled up in a little matting or sheltering behind a crude structure of cardboard, straw or tin.

"Lurid advertisements call people to patronize the latest films from Hollywood and Europe. Western materialism, strongly influenced by the atheistic philosophy of communism, merges with the superstitions of large

157

numbers of the people who still burn incense before the ancestral tablets and flock to the temples on special occasions. Hong Kong is a crossroads not only for trade but also for the conflicting ideologies which characterize Asian society today."

As accommodation in overcrowded Hong Kong was in short supply and expensive, the Adeneys' first home was a cramped apartment on the fourth floor with no lift. Climbing four flights of steps was a problem for Ruth, whose back still gave her trouble. She had finally had surgery for her slipped disc just before she left the States, and movement was still both painful and difficult. Fortunately a shop just across the road delivered her groceries, and a nearby shoe repairman soon became a friend and came up to the flat in response to Ruth's shout if she needed anything. Because in the heat and humidity clothes would develop mildew over a single night, Ruth used to spread things out in the sun whenever possible to get clothes thoroughly dry.

With the difference between the British (Hong Kong) and American school systems, Bernie had to have outside tutoring to help him with math, and Ruth had to help Michael in Latin—with only three years of high school Latin herself. Ruth's predominant memory of those early years is of her sons growing up and growing taller in the process. When the Adeneys moved into their next home around 1960, eighteen feet of youthful enthusiasm effectively filled the available space!

David's responsibilities were throughout Asia, but Hong Kong alone could have eaten up all his energies. What he found was revival. It had begun among students and was spreading, even making inroads into the wider population. David simply slipped into what God was already doing and made himself available to the people the Holy Spirit was quickening. Ernest Y. Lam, then a student and now an energy developer for the Bechtel Corporation in Arlington, Virginia, remembers those days. David, he says, was one of five men who worked together, all of them playing key roles in helping to disciple the hundreds of students being won to Christ in the spreading revival. The others he names were twins Gene and Dean Denler of the Navigators; Dr. Donald Chan, a professor in the medical school; and Dr. S. Y. King, Chairman of the Department of Electrical Engineering at Hong Kong University.

The resurgence of spiritual activity centered in Hong Kong University, the only university in the Colony. Suddenly there was new life in the

Christian Association. "Prior to David Adeney's coming to Hong Kong, we hardly knew what was involved in student evangelism," writes Professor S. Y. King. The Christian Association had been nothing more than a social club—Christmas parties, carol concerts, etc. No Bible study groups, no fellowship. With David's advice, we began to put our CA on a right evangelical basis. All officers had to sign a statement of their doctrinal faith, and the Association became the home base for reaching out to other students in the Colony."

"By the time I entered Hong Kong University as a lukewarm Christian," testifies Dr. Lam, "the CA had become a major organization and influence on the campus, claiming about ten percent of the school's 1500 students. The key rival group [besides the more liberal Student Christian Movement] was the Chinese society, which was dominated by leftists. The spiritual battle between the two was fierce. Both worked hard to attract the rest of the students to their camps. Scheduling of competing events was common. Mr. Adeney was always our much sought-after speaker, mentor, and friend."

Ernest Lam was one of the first students in Hong Kong David was to encourage towards God. "To us Mr. Adeney was not just a preacher who talked about Jesus. He bore the likeness of Christ. He was enthusiastic to talk about the one he put his trust in. He spoke of Jesus as one he knew intimately. He demonstrated that it was possible for a mortal to take on the likeness of the Divine One. We who considered Hong Kong University to be an elite school were impressed by how Mr. Adeney had traded potential fame and wealth derivable from his prestigious degree from Cambridge for a life living for Jesus.

"I have come to know perhaps hundreds of Christian workers. Mr. Adeney is one of the very few who has that rare quality of making you feel that he is taking you into the presence of Jesus when you engage in an ordinary conversation with him. His sermons come from his heart. It is impossible to listen just academically. They drive you to do something. You never leave unchallenged. Mr. Adeney turned this lukewarm Christian to rededicate his life to Christ."

One incident during a summer retreat in about 1957 stands out in Dr. Lam's mind: "The retreat was well attended, and the Holy Spirit was working mightily. People were saved, and Christians were dedicating their lives to God. Things were going well. All of a sudden, however, a CA member went berserk. He became possessed by an evil spirit. He yelled and spewed profanity and became totally wild. We panicked and didn't know what to do. Our non-Christian friends were confused and scared. We thought the whole conference was going to fall apart. Minutes seemed like hours as this person refused to be subdued. Some tried the standard biblical method of casting out the demon in the name of Jesus. Nothing seemed to work.

"We sought Mr. Adeney's help. While we waited, the man continued his abnormal behavior, moving erratically around in a room and cursing. Most of us stood outside the door as helpless spectators. One or two CA leaders were in the room, trying all kinds of ways to control the situation.

"When Mr. Adeney came, he quietly entered the room. Instead of directing his attention to the subject, he knelt down and began to look up and talk to Jesus. He was not even paying attention to the man. The way Mr. Adeney was conversing with Jesus convinced us that Jesus responded with his own presence. That seemed too much for the evil one to withstand. The man began to calm down. Serenity and normality returned, and the ministry of the conference was rescued."

David remembers how warmly the students welcomed him when he joined them in their rooms for Bible studies, not just at the Hong Kong University, but also at the various other colleges in the Colony which were eventually amalgamated into the Chinese University. "When David Adeney arrived, he came with a vision, a sense of urgency," remembers former student Michael Ho. "He had to coordinate and organize into a workable system an independent work so that it could continue on its own. He had to work against a silent opposition, suspicion from Chinese church leaders and school authorities.

"At that time," Michael explains, "there was a loose association of graduate Christians in Hong Kong, including local graduates and those returning from overseas. David inspired them into leadership to provide expertise, advice, prayer support, and financial assistance when necessary. This group, which later became the Graduate Christian Fellowship, became the locomotive of the local student witness."

Dr. Philip Chan, a young dentist who had just returned from studying overseas, was first moved by David's vision as the two talked aboard the Star Ferry. They were returning home after a meeting at Philip's church at which

David had spoken. As a result of that conversation, Philip became one of the leaders at the graduate prayer group then meeting on alternate Sundays.

Because David made a habit of making the most of such chance meetings, viewing them as God-arranged opportunities, in a short time he had gathered together several more committed Christian graduates, teachers, and church workers. And it wasn't long before the group began to get excited about what God might be calling them to do among students. From the outset the Graduate Christian Fellowship, as it came to be in 1957, had a special cohesion, a sense of family and friendship, which bonded its members together and remained an important ingredient in all that was subsequently achieved. "We were all connected," remembers Dr. Michael Ho, who joined the work later. "We became a family and felt the joy of witnessing and working together."

The second development in the Hong Kong student work was the opening of the Evangelical Reading Room later in 1957. Once again David was a catalyst in the process, having access to a quantity of books from the Evangelical Library in London. In the Reading Room young people not only had access to Christian books, but a quiet place to study and a meeting place.

Without funds, and knowing that the chances of finding suitable premises in overcrowded Hong Kong were very slim, David and the graduates welcomed the provision of a first-floor room at 2b Tak Shing Street, Kowloon, as an answer to prayer. "Through the introduction of Rev. V. H. Donnithorne ['Uncle Donnie'] of the West China Evangelistic Band, the landlady, a Christian, Mrs. M. Lee, offered the place at a reasonable rent," recorded Richard Tsao, one of the Christian graduates who has been a faithful supporter of the Hong Kong student work since its beginning. "She was glad to see her flat used for the Lord's work and later also made much needed contributions for its support. A brother in Christ, willing to serve as the first librarian and to stay in the rear of the flat, shared a good part of the rent and lessened the Reading Room's financial burden. Though the financial means, coming wholly from free-will offerings, looked tight, the Lord answered the prayers and somehow made ends meet . . . each month, every time." In such ways, the Graduate Christian Fellowship saw God at work in the first venture for which they became responsible.

Such was the first reading room's success that another one was opened on Hong Kong Island, purposely near Hong Kong University, so that Christian students could have easy access to it. Like its counterpart across the harbor, this room was also used as a venue for meetings. Both reading rooms made a strategic contribution to the development of the student work.

The third development in the growing movement among graduates and students was the establishing of a committee within the Graduate Christian Fellowship to look after the outreach in the secondary schools. The evangelistic rallies, such as Gwen Wong had held in the past, became the responsibility of the group; then summer conferences and workshops. With evangelism now a priority, the graduates majored on making the gospel known among the schoolchildren. With the Graduate Christian Fellowship, the reading rooms, and now the Inter-School Christian Fellowship, the foundations were laid for a national student fellowship, and in 1961 the Fellowship of Evangelical Students in Hong Kong became a reality.

"I was at first alarmed by these set-ups," confesses S. Y. King. "How were we to cope with so many activities? Yet this proved the real work of the Lord for student evangelism. I personally feel Hong Kong owes much to Adeney's pioneer work among students, many of whom are today playing a leading role in the church in Hong Kong and overseas." "Without David," agrees another student, "I just wonder how people would ever have got the idea of organizing student outreach." For his part, always concerned to give others credit and not to put himself on any kind of pedestal, David points to the hard work and dedication of the graduates and the students themselves. The beginning and growth of FES Hong Kong was a team effort.

Such growth was not without opposition. As Michael Ho mentioned, it came at first from some evangelical Chinese churches whose leaders felt they were losing valuable support. Young people who might otherwise be contributing to their churches were giving allegiance to another organization. David had to weather a lot of criticism of this nature in Hong Kong, and indeed in other countries, as campus ministries developed.

"If the blessing of God rests upon the work on campus," he countered, "not only will non-Christian students be won for Christ and added to the church, but Christians will be greatly strengthened and prepared for spiritual leadership. Their witness on campus will not prevent them from taking an active part in the work of their own local church, and they will also be enriched by fellowship with Christians from other denominations as they experience the true unity that is in Christ Jesus. . . . It is of course true that the work on campus may limit the amount of time that is available for church work, but surely the churches should recognize the strategic importance of the campus witness and rejoice that their members are being used in this way."

Hostility from some church leaders arose because of theological differences as well. When John Stott came to speak at an FES mission in Hong Kong in 1964, the Bishop of Hong Kong, who had always backed the more liberal Student Christian Movement, forbade Stott's participation at the last minute. Bishop Hall judged the visiting clergyman's theology "immature." In deference to the Bishop's authority over fellow-Anglican Stott, the mission was canceled.

Ever since he had been in Hong Kong, David had worked hard to keep communication open between himself and authorities hostile to IVF work. Indeed, he was always interested in dialogue with people of different views. Never one to exacerbate points of conflict, he tried constantly to break down barriers and establish common ground. After one meeting with Bishop Hall, he wrote in a personal letter, "There was at least an understanding that, while there were points of theological disagreement, we could recognize each other as fellow Christians. . . . " With typical warmth, he expressed his admiration for the sincerity and devotion of the Bishop. But while there might have been a genuine meeting at a personal level, there was little possibility of a more active cooperation. The theological differences were too fundamental.

Inevitably the students themselves felt the resistance to the influence of evangelicalism. School authorities in one school threatened several gifted pupils with expulsion just before they took their final exams because of their involvement in Christian activities. The youngsters had organized a number of meetings and were told they had to stop if they were to have any chance of furthering their careers. Though the pupils did curtail the meetings on school premises, they continued those outside, and seven of them were expelled. Despite this, all were eventually accepted into good schools to complete their education, and all went to the university. This was a significant encouragement to other Christian students to stand up for what they believed.

Like the ripples of a pool, the influence of Christian students in Hong Kong spread. The graduates who became teachers formed the Teachers Christian Fellowship, carrying on the work of the Christian groups from which they themselves had benefited, and nurses formed the Nurses Christian Fellowship. Both groups became part of the Fellowship of Evangelical Students.

David got to know innumerable students in making himself available to the mushrooming student groups in the Colony. And in doing so, almost instinctively he saw gifts and potential. His role as a facilitator in drawing out and aiming young Christians toward Christian ministry is illustrated by his friendship with Josephine So. David supported her in developing her journalistic gifts at Moody Bible Institute and Wheaton College in the Chicago area in the U. S. Then as she finished her training, he introduced her to Campus Evangelical Fellowship in Taiwan. There God used her to develop Christian literature for the growing campus ministries of CEF. By the time she underwent surgery for cancer of the thyroid, both the Adeneys and her sister So Yan-Kok were at the Discipleship Training Center in Singapore; so Josephine went to Singapore to recuperate. While there she took classes at DTC, and also managed to start a Chinese magazine for the local Fellowship of Evangelical Students. Seemingly healed of cancer, Josephine returned to her native Hong Kong with a vision to start a Christian magazine for teenagers. The magazine and ministry that she and other graduates developed eventually outgrew FES Hong Kong and became independent. "Breakthrough" is now one of the largest and most influential organizations in Hong Kong, with over a hundred staff and more than four hundred volunteers reaching out to young people. When Josephine died one Easter Day a few years after returning to Hong Kong, she had very clearly left her mark among Asia's students.

David gave Josephine every support, recalls Dr. Philemon Choi, a leader in the Breakthrough ministry from the start, for "one of his dreams was that there should be Christian literature for young people in Hong Kong." Dr. Choi himself testifies to David's influence and personal support as he turned his back on a medical practice to go into ministry. Several others contributing to the ongoing student work in Hong Kong today testify to similar encouragement.

Through such support from David a number of Asians first became involved in student work and later went on to give their services to the wider church. Ronald Fung was one. After graduating from Hong Kong University, he found his first publishing job through David's help. Soon afterwards, on David's prompting, he became the editor of *The Way*. Initiated by David, this IFES magazine was sent to Christian students in different Asian countries, its name reflecting its double emphasis—to point to the "way" of Jesus Christ and to promote witnessing to Asian youth. Ronald Fung went on to study theology in England and then in the United States before coming back to full-time Christian ministry in Hong Kong. Today Dr. Fung is a professor at the China Graduate School of Theology and, as the author of a number of Bible commentaries in both English and Chinese, is a strong influence in the theological world.

Chan Hay Him was one of the first staff workers at FES in Hong Kong. Hay Him remembers David's spiritual encouragement during those early days, and his and Ruth's practical support when he was ill. He also credits David with liberating him from a false concept of spirituality by showing him that humor was legitimate for Christians, something that was quite new for him at the time. Today Chan Hay Him heads up the Chinese Coordinating Center of World Evangelization, an international resource body working to promote prayer and support for the evangelization of the Chinese worldwide.

Chan Hay Him is still in touch with the Adeneys. But that is true of the majority of people with whom David has come into close contact over the years. David's capacity for correspondence, phone conversations, and flying visits are a source of amazement and gratitude among friends and colleagues. Without exception, it seems, acquaintances testify to David's personal concern for them and the significance of his encouragement. Dr. Ernest Lam wrote early in 1992: "Mr. Adeney's loyalty to his friends and the care he takes to maintain contacts with so many all throughout these years, all over the world, is quite remarkable. It can only come from a very genuine love and concern for his friends. His love for the Chinese is almost inexplicable."

From the very early days in Hong Kong David came alongside the students as if he were one of them. "He was always at our meetings, whether he was speaking or not, and would join us for a canteen meal afterwards even though the food was awful," remembers a professional woman, then a young student. "He often dropped into the reading room just to see us; so we always felt we could go to him for advice. If there was anything he could do, he would do it." This woman, married and carrying demanding responsibilities professionally, would still seek David's advice on a difficult decision today. "Nobody would have said he was a spiritual giant. The most impressive thing was that he gave himself completely and because of that people were moved to join him."

"One great achievement of Adeney's was that we never sensed a trace of foreigner in him," writes another long-standing friend and former member of the Graduate Christian Fellowship. "He was accepted a hundred percent as one of us. He had vision and action but above all knew how to delegate responsibility to others. He shared God's vision with you. He moved you by the love of God to accept the challenge. He encouraged you, but he left the work up to you. With God's enabling, he trusted that God could achieve his purpose through others as well as through him. We who were of little faith always got nervous in the beginning, feeling overwhelmed by the heavy responsibility and burden delegated to us, and sometimes we were even mad at Adeney for doing that to us. But as time progressed, God's work was accomplished in spite of our weaknesses and far beyond our expectations."

"His love for China is an inspiration to Chinese Christians," says Professor King. "With his fluent Mandarin, he was indeed considered as our fellow Chinese, apart from perhaps his high nose!" One of David's unique contributions among Hong Kong's students was to remind them of their roots in China and of their responsibility to their homeland, a responsibility at least to pray if not to offer themselves in full-time Christian service to their Chinese brethren in one capacity or another. "He repeatedly challenged the students in Hong Kong that missionary service is not the prerogative of the Western brethren," continues Professor King, who later became Vice Chancellor of Hong Kong University. "The great commission is meant for all Christians."

Alongside his IFES commitments David spent two years as part-time pastor of the interdenominational church he and Ruth had been attending, Emmanuel Church, where Ruth also led a Bible study group. The previous pastor had retired, and someone was needed to help until a replacement was found.

"During my time at Emmanuel I was eager to get young people more involved in the church; so I started a Junior Church Council. I also suggested to a few Chinese-speaking members of the church that we ought to have a meeting in Cantonese to cater to those Chinese people who lived in the area. As a result, they started a Chinese evening service which has now become much larger than the morning English service.

"One problem we faced concerned a young man who wanted to marry a non-Christian. As the church was not willing for the wedding to be held in church facilities, the man decided to have his wedding at a registry office. When I heard about this, I felt unhappy about his having a wedding with no Christian blessing. So at the last moment I got in touch with him and took one of the elders of the church and went over to the hotel where he was staying with his bride. We arranged for a little wedding service in the hotel room after the civil wedding. He then came back to the church with his bride and, I believe, both of them have followed the Lord faithfully over the years."

David also wanted to set the church bookshop to rights. He had received a letter from a young student at Fuller Seminary in Los Angeles, Wayland Wong, who was looking for practical experience in a church as part of his theological education, and wondered if there was a temporary post at Emmanuel. David suggested he come and take charge of the bookshop. Typically concerned to contribute to the young man's spiritual growth, David sent him to an IFES conference in the Philippines within a month of his arrival in Hong Kong and kept in touch when he went back to Fuller. Eventually Wayland came back to the Colony as a teacher and missionary. "Without David, I might never have come back to Hong Kong," he acknowledges.

Wayland Wong was the first to carry off one of David's secretaries, Clara Ho, as his bride. Along with Barbara Mak and Olivia Ho, Clara had been one of those behind the revival that wonderfully prepared the ground for David's mission in Hong Kong. When Wayland married her, he not only robbed David of an exceptional secretary, he set a precedent. When Vivien Knight, who succeeded Clara, met her husband Horace over a cup of tea at a meeting for Christian teachers which David hosted, it became a standing joke that becoming David's secretary was a sure ticket to marriage.

Frances Fung was the next on the list, although she waited until David had moved on from Hong Kong—accompanying him as his secretary—to fall in love and desert his service.

It was while Vivien Knight was his secretary, in 1964, that tragedy hit the Adeney family. She remembers the day the wire arrived. "I saw by his face that something was terribly wrong. Quietly he told me that his son-in-law, Arthur Lumm, had drowned in a swimming accident." Arthur and Rosie had been married just eleven months and were completing a summer school before going out together as missionaries to Thailand. Vivien protested when David, controlling his emotion, told her they would finish the letters that needed to be sent out that day. "Nothing interfered with what he felt he had to do. He finished the last few letters, quite composed, and then left me to get them in the mail."

"I was never so shattered as by that news," David recalls. "Art was Christlike, gentle, with a great love for the Lord. I learned what it means to pray without ceasing at that time, because every moment Rosie was in my mind. Paul's words about praying day and night made sense."

David was due to preach at Emmanuel the next day. "All that I ever believed was tested. I had to preach out of a confidence of the love and faithfulness of God and out of a hope of the resurrection."

Rosie came out to Hong Kong to spend time with her parents and decide what to do next, and while she was there, she attended an IFES conference at which she met one of the leaders of IVCF in the Philippines, Bel Magalit. She had been planning to go to Thailand on her own, but Bel persuaded her of the needs in the Philippines. In 1966, confident that God had prepared the way, Rosie went out as a missionary nurse with Overseas Missionary Fellowship to the Philippines and helped to start the Nurses Christian Fellowship.

The hard work and constant traveling, combined with the emotional stress of Arthur's death and Rosie's bereavement, took their toll on David and Ruth. Though Ruth's back was stronger now, her general health was fragile. Consulting a doctor for a bad sore throat, she was told she might have cancer of the ear and throat. As David had just left for a trip lasting several weeks, Ruth mustered the church to pray for her. She looks back on this time with gratitude to God because when she was checked by a specialist, he detected no cancer and prescribed a simple dose of penicillin.

Inevitably Ruth found David's absences difficult. "I had to be renewed again and again over it," she says. It was all the more difficult to cope when David's own health threatened to break down.

In 1965, while David was traveling in England and on the Continent, his lung collapsed. Between conferences at the time, he was visiting his brothers in England. His son Michael had joined him from his Stateside college, and the two of them were driving across London in a borrowed car when David was suddenly gripped by pain. Thinking his father was having a heart attack, Michael drove him straight to the nearest hospital, where the doctors pronounced that the only route to recovery was complete rest. Anything short of that would worsen his condition and put strain on the other lung. David accepted this reluctantly; Michael remembers him dashing off twelve handwritten letters from his sick bed! While he was in the hospital, David read and wrote prodigiously and took a pastoral interest in his fellow-patients. Among his many visitors were students from Hong Kong, India, the Philippines, and Uganda!

There had been an earlier warning that David's health was suffering under his heavy work load. After a speaking engagement in Hong Kong he had come home ashen-faced with a pain in his chest. X-rays had revealed congestion in the lung, serious enough but nothing to keep David in bed for longer than a few days. For several months afterwards David tired more easily than usual, yet still kept up his punishing schedule. "If you listened to your wife, you'd get along better," the doctor in Hong Kong had told him.

A few years later, David suffered a second lung collapse. This time he was in Germany for an IFES conference. He tried to make light of the pain in his chest and insisted he travel on to Switzerland to meet Ruth as planned. On arrival, however, he was rushed into the hospital. After his release, he was wonderfully looked after in the beautiful lakeside home of his good friend Dr. Hans Burki, the IFES Associate General Secretary for Europe.

But still David seemed to make little progress. Worried, Ruth telephoned his brother Harold, who advised that David should come back to Mildmay Hospital in England, where he had been treated before. Ruth was terrified on the journey that David would not make it. The doctors in Switzerland had forbidden him to take his dictaphone with him, much to his chagrin since he wanted to catch up on all the correspondence that had piled up while he was ill.

At Mildmay, the x-ray revealed David's lung to be in precisely the same state of collapse as it had been in 1965. Ruth was horrified. If the lung was still badly collapsed after the period of rest in Switzerland, how much worse must it have been at the start? David was forced to slow down for now, but would he learn his lesson? Ruth, knowing him so well, doubted it.

David had always paid a price for how his vision drove him. Though he was but one person among many whom God used in those Hong Kong years, he played a critical role. Says Dr. Ernest Lam: "Mr. Adeney left a special mark. I continue to be convinced that God sent him to Hong Kong in answer to the prayers of Clara, Barbara, and Olivia. They dared to pray for a revival, and a revival was sent. David Adeney was one who helped fan the little fire which the Holy Spirit kindled into a major fire."

16

International Fellowship

"The Lord put us into Asia at a most momentous time in the history of the world, and also at a most critical time for the growth of the church in Asia," David admits. The fact is humbling.

"At the time when the China IVF was formed," David observed in a letter to friends and colleagues, "90% of the non-Western countries were under colonial rule. By 1968, when I left Hong Kong, 90% of those countries were independent. The political map of the world had changed."

During the years David was working to establish national evangelical student movements in Asia, not only was he in China when communism swept over the country and ended the missionary era, but he was in Seoul, Korea, when the government was overthrown, in Tokyo, Japan, when the students were fighting the police, and in Hong Kong when communists staged a series of riots in 1967.

Not only were those years a time of unprecedented political transition, but it was also a time when universities were mushrooming everywhere and Asian student populations burgeoning. When David first visited Christian students in Malaysia in 1956, the University of Malaysia was no more than open fields and bare hills. In just a few years it had become a bustling campus. Post-colonial governments, seeking to establish their countries' own identities and needing to raise their own leaders, were pushing education. And Asian young people were clamoring for opportunity.

Growing student bodies created incredible opportunities for Christian witness and for influencing the future of young nations. David urged students and church leaders in the different countries to grasp these opportunities as he repeatedly visited countries on China's perimeter. "We are not satisfied with just seeing the numbers of students in IFES-related movements increasing," he told them. "We desire to see God raising up men and women with prophetic vision who will make an impact on their generation."

David had clear goals. He wanted to see the spread of the gospel rather than the spread of IFES, the name of Jesus honored rather than an institution gain recognition, dynamic Christians propelled into action rather than membership ticked off on a slate. His concern was reflected in the many articles he wrote for the quarterly IFES magazine. "We believe that God raised up the IFES in order to strengthen the faith of evangelical students throughout the world," he wrote in the winter of 1959. "But our primary loyalty is not to an organization but to the Lord Jesus himself." Two years later he was emphasizing, "The whole of our work exists . . . that university students may come to know Christ and then go forth in the mission of the Church to 'evangelize to a finish.' " The same missionary purpose comes out again in 1965. "Only if those who come to know Christ at the university are led into the fellowship of the church and prepared for effective Christian service will the evangelical unions be fulfilling their purpose."

The vehicle for this missionary purpose was of course the student movements. In order for the gospel to be preached, for Christian students to be effective in ministry, and for Jesus thus to be glorified—or seen—in the world, there had to be a starting point. Campus groups would provide the nurturing ground for wider spiritual impact. Thus, during the twelve years he was Associate General Secretary for IFES in the Far East, David threw his energies into the task for which he had been appointed, that of building national movements in countries where, in the early days, there was little or no evangelical witness. Hong Kong took up only a portion of his time.

David was largely starting from scratch. "When I came out of China," he recalls, "there were some Christian colleges in Asia, but they tended to be influenced by people of liberal persuasion. There was hardly any work of an IVF type, although it was just beginning in Japan and Singapore. There were very few evangelical Bible colleges or seminaries. If the gospel was going to spread throughout Asia, it was absolutely essential that there should be a strong evangelical witness established on the campuses of the Asian countries. That was the vision we were given when we went to Hong Kong.

"It was essential that there should be national leadership. The most important thing in any country was to pray that God would raise up leaders so that the work might become independent as soon as possible. As nationalism is always strong in the university world, only a work led by Christian nationals could hope to survive. Those chosen to lead the work had to be those with a firm, sound biblical foundation, men and women who knew the Scriptures and would be able to keep the whole movement going in the right direction."

In 1947, when IFES began, there were ten member movements around the world. Today there are over one hundred. When David and Ruth left Hong Kong in 1968, six national movements were functioning in Southeast Asia and a couple more were well on the way. Many different individuals were responsible under the hand of God for these developments, but—as in Hong Kong—David was often the catalyst and certainly key in giving personal encouragement to individuals who went on to play leading roles in the ongoing student work.

Campus Bible studies in the strongly Roman Catholic Philippines began in the early fifties. In 1956 a hundred students from ten campuses attended an evangelistic conference. With the dynamic help of itinerant IFES workers Gwen Wong and Mary Beaton, who gave vital training in Bible study and leadership, the IVCF-Philippines, under its first general secretary Ephraim Orteza, began to find its feet. By 1960 the IVCF was working on twenty-four campuses and beginning to establish a presence in the schools.

The route to building an ongoing student work among such young and inexperienced student leaders was training, an IFES emphasis that David fully endorsed and promoted. In the Philippines the main venue for training was Kawayan Campus. It was on this brand new camp site in 1958 that Isabello Magalit, later to be such a key student leader in both the Philippines and the international work, first met David Adeney. David was leading the second half of the four-week training course, and Bel, a young medical student at the time, clearly remembers his impact. "His message was that mere students could be used by God. He gave us a vision of what students can do." In a culture where students were normally considered too young and immature to be good for very much, this was significant. Such encouragement prompted Bel to begin leading a Bible study when he went back to university after the camp, and when he had completed his medical studies, he joined the IVCF as a junior staff worker.

Two years later, in 1966, David was again influential in Bel's life. Bel was thinking of leaving the student work to pursue his career as a doctor just at the time when the IVCF in the Philippines needed a new general secretary. David, who had got to know the young man over the years and seen his potential as a Christian leader, challenged him to think about full-time, long-term Christian service; Bel changed his mind and became General Secretary of IVCF-Philippines in 1968. He went from strength to strength. In 1972 he left a staff of thirty—having started out with three—to become Associate General Secretary for East Asia, following in David's footsteps. Ten years later he became a pastor in the Philippines, despite tempting offers to take his talents elsewhere. He is now putting his experience to work as the first Filipino President of the Asian Theological Seminary in Manila. The year that he spoke at the Urbana Missionary Convention in Illinois, he was the only speaker to get a standing ovation.

Finding those who have leadership potential was always important to David, and one of his considerable strengths. But he wanted others in IFES also to look out for people who might grow into strong leaders for God, then to nurture and encourage them.

When David saw leadership potential in someone, he committed himself to supporting that person in every way he could, keeping in touch, praying for him or her, counseling when counsel was needed. He stayed alongside that person as friend and mentor. William Girao, today a pastor and fine preacher in the Philippines, testifies to the significance of David's influence in his life in this way. Like Bel, he had reached a crossroads in his career after two years on the staff of IVCF-Philippines. His family responsibilities, taken very seriously in the Philippines, were inclining him towards a well-paid university post, but David challenged him not to disregard his Christian calling. Sometimes, he counseled, Christian workers had to pay a price as regards their families if they were really to be used by God. Following David's counsel proved to be a milestone for William Girao. He went on to study—with David's help—at the Asian Bible Study Center in Madras, India, and then devoted his life to a ministry as a pastor.

More than that, learning from David's example, William Girao has given priority not only to teaching and counseling, but to giving time to individuals. He pays tribute to David for not confining his friendship to the time when his responsibilities with IFES meant he had a duty to people in the Philippines. David has corresponded regularly, has always contacted the family when in the Philippines, and has prayed for them faithfully. This last has been the most significant support over the years for the Giraos: "Only eternity will tell how much these prayers have encouraged us. Even the thought that David and his family have been praying for us is a boost to our ministry."

In preparing people for leadership, particularly when he spoke at IFES training courses, David always emphasized the spiritual qualities needed in a leader. Unless the leader submits his life to God, he told his students, and is seeking in the power of the Holy Spirit to follow Christ through prayer and the study of Scripture, he has nothing of value to pass on to others. The first responsibility of a leader, David insisted, is to make sure his or her own relationship with God is sorted out.

From there, David felt, the main qualification for leadership was sensitivity—sensitivity first to the leading of the Holy Spirit, and then sensitivity to the needs and situations of those among whom they worked. Student leaders had to be, as he put it, "ambassadors of sensitivity."

David was aware that he was holding out a demanding ideal. "When we look at the standard which God sets before us, we can only say with Paul, 'Who is sufficient for these things?' " he wrote. "None of us would feel that we can measure up to the demands of discipleship which we find in the New Testament, and yet we dare not accept any lesser standard."

In Taiwan, the island off the southeast coast of China where the Nationalists under Chiang Kai-Shek set up their headquarters after the communist victory in China, David helped bring three people into student work, all of whom made significant contributions. When he first visited in 1956, he found that though missionaries were working among students in scattered groups, there was no campus ministry. David's first task was to find a Christian student to begin to organize a campus-based movement.

David's meeting with David Cha on the train between the capital city of Taipei and the city of Tainan, about a hundred miles south, was providential. This young man was a Christian graduate from China and already interested in working among students, having himself been converted through an Inter-Varsity conference in China before the revolution. He had come to Taiwan with the Nationalists in 1949, studied theology, and then had done a year's work among students in a large Baptist church. He was now wondering what he should go on to do. When he heard that David Adeney, whom he had known in China, was back in Taiwan and still involved in student work, he was determined to meet up with him to seek his advice.

David did not at first recognize the man who approached him on the platform at Taipei Station. It was, after all, ten years since he had seen David Cha. But when he found out who he was and heard his story, he looked at him with new eyes. Was this the person to lead a student organization in Taiwan? On the train down to Tainan, the two talked and prayed about the possibility, their excitement mounting with every mile. Dick Webster, a missionary at the center of student work in Tainan and the person David was on his way to visit, remembers that the decision was all but made by the time the travelers reached his home. David Cha went back to Taipei and began to seek out Christians at Taiwan National University. Through a bi-monthly magazine, he contacted a large number of other students who were then invited to summer conferences. From these conferences, groups were formed in several universities and colleges. And from these came the Campus Evangelical Fellowship, formally instituted in 1962.

With seven universities and fourteen colleges to get around to, David Cha found progress slow, especially since few Christian graduates stayed to help him. Either they were recruited into the army or they joined the mass exodus to the States for further study. Going abroad was considered highly advantageous in Taiwan, but fewer than five percent of those who left for the States ever returned.

David Cha also had the suspicions of the government to contend with; committed to its mission to rescue the mainland from communism and to restore the Republic beyond its present confines in Taiwan, the government was alert for signs of aggression from China. As a new student organization might hide communist influence, China Evangelical Fellowship was naturally suspect.

Within three years of the start of CEF, David Cha was due to go overseas for training, and it was clear that further help was needed if the campus witness was to continue. David Adeney recruited Gwen Wong to give the CEF a much-needed shot in the arm. As Christian training was still being done in English, Gwen began Bible classes in Chinese. This, she said, would sort out those who were really committed in their faith from those who just wanted to learn English. As a result, she saw a stronger core of believers emerge among the student groups, which also benefited—as did the missionary workers—from Gwen's thorough teaching of Bible-study methods.

The third person influenced by David and crucial to the student work was Chang Ming-Che, Professor of Chemical Engineering at Taiwan National University. David met him soon after his conversion to Christianity. "He had come to faith in midlife, journeying through Buddhism and agnosticism, and had been head of an oil company. After his conversion he felt he could be a more effective witness as a professor in a university, and he gave a lot of time to leading a Bible class for students at his church."

Professor Chang had been at first skeptical of the student movement on campus, believing that Christian students should be working in local churches. But with David's and Gwen Wong's encouragement, he gradually came around to seeing the value of the Campus Evangelical Fellowship. He became Chairman of the Executive Committee of the CEF and went on to lead the movement for twenty years, his teaching aimed at developing spiritual depth and commitment among students and staff workers. From these beginnings, the CEF has grown into a large, effective, and lively movement with significant literature, evangelistic, and training ministries.

David's influence in Taiwan on individuals was not confined to the student movement. One young woman remembers him because his preaching brought her to Christ. "David Adeney was one of the speakers in a [Presbyterian] summer retreat held at Sun-Moon Lake in 1958," she testifies. "One evening he spoke on the evidence for the resurrection of Jesus Christ. I was then able to see the love of Jesus Christ radiate from the cross. I realized that my disbelief was due to my prejudice. That evening the urge in my heart was so strong that I accepted Jesus as my personal Savior and my Lord."

"An incident which might sound trivial but which shows David Adeney's considerateness and sincerity happened just prior to the evening meeting," continues this now mature Christian. "The group was scheduled to go on a hike, and about forty minutes after we had started Mr. Adeney decided to go back. Asked why, he explained in a most modest manner that he

177

needed the time to pray and to prepare the sermon for that evening. I was amazed at his efforts not to discourage the rest of the party by holding back at the start. It would have been far easier for him to make an excuse and stay behind. His sincerity helped me to trust more in his preaching. His sacrificial behavior, which impresses me even as I recall it, taught me a lot about how to live a Christian life."

Alongside his official responsibilities, whether with Overseas Missionary Fellowship or Inter-Varsity, David has always taken the opportunity to preach whenever possible, believing this to be part of his calling before God and also loving its challenge. He has always enjoyed and thrived on preaching. Although he rarely found out at the time whether God touched people through his words, he often heard of blessing afterwards—sometimes years later when the person concerned encountered him again. This woman's memory of his contribution to the retreat also reveals something of the way respect for him has become so widespread, especially within the Chinese community.

Culture and circumstance created different problems in the countries where David was working. In Japan, where the KGK had been established for some years, nationalism clouded Christian witness. Recalling some of what he had seen in China, David stood strongly against the implications of this for the Christians: "Nationalism among Christians, if it is defined as love for country, is not wrong provided it is subject to the higher loyalty of the kingdom of God. Whenever it destroys true fellowship between believers of different races, it allows itself to become a tool of those who seek to destroy the church." With a tendency for the leadership of the student work in Japan to be in foreign or graduate hands, the problem was exacerbated. But a new wave of student initiative after 1962 eased the situation.

David sometimes found himself mediating between strong personalities. Such a situation developed in Japan. One of the early promoters of the KGK in Japan, Irene Webster-Smith was a woman of strong faith. Known as *Sensei*, she was the sort who had contact with the emperor and led a Bible class among members of the royal family. Though she lived in a fine old classical Japanese house, she generously let the KGK use it. When the KGK came to the place of needing a headquarters, she raised funds for it, then horrified many people by having her beautiful house torn down to construct the new building on the site. But what sent the high-spirited IVCF pioneer Stacey Woods through the roof was her inviting Campus Crusade to share the new quarters, when he had helped her raise funds for the building in the name of IVCF. Not everyone was happy either when Sensei made the front part of the property available to a McDonald's restaurant as a way to finance the upkeep of the complex as a Christian center. The on-going situation was a sensitive one, but it was not, of course, the first time David had had his hands full as mediator. The Tokyo Christian Center, with its sprawling, several-storied buildings is still the home of both IVCF-related ministries and Campus Crusade today, as well as a Christian bookstore and other ministries.

With its hierarchical patterns, Korea proved to be one of the hardest societies in which to establish a student-led movement. Shortly after David joined IFES, an Inter-Varsity movement was formed in Korea, but not on a firm footing. David's first visit alerted him to the underlying difficulties. "I felt somewhat uncomfortable, although I was welcomed and treated with great respect, because I realized the movement was developing from the top downwards and not from the students upwards. I was concerned about the future of the movement, and later on it did run into difficulties.

"The work in Korea has always been complicated by denominational and regional tensions, and unfortunately the church, in spite of its tremendous emphasis upon prayer, has had many conflicts and denominational rivalries. Nonetheless I was always impressed by the willingness of Korean Christians to endure hardship for the sake of the Lord Jesus. During the first student conference at which I spoke, though the funds for buying food proved to be inadequate, no one complained."

When the first leader of the Korean IVCF fell into spiritual failure, the movement sank miserably. In the vacuum another movement started. David tried to help both groups and enlisted Ada Lum, an itinerant IFES worker, to bring her teaching skills to Korea to help the students in personal Bible study. David worked hard to negotiate a joint conference for the two groups, hoping to achieve unity and fellowship. Everything seemed set. However, when he arrived at the airport on his way to take part in this joint conference, he discovered that each group had arranged its own separate conference, and, before he knew it, one group had scooped him up, the other his luggage!

Ada Lum, the young woman who came to help put the Korean IVCF on a more solid footing, remembers with both exasperation and respect

179

how David recruited her, originally for Hong Kong. He encouraged her to leave her work with InterVarsity in her home state of Hawaii to join IFES, but gave her no orientation when she eventually responded. He just told her to get her church to buy her ticket and then to write to the people in Hong Kong. Ada reckoned she could have done with a few more practical details. As she got to know David better, she saw that "detail" was not his forte; as far as he was concerned, if the motives were right and God was leading, the rest would take care of itself.

Once Ada got to Hong Kong, work opened up in other countries and David urged her to meet those needs too. So Ada found herself embarking on the itinerant ministry which took her all over Southeast Asia. "Those were the years when God was establishing evangelistic student movements in every Asian country where it was politically possible," she writes in her book, *A Hitchhiker's Guide to Mission*. "He was raising up his leaders everywhere for a new age in his churches in Asia, and they were calling for whatever help we could give them.

"No, IFES had no five-year plan for me, but it did have David Adeney, who was advance party and seed sower in new countries, trouble-shooter and counselor in emerging movements—a true Barnabas," Ada continues. "When in our travels we could meet at an airport or city, he would always be ready with three or four other possible assignments. Like his namesake, David was truly 'a man after God's own heart.' I usually trusted his judgments, and always he listened to my side of the story. For pioneering work, a relationship with such an experienced partner is far more important than a five-year plan."

OMF missionaries Paul and Maida Contento coordinated student work in Vietnam. At that time they were IFES associate staffworkers. David preached occasionally at evangelistic conferences there and saw the national movement take shape, although it did not officially come together until after he had left IFES. After the fall of Saigon in May 1975, the movement gradually dissolved, leaving those who had been so passionately involved in building it up with no further avenue to help except that of prayer. David and Ruth joined their prayers for Vietnam with those they constantly brought before God for the church in communist China.

In Thailand progress was slow; not until 1972, with the help of Ada Lum and two Christian university teachers, did the Thai Christian Students come together as a movement. Similarly in Indonesia, where Christian students had been active during the early years of independence, there was little coordinated work until 1971, when "Perkantas" was formed.

As David traveled around such Asian countries, the need for strong, national leaders in the church and among students became more and more apparent to him. He did not know it then, but his contribution to the developing student work in Asia was not going to finish when he left IFES. In some countries, again through individuals, his influence was going to be its most significant in later years.

Memories of David's work in India center around individuals such as P. T. Chandapilla, who was the first staffworker, and then became General Secretary for the Union of Evangelical Students of India, formed in 1954. "I had met him during his last year at Colombia Bible College in America," explains David, "and whenever I encountered him, I was inspired by his faith and devotion to the Lord. He accompanied me on many journeys and helped me to understand Indian life and culture. He and members of the UESI staff lived very sacrificially and insisted that the movement should trust God alone for the supply of its needs."

In seeking to stir a vision for the beginning of campus fellowships in Sri Lanka (then Ceylon), David had the help of the Bible Society secretary, who took him to universities to talk with students. One Sunday morning David spoke to the students in the university in Colombo. Afterwards the secretary drove him into the mountains to a city that claims to hold one of Buddha's teeth, Kandy, where David spoke again to the students at the university. Staying that night with a missionary in Kandy, David got up in the small hours to listen to the radio reports of man's first landing on the moon. "Next day as we were driving back to Colombo, I saw groups of country people gathered around someone with a transistor radio listening to the first 'moon walk.' It came to me with tremendous force that here were people listening to a voice from the moon who had never heard the voice of the Son of God. After ten years of research, expenditure of vast sums of money and some lives lost, modern technology made it possible for people on every continent to hear a voice from the moon. Yet Christians after 2,000 years still had not made it possible for these country people to hear the message of the gospel."

With his own deeply-rooted sense of being part of the worldwide family of God, David was concerned that cultural barriers be broken down among the Inter-Varsity groups. He rejoiced to see it happening at the joint conference in Hong Kong in 1958 which brought together IFES student leaders from seven different countries. "It was very clear that God had united us as one family in Christ, not only to discuss the work but to have real fellowship together. It was only the love of Christ which enabled Koreans, who had suffered much during the war, to have close fellowship with the Japanese. Indians who would not be welcome in Korea found that the hearts of their Korean brethren were open to them. Each national group had its own special contribution to make to the spiritual value of the conference. A young Japanese pastor, now on his way to do missionary work in the Philippines—where there was still a reservoir of prejudice against his fellow countrymen—rejoiced in the fellowship with Filipino delegates. We who were once strangers found that, having 'been brought near through the blood of Christ,' we were indeed fellow-citizens with the saints and of the household of God."

David fostered that Christian citizenship as much as possible. One of the reasons for starting *The Way* magazine in Hong Kong was to have a vehicle for exchanging news. He also encouraged staff to spend time with other national movements so they could learn from them and appreciate how God was working in Asia overall. David brought Maqbool Gill from Pakistan, for instance, to spend several months in east Asia to gain experience before he returned to his own country.

While the student movements in each country were finding their individual identity, David went to a lot of expense and effort to organize further international student conferences in Asia. He wanted the students to realize that they were part of a wider world. "Some people may ask, 'Is it worthwhile to spend so much time and money on a ten-day conference?' " he wrote after one mind-stretching gathering of students from all over Asia. "The answer is to be found in the tremendous value of personal relationships. The Chinese proverb, 'A hundred words do not equal one look' is certainly true when it comes to establishing fellowship between different countries. Delegates to the conference had read about the needs of student work in other parts of Asia, but it was only after being together for ten days that they really became deeply concerned about the needs in other countries."

In fact, fostering an interest among the students in needs beyond their own borders was inevitably one of David's priorities. He became increasingly concerned to encourage missionary vision. Since every missionary

Asians had ever known had come from the West, they were not used to thinking they might have a part to play too. Until Overseas Missionary Fellowship opened its membership to Christians of any color or nationality in 1965, Western missionary organizations did not usually take Asians onto their team as members, and there were almost no Asian sending agencies. To David, especially in the light of the increasing political tensions between the East and the West which were making foreign missionaries suspect, the need for Asian missionaries was urgent. "If the unevangelized millions are to be reached," he stressed, "the future missionaries will have to be Asians, Africans and South Americans."

Chua Wee Hian, a staffworker in Singapore when David was helping to build the student work in Asia, considers that David was ahead of his time in advocating overseas missions in Asia. He "sounded the trumpet," and Wee Hian was one of those to take up the refrain: "The task of world evangelism is not to be the monopoly of the Western Christians," he said at an IFES leaders' conference in Hong Kong in 1965. In 1968 Chua Wee Hian succeeded David as Associate General Secretary for IFES in Asia. Later he was to take over from Stacey Woods as General Secretary of the whole international movement.

Gradually, missionary concern became a more established feature of the national student movements in Asia. David gave an encouraging report in 1965 of the way some graduates had taken mission seriously: a dentist had started a Bible class and Sunday school in an eastern Malaysian city where there had been no gospel witness among the English-speaking people; a teacher was in the process of establishing a new Christian fellowship in a teachers' training college; a graduate working for the government in Sarawak was helping with evangelistic work in two fishing villages and at a home for leprosy sufferers; an engineering graduate in India had turned down a good job in order to take up a position as a teacher in a northern college where there was no evangelical testimony; a returning graduate to Vietnam was helping in the revision of the Vietnamese Bible.

The advent of missionary conferences in Asia during the 1960s and 1970s were signs of the shifting sentiment. In 1973 the Asian equivalent of Urbana in the Philippines brought delegates from all over Asia. Local sending agencies began to take shape, and one by one Western missionary organizations opened their doors to the increasing numbers of keen, dedicated Christians from Asia. David also urged those in professions to seek ways of contributing to the church if they were sent overseas, as was happening more and more with technical expertise being such a precious and exportable commodity.

Bel Magalit credits David with having developed a strong sense of cooperation among the different countries of Southeast Asia while he was working among them. He enabled them to see that they could do more together than apart. They were a "fellowship of equals." Christians in the different countries of Southeast Asia, Bel believes, enjoy a particularly strong mutual trust because of David's groundwork in the early years.

Evangelistic missions in some of these countries were among the most exciting events of David's time with IFES. In 1966 he led a four-week mission in the Philippines which was especially significant in its outreach to the huge University of the Philippines in Manila. Until then, no religious meetings had been allowed in the university buildings; Christian students had gathered for prayer and Bible study under the trees outside, nicknamed the "Christian trees." At the time of the mission, the IVCF had just been officially recognized by the university authorities, and while it was still forbidden to hold religious meetings on the premises, it was now permissible to give academic lectures concerning religious matters. David and a Christian professor from the university went to the dean and asked permission to give lectures about Christ. The dean was open to the possibility but rejected David's proposed lectures because the subjects were too religious. Fresh topics were worked out to the dean's satisfaction, and the mission went ahead. After that, school authorities allowed Christians to meet on campus.

From Manila the mission shifted to the island of Cebu, where David conducted nineteen meetings for students from nine different universities and colleges. This led to a spontaneous invitation to preach at the oldest Catholic university in the Philippines, San Carlos University, where the president gave David every support, believing that only through spiritual renewal could corruption in the Philippines be redressed.

David also remembers a mission to the University of Malaysia. "At the close of the mission a Christian student brought his cousin along to see me. Because of parental opposition, he had not been to a single meeting but he had a deep hunger for God, and that evening, as we talked and prayed together, he entered into true faith in Christ. In spite of persecution he maintained his faith and became a very effective witness for Christ. He later married a fine Christian woman, and today both his parents have become Christians. He himself became a leader both in the student work and later in his church. Today he teaches in a college and continues to be active in the service of the Lord Jesus."

David recalls such occasions, and indeed the whole of his time in Asia for IFES, with characteristic gratitude to God and appreciation of the many people with whom he worked. "I really feel that God's great gift to us was the raising up of leadership. Also, certainly to me, the privilege of friendship with some outstanding men and women of God meant a great deal." He adds, "My life was greatly enriched by the experience of serving on the IFES general committee. It was a tremendous privilege to work with leaders of the student work around the world such as Dr. Martyn Lloyd-Jones, Oliver Barclay, Samuel Escobar, and many others." If the qualities and friendship of everyone David has known over the years were mentioned in this book, there would be no room for his own story. He rarely refers to anyone without words of appreciation and gratitude.

David traveled widely during these years with IFES. It was not unusual for him to take up opportunities in Australia, Europe, and across most of Asia in one gallop. Europe came into the picture because of the IFES committee meetings he attended. His journeying was credited by some as apostolic, notably Douglas Johnson in his history of the IFES, but those nearer to him knew how enormously costly his travels and ministry were.

As much as David relished the work God had given him, the days prior to major trips and demanding ministry opportunities were invariably days of personal battle. Always fearing inadequate preparation and a loss of spiritual power, he agonized over his messages. Though he may have given a message many times, he always spent time before God and in his Word to make it fresh, making new notes and seeking assurance that it was God's word for this time. He struggled with the weight of being worth others' trust and expectations. He feared failure. He would get so low

185

sometimes as to be almost ill. And the closer he came to leaving home the harder the leaving became.

It wasn't that David didn't know the answers to his struggles intellectually. But he seems to have had to grapple with his own inadequacy and to find fresh faith to grasp God's sufficiency over and over. It was spiritual warfare on a very private level. It is a battle he still fights today.

Interestingly, however, once David had said the painful good-byes and had stepped into the world of travel and ministry, the tensions melted, and he was free to serve, whether in a committee meeting, in the pulpit, or in personal conversation. His battles have not been against God, but against self and all the forces that would make his weakness a source of failure rather than of strength.

One advantage of the trips David had to take for his work was the opportunity to see his children. Once the four children had left home and were scattered in different parts of the world, David's travels often took him within visiting distance of each of them and other members of his family as well. And sometimes Ruth was able to go with him. This built strong ties among the family. Even though John, for instance, has spent years in Germany as a computer engineer, he has been as close to his parents as any of the four.

But how did David's regular absence affect the children in their younger days? Loyal to their father but also sincere in their assessment, the Adeney children do not consider themselves deprived. Though John for one did not like being away at boarding school, Rosie and all the boys remember being very loved and secure during childhood. As with David's own mother, Ruth was the mainstay at home and filled as far as she could any gaps that were left by David's absence. When he was home, he made up in quality what was lacking in quantity of time spent with his children. "It tended to be that when he came home, we all loved him, and Mum got the rough end of it because she had been the one left to do everything. But even though Daddy had to be away traveling so much, he always showed us how much he loved us, and we always knew how much he loved and cared for us," Michael agrees. "He has always taken a great interest in us, giving us a lot of support and prayer." When the children were small, David's pirate stories at bedtime were coveted. One Bible story and one other story were the evening diet; unashamedly the children enjoyed the "other" story the most.

"I don't believe that you should never do things that are detrimental to your family," says Michael. "You can't avoid the fact that taking up the cross will affect your kids." He goes on to suggest that the modern emphasis on family priorities brings people home from the mission field when perhaps they should be prepared to make sacrifices and trust God for the outcome. In any case, it was not as if he and the other children suffered unduly from their parents' commitment to missions. Michael judged that traveling, and the opportunity to meet interesting people of all nationalities broadened his thinking and gave him a stronger foundation for adulthood than he might have had otherwise. Even at college, when friends were rebelling against a narrow upbringing, he realized the advantages of his own background.

All the children enjoyed the excitement of traveling in different countries. Rosie remembers feeling sorry for other kids who just stayed at home in the summer when her family went all over the place. The summer camps were a highlight for her, "mountain-top experiences" which fed her Christian faith. But she also remembers hoping that one of her classmates did not see the family kneeling down after breakfast for morning prayers as he went by on his way to school. She was afraid he would kid her about it later.

The youngest son, Bernard, while also remembering happy childhood days, struggled the most with the missionary zeal of his parents. A sensitive child, he felt he could never live up to the ideals his father espoused. John felt the same way. While David did not consciously put pressure on his children, he obviously felt they had as great a responsibility as anyone to seek God's call and respond to it. Knowing that their father longed to see servants of God raised up to make an impact on their generation, both John and Bernie felt this a standard of perfection that was out of their reach. Bernie particularly felt he was living in his father's shadow, as David's reputation increased as Bernie grew up. The pressure to conform, to behave appropriately, seemed too much, and for a while during his teenage years he escaped into rebellion. The turning point came at an InterVarsity camp in the States one summer, when Bernard recognized that he was free to make his own choices, and that his relationship with God was an independent one and not something imposed from outside.

Towards the end of David's time with IFES in Hong Kong, the two older boys were in the States completing their college education, Rosie

187

was a missionary with OMF in the Philippines, and Bernie was at school in Taiwan. Bernard recalls the importance of the weekly letters from his parents. When he made the decision while at university to marry a post-graduate student without consulting his parents, it is his father's letter—containing his consternation but also a loving concern—that Bernard particularly remembers. The understanding and care it contained moved him deeply and drew the two closer.

When David handed over his work to Chua Wee Hian in 1968, he was convinced that Wee Hian, with his gifts in leadership and teaching, was just the person for the job. It had always been his conviction that an Asian should take his place, and now the right successor was moving into place.

In the year he spent working and traveling with David in preparation for his new job, Wee Hian learned some lasting lessons from David's example. The first thing that impressed him was the way David always introduced him as his co-worker. It was in fact David's habit to consider all his colleagues as co-workers, taking his cue from Paul in his New Testament letters. But such an attitude surprised Wee Hian. Few people, especially in Asia, paid so little attention to their position in the hierarchy of society or workplace. David went even further by asking Chua Wee Hian to call him by his first name instead of Mr. Adeney. Again, David asked this of all his colleagues and again it went against Chinese culture which dictated respect for elders. Some could not bring themselves to call David by his Christian name and persisted with "Mr. Adeney."

Another unusual quality Wee Hian noted in his senior colleague was a willingness to confess failure. This too was very un-Asian. In Singapore the emphasis on success was particularly strong; Wee Hian had been used to the idea that if you did not succeed, there would be somebody after you who would. It was normally in everyone's interest to paper over the cracks of difficulty and to maintain at least an appearance of competence. Wee Hian saw David as "a breath of fresh air" in being willing to show weakness and admit mistakes. "He made an impression on people by being willing to confess. They warmed to him." People found it helpful that a mature Christian leader should admit he had weaknesses; it put their own into perspective. If they were inclined to think they were not good enough to serve God in any active capacity, David's example enabled them to see that everyone, Christian leader or not, had human weaknesses and was in need of God's grace. It was through God's grace alone that anything would be accomplished, and not through so-called human success. "David taught people how to cope with failure," says Chua Wee Hian.

A saying of David's that Wee Hian has always remembered is, "The greatest sin is not falling but the failure to get up again." David knew that all Christians "fall" or make mistakes and taught that as soon as failures or sins were confessed, they could be left behind and the Christian life continued. If failures were not confessed, he told the students, the Christian would stay defeated by them and cease to be useful in furthering God's kingdom on earth. Chua Wee Hian acknowledges that many Asians are indebted to David for his emphasis on confession: "David hates hypocrisy and champions honesty. I think some of that spirit has rubbed off on us."

In 1968, with the formal handover to Chua Wee Hian complete, David and Ruth left Hong Kong. But they did not leave Asia or the work among students.

17

DTC: A Terrific Gamble

For a few years prior to David's leaving Hong Kong, an idea had been simmering among the leadership of Overseas Missionary Fellowship, concerning theological education for graduates in Asia. Its main proponent was the man who had been in charge of all OMF's missionary work across Asia since the withdrawal from China—Arnold Lea.

Like many others intimately acquainted with Asia, including David, Arnold Lea fretted at the lack of theological education in this vast continent, and at the prevailing liberal emphasis in those colleges which did exist. The only interdenominational evangelical school which offered a theological education at graduate level in Asia was Union Bible Seminary in India. Not only was India a long way to go for Christian graduates living in East Asia, the alternative was worse: to travel to Europe or the States for theological training. Besides being beyond the means of many potential students, seminaries in the West taught theology in surroundings and in a manner unrelated to Asian culture. Not only so, those students who did travel to the West to study would often stay in the West, leaving the church in Asia no better off.

OMF had provided finance and personnel for a number of different Bible training projects since shifting its operations to Southeast Asia. But Arnold Lea's vision was new and creative, a step beyond. He envisaged a small training center, restricted to perhaps fifteen people, with students and staff living and working closely in community. Because its goal would be preparing students for effective Christian ministry, personal discipleship and practical work in churches would be given as much importance as academics.

191

Lea's colleagues took up the idea enthusiastically. By January 1967 they had secured an agreement with Singapore Bible College, an evangelical undergraduate college with whom OMF had close links, to accept the new training center as its graduate arm. If all went to plan, the Discipleship Training Center, known from then on as DTC, would open in the autumn of 1968.

The pressing need now was for someone suitably qualified to lead DTC. The first dean had to be someone who was in sympathy with the vision for the training center, and at the same time prepared to bring independent creativity and direction to its day-to-day running. The ideal, OMF agreed, would be for a missionary couple to take responsibility together.

The obvious people for DTC were David and Ruth Adeney. David had supported the idea of graduate-level training from the beginning. In fact, with David's regard for the Missionary Training Colony and Pastor Yang's Spiritual Work Team, it is hard to believe that David didn't plant some seed thoughts among OMF leadership during the years he was traveling around Asia. He doesn't remember. In any case, he couldn't have agreed more with the essentials of the proposed scheme, based as it was on the model of Christ's training of his disciples.

"I am most interested in the tentative draft of the discipleship training for graduates," he told Arnold Lea, writing his reply between visits to the Philippines and Korea in February 1967. "Ruth and I feel that we should accept your invitation to serve in this work."

As enthusiastic as he was about the intimate, small-group approach to theological training, David was less sure about the proposal that all DTC students take the London University Bachelor of Divinity degree over three years. Being locked into a degree course seemed restrictive, as he pointed out to Arnold Lea in his letter of acceptance. For one thing, it asked for a commitment of three years when some students might prefer to come for a shorter time. More important, it was a program of study that might not serve the best interests of Asian Christians because it was oriented to the West. David also worried about the balance in the allocation of time to specific subjects. Was biblical language study really necessary, for example, when some students would have a hard enough time as it was completing the course in English? Was it wise to pay a lot of attention to modern methods of biblical criticism when it was important to maintain a high view of Scripture as the inspired Word of God?

David was concerned that placing too high a priority on academics would threaten the real aim of the training center—preparing men and women for Christian service in the church in Asia. He was not against high academic standards, he assured Mr. Lea, but, he said, "We dare not sacrifice effective training for the sake of the prestige of a certain degree." He was even more emphatic in his next letter: "If this course is to be just another seminary, then I feel very doubtful whether I should accept responsibilities in it."

To appease David, at least for the time being, the decision-makers made provision for graduates to come for a shorter course if they preferred, and for students to take the degree in parts if necessary to ease the pressure.

David felt strongly that it was vital to have Asians on the staff. He also suggested that visiting lecturers should be invited from various Asian countries as well as from the West, so that the students would not only benefit from the rich variety of teachers but could learn about needs worldwide, especially in Asia. Arnold Lea wholeheartedly concurred with both these ideas. As the two men developed the vision for DTC, they were "sparking each other off," to put it in Arnold Lea's words.

David had one more request: Could he be free to continue his international student work? "The Lord has given such wonderful opportunities in student meetings," he explained to Arnold, "and I feel that it will be important for me to keep in touch with the student work in each country." Yes, it was agreed, vacations would provide time for this.

As excited as David was about the prospect of DTC, he was also anxious. It was characteristic of him, after he had taken something on, to wonder whether he was really qualified to do it. "I think I am the kind of person who feels that if the Lord opens a door, you should go in through that door," he said later. "I felt DTC was the door God had opened . . . although I felt very unfit for it and very nervous about how it would all work out. Perhaps one of my failings is that I find it much easier to say yes to an invitation than to face up to how to fulfill the obligations that come with acceptance."

Because David is not a person to minimize demands or to lower the standards of his own ideals, there are no easy ways forward for him. DTC suddenly presented a daunting prospect. How would he react to staying for so long in one place? Could he manage teaching students long-term, rather than just for a week or two at a conference? Would his relatively limited academic qualifications be up to the challenge of running a graduate-level theological college? His anxieties littered the pathway ahead with doubt—especially when Ruth's back began giving her trouble again.

The doubts became a full-blown crisis when, quite out of the blue, IVCF in America offered David another job. Would he take responsibility for the western states, counseling staff, speaking at conferences and ministering to Asian students in the area? Seemingly tailor-made for David's gifts and experience, the offer threw David. Should he be accepting this position instead of the one at DTC?

"I quite realize that this invitation may be a sidetrack," he told Arnold Lea. "I am afraid you may feel rather upset because of this apparent vacillation. I have sought to examine my motives very carefully in this whole matter, and I feel that the Lord must have some purpose in bringing this new call to us in order that we may be cast completely upon him and come to a clear conviction regarding the work that he has for us to do during these next years."

Arnold Lea mustered all his patience for his reply. He pointed out that David and Ruth's acceptance of the invitation to DTC had been the green light to go ahead and that it was already coming together with David's stamp on it. To go back now was difficult to envisage. Even the students were likely to come because of David's drawing power. As a final twist of the arm, Arnold reminded David that he would be training people who might be key leaders in Asia.

Eventually David and Ruth were fully convinced that it was right to go to DTC. "The Lord has given a sense of peace in turning down the IVCF invitation," David wrote to Mr. Lea in June, "and a real conviction that he wants us to have a part in raising up workers for the church in Asia."

With this assurance, staff and students could be recruited in earnest.

Arnold Lea had been right in thinking that David would attract students to DTC. In touch with a great many young people through his work with IFES, David could spread the word easily. He could also look out for individuals who might benefit from the training and encourage them to come. Some David approached were already considering further training; to be able to study with David was an added draw. For others the personal invitation was a vote of confidence that encouraged them to take up the challenge. In this way most of the fourteen applicants for the first year were hand-picked.

Arnold Lea's original idea had been for no further intake of students until the first group had graduated, but with applications still coming in as the start of term drew near, it looked as though this would have to be modified. David had never really been in favor of it anyway. "Personally I hope that the door will not be closed to the possibility of taking new people at the end of the first or second year," he had told Arnold in another of his lengthy letters. "Unless we are truly flexible and are willing to follow the leading of the Holy Spirit of God in setting up a course which will meet the needs of Asia today, I feel that we will not gain the confidence of Christian graduates."

Finding qualified teaching staff who would be willing to share fully in DTC's community life presented a challenge. People who were used to both privacy and privilege in a profession might balk at the thought of living under the same roof as their students. Nevertheless, two couples responded positively to David's invitation: Doug and Beryl Anderson, active in Presbyterian church work in New Zealand, and Fred and Jeannie Woodberry, former staffworkers in New York with the IVCF. Tan Che Bin, in the middle of a Ph.D. program but willing to give two years of his time to this new venture, completed the full-time staff.

What about premises? It was Ernest Poulson of the Singapore Bible College who found the two properties for rent in Kings Road, each containing two flats and conveniently situated next door to each other in the same compound. Perfect—except that the houses were in a flood-prone area of Singapore. Since everything else was in their favor, including low rent, the lease was signed.

As David thought about the goals he wanted to set for DTC, he referred back to the models of the Missionary Training Colony and David Yang's Spiritual Work Team again and again. Both emphasized spiritual development. This would also be the emphasis at DTC, maintained through the same disciplines of prayer, Bible study, caring for one another, and going out to preach and serve others in obedience to Christ's command. As for the teaching he hoped to offer, Asian studies would be high on the agenda along with Bible study, so that students could be equipped to serve the Asian church effectively. On the academic front, he was still convinced that too much store should not be set by paper qualifications, and managed to change slightly the planned course of study for the London B.D. Instead of working towards this over three years, the students would take a two-year course leading to the slightly less demanding Diploma of Theology, also offered by London University. Then if they wanted to pursue the B.D. after a further year's study, they could elect to do so.

Though the two- or three-year option was an acceptable compromise, won after considerable debate, the matter of the course of study DTC should offer remained a bone of contention among different interested parties for many years. Almost seven years later David wrote to the council members —using most of a two-sided, single-spaced letter on foolscap paper—to argue his concerns that the pursuit of degrees could undermine emphasis on spiritual qualifications for Christian service. Again he voiced his worry that a degree program would force the students into a stereotyped course of study unsuited to the needs of the Asian church. He wanted desperately to retain flexibility, to be free to be creative in planning DTC's curriculum, and unhindered in giving DTC diplomas to spiritually qualified students with different academic abilities.

"I would rather see us free to be led by the Spirit into new experiments and perhaps constant changes in our curriculum and methods than to have to conform to an accredited and fixed degree program. This involves striving for a complete freedom in our fellowship, realizing that we, staff and students, are learning from each other. Even though there may be dangers and sometimes failures in this type of training, we believe that God has called us to it and so pray that the value of DTC may be manifest, not by degrees and diplomas . . . but by the quality of students' lives and the service they render as they go forth into the ministry of the gospel."

As the pattern of the new Discipleship Training Center was taking shape, David was setting himself high ideals. Still nervous about carrying them out as 1967 came to a close, he was heartened by John 17. "I have been impressed by three phrases: 'the work you gave me to do' (verse 4); 'those whom you gave me out of the world' (verse 6); and 'the words you gave me' (verse 8)," he wrote in his end-of-the-year prayer letter. "Our calling, our fellow-workers and our message are all from God himself, and only through the help of the Holy Spirit can we possibly fulfill the task committed to us."

How did Ruth feel about yet another move when her health was none too good, and she and David were going into something so totally new? "It was an adventure. We weren't sure how it would turn out. I think David could be described as always someone with a vision. He had a vision for one thing; when that seemed to finish, there was always some new vision. That's rather contagious in a way. Visions are always contagious."

But would it work?

That was the one remaining question in September 1968, when DTC began. Some had their doubts. Alan Cole, a missionary who had experience both in teaching theology and in organizing training for Christian service on the mission field, was very skeptical about the possibility of achieving a high academic standard alongside a successful community life. "You're just not going to be able to combine the two," he told David. "You are trying to do the impossible." Jim Nyquist saw DTC as "an interesting blend of who David is," bringing together his commitment to the Chinese and to Asia, his concern for students, his loyal relationship with OMF, and his vision to raise up indigenous Christian leadership. But Jim too wondered what the outcome would be. No one really knew. It was an experiment after all. A lot was being asked of staff and students simply in living together, never mind everything else. What kind of situations would develop when people from so many different cultures came together under one roof?

It all remained to be seen. As Arnold Lea put it, DTC was "a terrific gamble."

A great encouragement from the start was the quality of commitment among the new DTC students. They all testified to how God had led them to apply, and for some this had entailed considerable self-sacrifice. "You start something new, and it is not only you who are taking risks," David said. "The students are also taking a risk, coming into something that is quite unknown. They themselves have to have a pioneer spirit." Evidence of such a spirit among the students thrilled both him and Ruth, and quickly drew everyone together in a common bond.

Ogawa-san from Japan had been studying in Tokyo for a Ph.D. in physics under a professor who was a Nobel Prize winner. He was introduced to David because he was thinking of continuing his studies in the States and wondered if David could put him in touch with any Christian student groups. Instead, David planted the thought of his coming to DTC. "I can't invite you," David told him, "but if you are confident that your coming is from the Lord, and you have faced up to what the opposition might be, then we would be happy for you to come." His uncompromising stand on knowing God's call might have lost DTC a very promising student; but if that had been the case, David would have been satisfied that God had not meant Ogawa-san to come. As it happened, counting the cost did not put Ogawa-san off. Quite the reverse. He gave up his studies, a prospective marriage, and the support of his family to come to DTC, so convinced was he that God meant him to be there.

Another student, Lim Fong Jwong from Malaysia, came up against opposition from his mother; she was so horrified at the prospect of his studying at DTC that she threatened to commit suicide if he went. Lim Fong Jwong and the Adeneys committed the whole situation to God in prayer and waited for him to open the way if this was his will. Eventually the mother was asking when Fong Jwong would be off to Singapore.

Eight different countries were represented by what affectionately came to be known as DTC's "first batch." Two women came from Hong Kong: Spring Ho, a secondary school teacher, and Frances Fung, who had been David's secretary and was to continue giving him secretarial help. As Spring Ho had lived most of her life within a square mile of Hong Kong, coming to Singapore was a courageous step. It was also the beginning of a realization that God was calling her to overseas missionary work.

Two families came from Taiwan: David Chen Liu, a China Evangelical Fellowship staffworker for five years, with his wife Dorothy and young son; and Morley and Sophie Lee, also actively involved in CEF, with their two young children. Robert Hu Yueh-Ming, who already had two degrees, completed the contingent from Taiwan.

Lim Fong Jwong was one of four students from Malaysia. Jeanette Hui recalls how three different people put the leaflet about DTC into her pigeon hole at the University of Malaysia, too much of a coincidence to be ignored. When she learned from David that graduates from the university were willing to support her financially, she felt sure God was leading her to DTC. It seemed that these Malaysian graduates had been praying that someone would go, and Jeanette's name had kept coming to them. Another student, Lucy Tan, had planned to train for Christian ministry but had been waiting to finish financing the education of her younger sisters.

198

Now the time was right, and she willingly paid the necessary fee to the Malaysian government to release her from her teaching contract in order to come to DTC. Another teacher, Loh Soon Choy, was the fourth Malaysian student.

Jonathan Parreno from the Philippines, a staffworker with the IVCF, and John Ting, an Australian-born Chinese and schoolteacher in Australia, completed the first intake. Within a few months a girl from Indonesia, Lydia Giok Lan, and a scholar from Korea, Seyoon Kim, had also joined the DTC family.

The early days were heady with excitement and activity as the students got to know one another and embarked on their studies. The proximity of the two houses, one allocated to the women with David and Ruth, and the other to married couples and single men, enabled a close sense of community which was fostered by shared meals, joint lectures, and everyone giving a hand with the household chores. Monday evenings were reserved for a special time of fellowship, when everyone came together to talk, pray, and generally enjoy getting to know one another better.

Alongside the teaching given by the full-time staff, lectures were given by people from OMF such as Denis Lane, who had succeeded Arnold Lea, and by others from all over the world. David had planned this carefully. He made the most of his many international contacts to bring a breadth of expertise and experience to the students. "One of the greatest strengths of DTC was education in international cultures," remembers Seyoon Kim, the student with a keen intellect from Korea. The special lectures were only a part of this, albeit an important part, since students and staff learned a great deal just from living in an international community and having to relate to people from different cultures. Exposure to Christian ministry around the world also challenged the students about where they might go on to serve God, again a crucial element in preparing them for Christian service.

At the weekends, students tackled their practical assignments. A great deal of time and prayer went into choosing these assignments. Most of the ministries in which the students participated were pioneering ones. Ogawa-san decided to work as God led him among a community of Japanese he discovered on the large new industrial estate of Jurong across the causeway in Malaysia. First he found some Christians, who welcomed him with open arms. Then he began visiting other families just to make their acquaintance. Before his first year was out, he had begun a Sunday school class and was reading the Bible with several people who were interested in Christianity for the first time.

Spring Ho from Hong Kong, working with Robert Hu, had to overcome shyness and skepticism when she visited people who lived in the area of her church. "My heart thumped with apprehension and uncertainty as Robert and I set out on our first house-to-house visitation," she wrote in the DTC magazine, *Asian Challenge*. "We met two boys on the staircase. Before we left them, the Roman Catholic boy agreed to have Bible study with us the following Sunday. The other one would not commit himself to anything. We knocked at those doors again. Disappointment! Even the Roman Catholic boy did not keep his word. Why, Lord?

"Robert suggested that we should visit the 'non-interested' boy. 'What's the use?' I argued, 'he isn't interested.' I dragged my feet up those steps. To my surprise, the boy invited us into his house. Robert suggested Bible study to him. I heard my own disapproval within: how can you force this on him? Yet he agreed. An unexpected three-quarters of an hour of studying God's Word followed. We had Bible study with him for five consecutive Sundays. Then he departed for Australia. God has his own timing for everything. The seed is sown."

Monday was always a day of rest after the busy weekends, a time for personal prayer and study. David himself often went early in the morning to the nearby Macritchie Reservoir, a beautiful stretch of water set in a park. There he enjoyed his favorite form of exercise, walking, while also pouring his heart out to God. One of his colleagues has a vivid memory of David walking round the reservoir with his arms raised in worship. David often encouraged others to come with him to the reservoir, especially if discussion was needed about something. He found the open air more conducive to serious talking than the confines of a room, though he was assiduous in arranging private hour-long meetings every week in his small office with each student to keep closely in touch.

Volleyball was the most popular form of recreation at DTC. Every day the Kings Road neighborhood echoed with the splat and thump of the ball and the shouts of students and staff on their makeshift court. David joined in with a readiness that impressed the students—in Asian cultures, the head of a training college would rarely be seen cavorting around with his students. "Physically, he wasn't quite up to it," recalls staff member Doug

Anderson, knowing that David had barely recovered from his collapsed lung, "but this he would good-humoredly deny."

It was not long before the inevitable consequences of living in an area subject to flooding disrupted life at DTC. The very first December, heavy rains coincided with a high tide and brought rising water. In the middle of the night the barks of the little dog, Brownie, a stray that had been adopted by the students, woke everyone up to discover the water already swirling into the lower rooms. Several students, still bleary-eyed, tried to hoist the piano out of danger but lost their grip at the last moment and watched in horror as the instrument sank into the murky water. Needless to say, the piano was never quite the same again. In the kitchen the students could not work fast enough to save all the food and electrical appliances, a loss which was keenly felt as the morning dawned and everyone realized they were very hungry. It took an enterprising individual to find a source of electricity and prepare breakfast with what had been salvaged. Eggs and rice had never tasted so good.

The real work began when the water drained away. Everything was coated with a thick, sticky layer of mud, the walls and furniture had to be washed down, the rooms swept out. David donned shorts to wade into the filth with the rest of them, cheerfully noting that, in spite of all the inconvenience, the flood brought everyone closer and got them working well together. As Ruth remarked, "We sort of called it discipleship training and tried to make the best of it."

After the early weeks of excitement and settling into a new routine, some of the tougher realities of living in community began to emerge. Instead of finding it easy to get along with their fellows at DTC, both staff and students discovered how difficult close relationships could be. Personality differences surfaced and resulted in painful clashes. Cultural differences lost their fascination and became barriers instead. For some, language difficulties added to the frustration. Misunderstandings arose, people were hurt, and suddenly the idea of living together did not seem so appealing.

The Monday evening meetings always reflected the mood of the community because there everyone was encouraged to speak his mind. "If anything goes wrong in our fellowship, we must bring it out into the open," David told staff and students from the beginning. Asians in particular were not used to baring their souls in this way and found it difficult. The idea itself was a source of tension. At first the meetings were lively affairs, enjoyed by all. When tensions mounted, the meetings became slow, dulled by awkward silences as few were willing to say very much. On other occasions, David's encouragement that all be honest about their concerns or difficulties resulted in painful confrontation. Though everyone learned lessons about confession and forgiveness, the process was hard.

David bore a great deal of the burden. He was the one to whom everyone brought individual troubles because he invited them to do so. His weekly sessions with the students laid bare some of their deepest struggles. Sometimes, particularly in later years, the complaints voiced were against David himself for the way DTC was run. "We turned his hair white," some of the students agree contritely.

"We deliberately placed ourselves in a very vulnerable situation by saying we were going to live together as a family," David commented when he looked back on his time at DTC. "It was a costly thing to enter into this kind of fellowship." Just because it was costly did not mean it was misconceived, however. David remained convinced of the value of living together as a community even during the most painful times of conflict. "Confrontation could be the means by which the Holy Spirit molded us for future ministry," he said.

One incident reveals how easily difficulties arose because of differences in culture and religious sensitivity. One of the students who came to DTC in its second year had to go home to Japan within a few months because his mother was seriously ill with cancer. While he was away, his friends at DTC prayed for him and his mother. Slowly her health improved, and when the student came back, he brought gifts of delicate, handmade paper dolls from his Buddhist family, sent in appreciation for the prayers that had been said. The dolls were unquestioningly accepted by everyone except one of the girls, who worried that they were linked with Buddhism and the spirit world in a way that was potentially harmful. At the next Monday evening fellowship meeting, she voiced her concern. The others were astonished. How could she see anything wrong in paper dolls? Besides, as the dolls were a gift, it would be ungracious to reject them. She stood her ground, insisting that Christianity and Buddhism did not and should not mix. The argument became heated, and finally it was agreed that the dolls should be burned. Some of the students had come round to the girl's way of thinking, while others were happy to acquiesce to her wishes since she felt so strongly about the matter. The student at the heart of it all sensibly did not take the rejection of his gifts as an affront.

David, sensitive to every ripple on DTC waters, found the incident very painful. He was upset by the heated confrontation between the students, partly because there seemed little he could do to prevent it. He felt his responsibilities so keenly that it was easy for him to feel he was failing when things did not go smoothly. He also identified closely with each student in his or her growing pains, so he struggled whenever one of his students did. The suffering he took upon himself in this way cost him dearly every day. For this reason as much as anything else, the DTC years were among the hardest of David's ministry.

All who know David well acknowledge that he is a lover of peace. He goes to great lengths to avoid conflict, believing that little can be achieved by it. "I find it more effective to pray for people than to confront them," he told one of the staff at DTC. Staff and students lamented at times that he was too soft on some of the more persistent trouble-makers. Tougher discipline might have done them good.

But it was a matter of opinion. David wanted to treat the students as adults, not to subject them to rules or dole out punishments when they had a bad day. Some of them, however, had a lot of growing up to do. They certainly did not always treat David with the respect he showed to them. Charles Christano, a student from Indonesia who joined DTC in its second year, once overheard a particularly vehement outburst against David and could not bear to see the older man taking it all so quietly.

"You shouldn't let them say these things to you," he told David afterwards, keenly aware of how hurt the DTC dean was.

David shook his head. "Charles, the Lord is honing parts of my life." It was a point David made time and again.

One of the greatest heartaches suffered by all at DTC in its early years concerned one of the lecturers. The theology of this man turned out to differ from evangelicalism in some fundamental ways, opening up the whole thorny issue of what was an acceptable viewpoint and what was not. The teacher was an able, popular communicator, much appreciated by both staff and students, but the conclusion of those responsible for DTC was that his teaching was not helpful to the students. Complaints were also coming from some of the churches where he had been speaking. David had the difficult task of asking him to leave. He wrote to the lecturer: "I want to tell you again how deeply grieved I am that this matter has arisen and how I long to find some way which will make it possible for you to remain with us.

"You know how much I have counted on your fellowship and help in the work. I felt the need of a man who would teach the students to love the Scriptures and through the ministry of the Word apply the message of the Lord that would speak to the spiritual needs of the students. I feel that you have been doing this. You have brought blessing to the lives of many of the students.

"The problem lies in the fact that we are also responsible to prepare the students to give a clear presentation of the gospel of our Lord Jesus. Now we find ourselves in disagreement on certain facts which affect the very basis of the gospel such as the atonement, the position of man since the fall, and the place of faith in the purpose of God. If we held only slightly variant views, these would not be such a problem, for we certainly do not expect everyone to have exactly the same theological views. It seems, however, that you feel very strongly that the majority of evangelicals are mistaken in the construction that they place on many of the passages of Scripture.

"I am sure you realize that when those who sponsor the DTC hold strongly to the generally accepted evangelical interpretation of the gospel . . . and you . . . are teaching something completely different, it creates a very confusing situation. It is for this reason that with great sadness of heart I have come to the conclusion that it would not be right to ask you to teach the New Testament Survey course next year."

As with everything at DTC, this issue was out in the open, and all participated in the process of thinking and praying about what should be done, and all felt the pain of a broken relationship. Inevitably, opinions differed as to the right course of action, and it was a long time before the matter was laid to rest.

Whether difficulties grew out of circumstances or the daily demands of living in community, the outcome was very significant. The conflicts were a form of training in themselves. As David Chen says, "The most important lesson we learned was, as a community of different brothers and sisters from different backgrounds, to practice genuine Christian love, patience, and forgiveness. Having to overcome cultural barriers and difficulties made a valuable contribution to our later ministry." Once the students had learned to get on with each other, the lessons were good for life. "By the time we finished," another graduate points out, "we had gained confidence that we could work with all kinds of people."

All the students testify to the benefits of what seemed hard at the time. "The challenges and tensions provided an excellent situation to make or break ordinary mortals whose ambitions were selfish or purely academic, and who were happy only with a highly structured program," Loh Soon Choy says bluntly. The "breaking" was part of the "making." As Ogawa put it, "All of us were under the training of the Lord."

Holidays could also bring testing. A Singaporean graduate of the Polytechnic came to DTC to fulfill a promise to God to seek Christian training after two years in a very good job with a high salary. All went well until the Chinese New Year's holiday, when all the students who lived nearby went home. His time at home was miserable. Family and friends criticized him for giving up a good job. His sister wouldn't speak to him. People asked him, "Where is the car you used to drive?" Even a member of his church said, "You used to be able to give far more to the church when you had a good salary."

After the holiday the young man, obviously depressed, went to David's office with the question, "Did I make the right decision in coming to DTC?"

"I can't answer that question," David told him kindly. "You must return to the word that God gave you when you came to DTC."

A few days later at the Monday-night fellowship meeting, the student told of the experience at home and of his talk with David. "Mr. Adeney did not say much to me," he testified. "He told me to go back to the message God had given me through his Word. I followed his advice, and the Lord has given me his peace." The young man finished his course at

DTC and later served on the staff of the Fellowship of Evangelical Students in Singapore, and eventually became one of the pastors in a large Chinese church in London, England.

Morley and Sophie Lee remember the two years at DTC as a highlight of their lives. Their background in Taiwan had given them a narrow outlook on life which DTC, and David in particular, did much to dispel. Morley had not been to the cinema for ten years, for example, such levity being frowned upon among the Christian community in Taiwan. It was only when David persuaded him to join in a DTC outing with the children to see *Snow White and the Seven Dwarfs* that he began to relax over such matters. "From that moment," he recalls, "I started to develop a Christian world view for myself."

The suggestion of an evening out at a film was typical of the way David and Ruth sought to surprise or entertain the students. They often treated them to a meal out or bought them little gifts. They rarely spent money on themselves but delighted to give it away to others. One of the teacher's wives recalls that a sum of money mysteriously appeared in their bank account just when they had to pay an unforeseen bill. She could not think of anyone but the Adeneys who knew the money was needed. "We were just sent a gift, so thought you might like to enjoy it with us," David might say by way of explanation when he took a student out to tea, or "I have just heard about a new restaurant and wondered whether you would like to come and try it with us." He loved to do new things himself and it was natural for him to invite others to share in the fun.

In fact, the capacity to keep up with a constantly changing world, open at all times to new things, is one of the qualities that has kept David young at heart and enabled him to go on identifying with young people. At DTC, while his age and head of white hair commanded respect according to Asian culture, the students did not find him distant. "We never felt he was old, never felt the gap," one of them said.

One of Sophie Lee's enduring memories of DTC is of Ruth. Sophie helped her with the domestic chores and saw what a heavy burden Ruth had to carry at times. On one occasion, after she and Ruth had disagreed over a small matter, Ruth came up to Sophie later and gave her a hug, saying quietly, "I'm sorry; I think I was wrong." Ruth's generosity and willingness to admit her fault touched Sophie deeply, all the more so because Ruth often appeared to be more tough than kind as she juggled several responsibilities and tried to look after both David and herself.

David always said that the value of any student work would be apparent only after ten years. Not before time had gone by would the lasting achievements be seen in lives dedicated to Christian service. It is a testimony to DTC, as well as to the quality of the students, that almost all have gone on to serve God in some Christian ministry. Many graduates, such as Morley and Sophie Lee, who returned to work with the Christian Evangelical Fellowship in Taiwan, went from DTC into student work, at least initially. Others went into the pastoral ministry or became missionaries. Some, such as Seyoon Kim from Korea, went on to further study and then to teach theology. Of these, several have come back to DTC either as full-time staff—John Ting and Jeanette Hui to name two—or as visiting lecturers. Frances Fung, in the time-honored matchmaking tradition, went from being David's secretary to being John Ting's wife, so also returned to DTC.

The ten-year test can be extended to twenty years in the case of the first DTC graduates. Ogawa-san went back to Japan to pastor a church there, and later joined OMF and spent eleven years serving God in Indonesia. Now he heads up the Evangelical Free Church in Japan. David and Dorothy Chen Liu went to work among Chinese communities in Europe before returning to Singapore as missionaries with OMF to work on Christian broadcasts for the Chinese Mainland. Fong Jwong returned to Malaysia as a pastor. Lucy Tan, devoting herself to the ministry of intercession, set up a prayer conference center in Malaysia. Spring Ho became an OMF missionary, but was tragically killed in an air crash early in her ministry in Indonesia. Another who died early, of cancer, was Dr. Nghakliana, who came to DTC older than most students, but whose gracious manner and deep love for the Lord Jesus endeared him to all. After graduation he became a member of the Bible and Medical Missionary Fellowship and was appointed traveling secretary for the Christian Medical Fellowship of India.

Seyoon Kim came to DTC from one of Korea's top universities, a young man with a strong personality and a temper to match. "Seyoon spoke terrible English, but was a great worker," smiles David fondly. "Though he couldn't take the London D.Th. exams at DTC during his first year, at the end of his second year he took both parts in one sitting." After gaining his B.D. at DTC, Seyoon studied for his Ph.D. under the celebrated evangelical scholar, Professor F. F. Bruce, in Manchester, England, then took further studies in Germany. Today respected as a teacher and writer, he is back in his native Korea lecturing at the Asian Center for Theological Studies in Seoul. He writes: "Although David did not have a great trust in theological scholarship, he, together with OMF General Director Michael Griffiths, encouraged me to pursue further studies in theology and made all the arrangements, including the financial support, for my studies in England.

"While I was studying in England and Germany," Seyoon Kim continues, "David persisted in acting like a spiritual father to me. He often wrote to me and undertook long trips to visit me, in Manchester or Cambridge. Through his letters and visits, he always encouraged me and reminded me of the need of practical ministry. He always emphasized the need to serve the church in Asia. I can hardly recount all the help I received from the Adeneys. In the preface to my first book, *The Origin of Paul's Gospel*, I expressed my gratitude to them for acting as my "spiritual parents." That best sums up my appreciation of our relationship. Their care for me was truly that of parents for their son. It was a privilege to have David as the preacher at my wedding. He has been a faithful mentor."

All who came through DTC during the years the Adeneys were there testify to similar support from David and Ruth. Seyoon Kim adds that David has many "sons" besides himself: "It tells a lot about his capacity to love that he has helped so many young Asians in so deep a way that they all regard him as their spiritual father."

The Adeneys initial commitment had been for three years, the time originally envisaged for disciplining a select group of students. But at the end of three years the "terrific gamble" was already showing its worth. Further students, it was decided, would be accepted on a yearly basis.

In 1971 DTC became independent of Singapore Bible College and moved to the old OMF language school in a quiet, flood-free residential area of Singapore. David and Ruth moved out of the community to a small flat nearby so Ruth could benefit from a little more privacy and quiet. Both continued to be closely involved with the student family, with David spending almost as much time on the premises as he did before, and Ruth maintaining among her other responsibilities the Bible study she had with the domestic staff. Both of them ate main meals in the community dining room.

Among the new students in 1971 were the Adeneys' son Bernie and his wife Fran, the first Western students at DTC, attracted by the emphasis on community at DTC and its unconventional approach to theology. "Like everyone," Bernie admits, "I came with very idealistic notions about community and wanted to leave in the first year, but in the end the experience was very positive."

Also in 1971 two new staff joined DTC, Howard and Roz Peskett; David had already identified Howard as his likely successor as dean of DTC.

Howard Peskett was a student at the Hebrew University in Israel when he first met David, having been Senior Hebrew Scholar at Cambridge University. David had sought him out especially to ask him to consider a teaching post at DTC, and after a period as a curate in England, Howard agreed to come to Singapore.

The new staff member and David were alike in the high standards they set for themselves. But they were very different as personalities. Howard, a very organized person, found David's notorious disorganization hard to live with. His exasperation was kindled at staff meetings when David never had an agenda and often left decisions open-ended. Another member of staff, Peter Yuen, had already tried to bring some order by taking minutes of the meetings, but it seemed these were of limited effect since David often forgot about them and went off on another tangent anyway. On one occasion the inefficiency of the meeting became too much for Howard; all his strong feelings came out in a burst of criticism against David in front of all the other staff.

In an Asian context, such direct confrontation was very shocking, and Howard regretted his temper almost at once. When he was called into David's office, he expected to be given a thorough and deserved dressing down. "Instead," recalls Howard, "David apologized profusely to me for making things so difficult. I just broke down. He could have heaped blame on to me, but instead he took it on himself. It was very Christ-like. That sort of thing inspires loyalty."

True to his intention, David took every opportunity to fulfill international engagements while at DTC. Even before his furlough with Ruth in 1972, he managed to get as far afield as India, Burma and Ceylon, Australia, England and Switzerland, and several countries in the nearer vicinity of Southeast Asia—mostly for student conferences. At DTC, the acronyms of "CIM" and "OMF" took on a new meaning when applied to David: CIM stood for "constantly in motion," and OMF for "only much faster" or "only more frequently."

The six-month furlough, during which Howard was acting dean at DTC, was a further opportunity to squeeze in as many different countries and activities as possible. In June, David was speaking at a series of meetings at the University of Malaysia. July saw him and Ruth in Manila for Rosie's wedding to fellow OMF missionary Ken Chandler, and also to catch up with their son Michael and his wife Miriam, who had been studying and working in Manila for the last three years. The next port of call was Taiwan for a student conference, then on to the States for two intensive months of meetings arranged by IVCF. "Almost every weekend I speak five or six times in addition to spending hours talking to students in groups or individually," David reported in a letter. A few days were also snatched with son John and his family, based in the States, but also traveling to and from Europe as John pursued his career. At the end of the six months, David and Ruth came back to Singapore via England to visit family and friends there.

David was in his element during such a time. He confessed that one of the greatest difficulties he had at DTC was being limited to ministry to one small group of people. "He was like a bird with his wings clipped," as one student put it. It was a physical release when he could get on a plane again.

Maintaining such a hectic lifestyle laid David open to some affectionate teasing at DTC. Howard Peskett did a skit at one of the Monday fellowship evening "fun nights" in which he acted out a scene of David receiving the mail, a moment in the day which was always a highlight for David. Looking as serious as David did when sorting through the letters, Howard made his way through an enormous pile from a dozen different countries, shaking his head at such a "small" delivery. He opened one letter from Hawaii, an invitation to speak at a conference. The next was from Alaska, announcing a meeting for the day after the Hawaii conference. "Hmm, perhaps I could just do it." Then came an invitation from Antarctica. "That would be interesting; I have never been to Antarctica. . . . " His audience was helpless with laughter, no one more than David himself.

As soon as Howard was comfortable about taking on the full responsibility of DTC, David prepared to move on. The issue of DTC's academic status was still being debated. The London Diploma had been dropped to make way for DTC's own diploma, purposely designed to be relevant to the Asian setting and to Asia's needs, and while students were usually quite happy with this during their time at DTC, afterwards some of them felt they were at a disadvantage without a recognized qualification. David understood their concern, but he could not change his heartfelt conviction that letters after a person's name were not what counted.

"In today's world, and in Asia in particular, where such a high respect is paid to paper qualifications, perhaps it was a hopeless ideal to expect young graduates to give two years of study and not receive any outward endorsement of what they had done," Denis Lane reflected when considering the whole academics debate. He was not regretting the route DTC had taken so much as acknowledging the difficulties that came with it. For his own part, along with Arnold Lea, he felt DTC had achieved exactly what they had hoped it would. It was offering an alternative theological education to equip people for effective Christian service. All the evidence pointed to this having worked. DTC graduates were occupying positions of Christian leadership all over the world.

Every student was special to David, but no one would forget Makino-san. This Japanese student arrived at DTC with very little knowledge of English, a mischievous sense of humor, and a conscientious determination to make the most of this opportunity to study. He was the one to tease Ruth and make her laugh when she was exasperated; to tick off his fellow-students when they wasted time complaining about the teaching at DTC instead of getting down to studying; to surprise everyone by passing his exams when they had observed him enjoying himself so much. One of the first Asians to join OMF, he worked in a church in Japan for a while and then among students in Thailand for eleven years. Today he is in charge of the orientation and training of new OMF missionaries in Singapore.

Tonglaw Wongkamchai, another DTC graduate, has given his life to the church in his native Thailand, first among students, becoming General Secretary of the Thai student movement, and then as a church pastor. He is widely respected in Thailand as a key Christian leader. "I want to give my attention to people above all," he says, acknowledging his debt to DTC for all he learned there.

Samuel Lee also went to Thailand to work among students, having been one of the more rebellious students at DTC. He remembers being encouraged by David's saying to him that sometimes God's work in a person's life is not evident at once.

Charles Tan Christano from Indonesia, considered a risky applicant by some of the DTC staff, became a pastor of one of the Muria (Mennonite) churches in Indonesia, and served a term as chairman of the World Mennonite Central Committee. Another DTC graduate to continue serving in Indonesia is Iman Santoso. After working with Perkantas (the IVCF-related organization in Indonesia) for a time, he gained a D.Min. degree at Fuller Theological Seminary in California, then went on to study Islamics before returning to Indonesia. Iman Santoso is known widely as a man of prayer.

Part of the success of DTC in preparing people for ministry came from David's capacity to see and bring out the best in even the most unlikely candidates. Ellie Lau is a case in point. "When Ellie first came to DTC, she was wearing a T-shirt that said, 'The devil made me do it!' " David recalls with mild chagrin. He had known Ellie as a little girl at Emmanuel Church in Hong Kong. By the time she came to check out DTC, her home was Canada, and she had been serving with the Peace Corps in Indonesia. Ellie came to DTC solely because David persuaded her that it would be good for her and she would be good for DTC. "He felt that about every student," says Ellie, "but it was very genuine. He allows people to feel their personal worth."

When Ellie first visited the Adeneys' home in Hong Kong, she burst out with characteristic directness, "As Christians we can evangelize Hong Kong now. We don't need you; you might as well go." What astonished her at the time was the way David took in what she said without arguing.

It had been the same with her father. Seeing his children becoming Christians one by one, he had blamed David volubly for four hours in the family home without apparently incurring any wrath on the part of his quiet listener. David's gentle serenity eventually won her father's lifelong friendship.

Ellie was no less outspoken on the subject of DTC. "It's pie in the sky to think you can get Christians together and loving each other," she told David when he invited her to come. As he still encouraged her to join the group of graduates at DTC, she did, warning him that she might not become a full-time Christian worker.

Once there, Ellie systematically broke all the rules. She used to hate going to see David when it was her turn to chat with him because she was always in some kind of trouble. "I would complain; he would listen and pray. He would understand." She thought he was far too busy to spend such time with the students, and it seemed ridiculous that he should go on doing it. "But he did, and it made you feel fantastically special."

At the end of her two years, Ellie resisted going into full-time Christian work to the last. "I prayed that I would not go into student work, but my prayers were not so strong as David's!" laughs the one-time rebel, now a full-time student worker. "It is because he tries his uttermost best," she says of David, "that he inspires others to be the best that they can be." And Ellie has given her best as assistant traveling secretary for IFES in Asia, teaching Bible study methods and talking up missions.

Ellie's "boss" is Otawa-san, IFES's Regional Director for East Asia. The eldest son in a prosperous Hokkaido family in Japan's far north, Otawa was expected to take over the family business. In spite of the opposition of his father and his devoutly Buddhist mother, he came to DTC and today represents many DTC graduates who serve Christ at great personal cost.

A few years after he left DTC, David was awarded an honorary doctorate from Wheaton Graduate School in recognition of all that had been achieved at DTC. Peter Yuen, former member of DTC's staff, had suggested he be given the honor. David, embarrassed to be singled out in such a way, was nonetheless pleased to be receiving his doctorate alongside Jeanette Hui, who was receiving her M.A. from Wheaton at the same time.

"I hope my friends will not use the title 'Dr.,'" he said in a letter sent out widely to his correspondents afterwards. "I have to accept it when used in public gatherings, but it certainly is not necessary among friends and fellow workers." He was anxious to take the spotlight off himself and shine it instead on the one who, as far as he was concerned, was responsible for everything that had been achieved at DTC, the God whom he served. "Anything that has been accomplished has been only by the grace of God. The trustees of Wheaton College knew very little about my weaknesses and failures. They said they wanted me to accept the degree in order to emphasize the fact that Wheaton still considers missionary service as very important, and wishes to demonstrate the value they attach not only to academic achievement but also to work done for the kingdom of God. I can only pray that people may glorify the life of Christ who dwells within a very weak human vessel. I must also bear witness to the fact that all that has been accomplished through DTC is due first to the work of the Holy Spirit in choosing and equipping those who have come to us, and second to the spiritual gifts and faithful service manifest in the lives of my fellow workers and those who continue in the work."

David's "sons and daughters" are contributing godly leadership to the church of Jesus Christ. DTC graduates are general secretaries or staffworkers in IFES-related movements in Thailand, Taiwan, Hong Kong, Japan, Korea, Indonesia, and beyond. Graduates pastor churches in Japan, Taiwan, Hong Kong, the Philippines, Thailand, Malaysia, Singapore, the United States, Canada, Australia, and Great Britain. Theologians among them are teaching in Korea, Malaysia, Singapore, and the United States. Jonathan Parreno, now a major in the U.S. Army, has served as chaplain for many years, including stints in Korea and Germany.

DTC has so far continued along the same lines on which it began. The vision behind it is still compelling. Its mix of community life, practical training and theological study is unique, found in no other academic institution in Asia. "God has used DTC and David Adeney as a protest reform movement within theological education," says Jeanette Hui, graduate of DTC and teacher of theology. Former student Lucy Phua summarizes both the difficulties and the rewards of living in community when she says: "Living at such close quarters opened my eyes to the frailty of the flesh and the reality of sin even in the best of Christians. But it also restored hope in the gospel when I saw broken relationships mended, sins forgiven, and situations worked out."

It was for this, a deep awareness of both human frailty and the grace of God, that David held on to his ideals. With such an awareness, Christians were equipped in the best way possible for service in God's kingdom.

18

All That Really Matters

Completing eight stretching years at the Discipleship Training Center, David and Ruth Adeney officially retired in 1976, forty-two years after the China Inland Mission accepted David in spite of the doctor's "poor-risk" evaluation.

Not that David entertained any thought of stopping. Even as he passed his eightieth birthday fifteen years later, he continued to fill up the corners of his days with matters of the kingdom of God. The fire still burned.

But in their retirement years the Adeneys were to face some of the deepest struggles and greatest delights of their lives.

Once David had handed over DTC's leadership to Howard and Roz Peskett, David and Ruth left Singapore, not for home, but for Hong Kong. David had agreed to teach for six months at the new China Graduate School of Theology started by Jonathan Chao. While Ruth at least was looking forward to settling in the States afterwards as planned, both she and David savored the chance to withdraw slowly from their work and their friends in Asia.

"I had known Jonathan Chao for quite a long time, and we had often discussed his vision for the school," David explains. "He was busy gathering together faculty members, and when CGST finally started, I had the privilege of speaking at the inaugural service. I was teaching the book of Acts, and really enjoyed that time with the students there. We were living in one of the new high-rise districts in a building of over twenty stories, and participated in a Bible study group started by a friend in a neighboring building."

David and Ruth finally made the break with Asia, at least in terms of living there, when they moved to Berkeley, California, in 1977. They chose Berkeley not only to be near Bernie and his family, who had also settled there, but because of the city's concentration of students and Chinese. The University of California, high in the hills of Berkeley above the beautiful San Francisco Bay, was one of the largest and most influential in the country. Chinese ranked high among the school's many Asian students. As many as a hundred Chinese churches dotted the Bay Area. David saw Berkeley as a strategic place to continue a ministry both to students and among the Chinese. And this is what mattered to David—to be in a place where he could go on being useful to God. The proximity of a couple of international airports didn't hurt either!

The first days in their new home left little doubt in the Adeneys' minds that they were in the middle of a mission field. "Coming to Berkeley was a kind of culture shock," remembers David. "Soon after we arrived I spoke at a meeting in the Logos Bookstore on the famous Telegraph Avenue, where a lot of student demonstrations took place. On the way to the bookshop, we passed a group of yellow-robed Hari Krishna monks beating their drums and chanting. Then, during the meeting, there was an uproar outside as a group of people who called themselves 'the New Paganism' danced round a golden calf!"

No wonder then, through Bernie, that David and Ruth became involved in the Berkeley Christian Coalition, part of the Christian World Liberation Front, which sought among other things to campaign against the mystical philosophies and cults which were ensnaring so many young people at the time. Bernie and Fran were among the leaders of the Coalition, particularly in the informal house-church set up to accommodate street people who felt uncomfortable in a traditional church. The Coalition also organized housing for the homeless, and at one point was running several homes and a ranch where the disadvantaged were helped to start a new life. Though a completely new ministry for David and Ruth, they gladly helped wherever they could in response to their son's invitation. David contributed mainly by preaching at the house church, counseling those who came to the church, and being available to the staff of the Coalition, who were glad to have an older, experienced advisor.

David could have become more involved, but his time was increasingly taken up with other considerations. "Actually I have three jobs," he informed his friends, "representative at large for the Overseas Missionary Fellowship, honorary staffworker for the IVCF, and part-time worker with the Berkeley Christian Coalition." His continuing connection with both IVCF and OMF meant frequent absences from Berkeley for conferences and meetings across the States and beyond. In addition to this, invitations were now coming for him to speak at Chinese churches.

Feeling more and more squeezed out, the staff of the Coalition at one point asked David to consider declining some of his other opportunities in favor of spending more time with them. Reluctantly David agreed, and he drafted a letter of refusal to the latest batch of invitations. When the staff met again, David confessed that he had not been able to send those refusals. "After a while," recalls one of the staff, "we realized that his heart really was with the Chinese and the Chinese church, and to hold him back was both futile and disobedient to the call that God had given him."

Having been instrumental in its founding, Bernie was also very much involved in another arm of the Coalition, a small study center in Berkeley called the Crucible. This center for training lay people in theology became New College Berkeley in 1977. The dean and founder, David Gill, invited David Adeney to serve as both part-time professor of missions and informal "chaplain" of the college. As recently as the winter of 1991–92 David was still teaching a course on the church in China.

"As chaplain, David was uncomfortable with official titles, because his busy itinerant speaking schedule kept him from being as available to students and faculty as he would like," explained David Gill in 1988. "However on an informal basis he has had a tremendous impact on our spiritual life. Throughout this past year, for example, he has been part of a small prayer and fellowship group of five local Christian men in leadership positions, including myself. We meet one morning per week, and David's influence has been very important."

After some temporary living arrangements, David and Ruth settled in a small bungalow on quiet, residential Grant Street. They were soon welcoming countless visitors for coffee, a meal, to stay the night, or indeed for however long was needed. They even adopted a Chinese "son" for a while, giving him a home and helping him with his education in the States. Their own grandchildren, of course, were regular visitors, particularly Bernie and Fran's three children, who lived a mile or two away. So it was rare that the house was quiet except when they were away.

"Hundreds and maybe thousands of people count David as a close friend," says one of those friends from Berkeley. "People from almost every continent seek him out when they come to the Bay Area. His and Ruth's hospitality is legendary. Whether their visitors are world-renowned scholars or Christian leaders, or unknown pastors and evangelists, David relates to them warmly, and they rightly feel that he is a personal friend."

Years of keeping close touch with so many people means that the Adeneys' mailing list is very long, the phone calls numerous, and the visitors a way of life. Daughter Rosie used to laugh at how, when she was staying with her parents, the phone always rang before breakfast, a popular time for international callers. "He is a faithful friend," says Jim Nyquist, echoing the words of many. "If I ever need to talk, I know I shall find a listening ear and understanding heart in David. We often pray together, even over the phone. He is a wise counselor."

Sometimes the actions of their host puzzled new Western friends. An American member of the house church once said to colleagues, "You know, there is something very strange about David Adeney. Every time I leave his house, I say good-bye to him, and he follows me out. I think he has something he wants to talk to me about; so I stop and look at him, waiting for him to say something. But he doesn't have anything to say. So I start walking again. But he keeps following me. So I stop again. Still he doesn't say anything. This happens at least three or four times until I get into the car and drive away. He follows me all the way to the car!" His friends laughed and explained that this was a Chinese custom. The guest was supposed to insist that the host come no further, but the formality would be enacted until the guest left. This was only one of many Chinese habits David had imbibed over the years. Such was his identification with the Chinese that they sometimes liken him to an egg, white on the outside but yellow on the inside. Several describe him affectionately as more Chinese than the Chinese.

The house on Grant Street is simply furnished, with a dining room table large enough to seat a dozen or more, and a spare bedroom which is a sitting room by day. There is a cozy, cluttered feel about the comfortable living room, where shelves and walls are full of mementos of friendship. Simple gifts, lovingly given from friends, are David and Ruth's prize possessions. In David's study, which overlooks the patch of garden where Ruth tends asparagus plants and where David grows the roses he loves, the piles of paper and haphazard shelves of books betray David's inefficient filing system. Above his desk, by contrast, is a carefully arranged panel of photos depicting some of the many friends for whom David faithfully prays.

The study is where David prepares the many messages he is still invited to give. Even those messages given many times are freshened with further Bible study and prayer, and always kept open to the Holy Spirit's leading. Once David had already sent in the script of his message for one of the plenary sessions for Urbana 1979, when he felt he should talk about China instead. The change threw the interpreters, left without matching scripts, but God used that message to aim quite a number of young people to go to China as teachers. The original message, "The Lifestyle of a Missionary," was printed in *His* magazine and later included in the handbook, *Perspectives on the World Christian Mission,* used all over the world and even being translated into Tagalog in the Philippines.

Another time, the Holy Spirit led David to stay with a message he wasn't sure of. In the late 1970s, the Adeneys were at Gordon Conwell College in Boston for an IVCF conference, during which David was giving a series of messages in the evening meetings on "Men of Faith" from the Old Testament. Not quite sure about his message on Enoch, he talked with some of the staff about the possibility of changing the message that evening. Eventually, however, he decided he should go ahead and speak on "Enoch, the Man Who Walked with God" as planned. He was in his room making last-minute preparations when a staffworker and a policeman came in. The serious look on their faces told him immediately that something was wrong. Tom Hoppler, they told him, one of the most loved of the staffworkers, had gone out jogging that afternoon, and someone had just found his body at the roadside. Apparently he had died of a heart attack. David gave his message on Enoch that night—the man "who walked with God, and he was not, for God took him." Long afterwards at Tenth Presbyterian Church in Philadelphia, Tom's widow Marcia came up to David, thanking him for his letter after her husband's death, but especially for his sensitivity to the Spirit in staying with the message on Enoch. That, she said, had meant so very much to her.

In 1983 David found himself struggling with depression. "I sometimes wonder if there is something about the atmosphere of Berkeley," he confided in a letter to Howard Peskett at DTC. "Perhaps it is that I am entering into a new kind of spiritual conflict which comes with old age."

The trigger for this difficult time was David's appointment in 1979 as president of IFES. The honor placed what seemed a heavy burden on his shoulders. In such a position of public office, David was very conscious of the need to live an exemplary Christian life so that the young people who would inevitably look to him as a model would have no reason to doubt the grace and goodness of God.

Having always desired to reflect the glory of God in his life, David realized more than ever how vulnerable he was to temptation and sin. In a letter to a close friend he confided: "When I was told after the appointment had been made that I was elected president of the IFES, I realized that it was a great temptation to pride, to which I have often succumbed. I wish that my motives were entirely for the glory of God. I know that I constantly need cleansing in this matter." The appointment was even more upsetting to David because he had not heard about it before the announcement. The communication had never reached him. He had to deal with it as a *fait accompli,* instead of having the chance to pray and prepare himself.

When he was elected to a further four-year term of office, he did not find things any easier. In another personal letter he wrote, "I sometimes fear that through lack of faith I might dishonor the Lord. It is a responsibility to hold this position, and I long that my life might be a testimony to the grace of God till the end." These words indicate the real source of

David's depression: his longing to serve God faithfully until the end of his life, a longing so fervent that he feared he would not manage it.

David's friends tried to reassure him. None could see how a person who had so far led a life of such notable discipline and faithfulness had any reason to fear dishonoring the Lord.

Yet David could not shake off his awareness that none were exempt from the possibility of falling. "Many people have good beginnings; few have good endings," the Chinese pastor Wang Ming Dao had said, words David had never forgotten. Now they haunted him. He had seen fellow Christians reach the end of their lives despairing, some of whom he had admired greatly. Surely the same thing could happen to him. He had known people, some very close to him, who had stopped giving their best for the Lord in their later years. That was the last thing he wanted to do. But suppose his energy gave up, or the invitations stopped coming?

David knew it was his own weakness that let such thoughts overwhelm him. Faith told him he would be "kept to the end." But having been so used to achieving goals for God, the possibility that there might be little left for him to do filled him with a kind of dread. One reaction was to book up his time even more than ever.

David knows his own temperament. "In current terminology, I would be described as someone who has been driven, with a constant vision of a work to do which I must accomplish." His daughter Rosie summed him up like this: "He has a great love for people and a great love for the Lord. I think the combination of the two is what has really driven him. He wants to really accomplish something. He seems to need and want to feel that he has made a significant impact for the Lord." But had he accomplished things for the kingdom? This was the question which filled him with uncertainty and made the doubts gnaw at his faith.

When the darkest period of depression was past, David detailed some of his reflections during this time in a letter to a few close friends. "I am doing this because I feel I need your fellowship," he said at the beginning. He had always valued close contact with his friends, not just for their sake but for his own. He had an inbuilt desire to communicate. No decision had ever been taken without consulting a number of people, no difficulty endured without the burden being shared with another. It is, he felt, what the family of God is all about, sharing one another's burdens, rejoicing with those who rejoice, and crying with those who cry. It was far too easy, he told his friends, to enjoy friendship and fail to share in the deeper things of the Spirit. He hoped that those who received his letter, many of whom were also "in the latter half of life," would respond by telling him something of their experience of God's presence.

"I know there is a great danger in being introspective," David wrote. "Over a year ago, I went through a time of depression. I thank God that he has brought me out of that period of darkness, and I enjoy much more confidence in the Lord. I think I am learning a little more of what it means to rest in his grace. At the same time, there is much dissatisfaction with myself. I know the difference between reputation and character. I am humbled when I meet people who regard me as an example of faithfulness to the Lord. If people have been helped through messages I have given, it is only by the grace of God, for they do not know the weaknesses and failures in my life. I have been far too busy, and have found it hard to relax and enjoy the good things that God has given. I love to get out into the country and greatly enjoy the beauties of God's creation, but I do it far too little. I know that the pressures of work in my life have not made it easy for Ruth and my fellow-workers.

"But why am I writing like this? Partly because I want to think through what there is of lasting value in life. It is not that I want to boast of anything that has been accomplished, but Ruth and I do need to be confident that we are fulfilling God's purpose for our lives. . . . I wish I could have spent more time in true worship and communion with Christ. My morning time of fellowship alone with God and family prayer, when Ruth and I intercede for our children, OMF, IFES, DTC and other friends, still has priority in our lives. I hope that this fellowship with the Lord may grow deeper as the days pass by. It is the assurance of his resurrection, his living presence, and the hope of seeing him that is the foundation of our lives.

"Then there is the question of the value of one's work. The Lord's call at the beginning of my life was to have a part in what God was doing in calling out a people for himself in China. I think the main motivation since the time when we went to China in 1934 has been to see the Lord Jesus glorified. I realize the constant insidious danger of seeking to glorify my own name. . . . I trust that it has helped to mobilize a prayer task force supporting the Chinese church. I know from my own experience how difficult it is to maintain a disciplined, continuing fervent intercessory prayer for the work of the kingdom of God overseas. But only the faith that this ministry of prayer is vitally important can really give value to the work which we have been doing. It is not a matter of other people appreciating the work. It is the need for the deep inner conviction that this is a work which is truly pleasing to God."

This was surely the hub of the matter. When a person has spent a lifetime in the service of his Lord, how shattering it can be to wonder if it has all been directed to the right end, whether it has really achieved all that could have been achieved. Even more so if one is conscious of others' sacrifices having been made alongside one's own, as David was of Ruth's and those of his fellow workers.

Years later David was still thinking in this vein. After enumerating his activities in a letter to Dr. Dan Bacon, OMF's National Director in the U.S., David concludes: "Actually, Dan, I feel rather badly listing all these things because the value of one's life and work does not consist in the number of public activities. I have not taken enough time for what Madeleine L'Engle calls just 'being,' and I know I have often been driven by the pressure of the work. I do pray that some of what has been done may be acceptable in the Lord's sight, for that is all that really matters."

Then, as a postscript to his letter to Dr. Bacon, David quotes a bit of poetry of unknown origin that Howard Peskett passed on to him:

> O Master Workman, if Thou choose
> The thing I make, the tool I use,
> If all be wrought to Thy design
> And Thou transmute the me and mine,
> The noise of plane and saw shall be
> Parts of the heavenly harmony,
> And all the din of working days
> Reach Thee as deep and peaceful praise.

In the midst of all his doubts and hesitations, David continued to do what he felt he must. For all his fears about giving up, he has never shown himself anything other than extraordinarily able to keep going, to "press on to take hold of that for which Christ Jesus took hold of me" (Philippians 3:12), in the words of the apostle Paul.

And where David was most active in these "retirement" years was actually in China. Things had come full circle since he first sailed for Shanghai in 1934, and once again he had access to the country which had claimed so much of his love and loyalty. The China trips were to supply some of the highs in these latter years.

19

China Opens

Early in the 1970s, information about what was happening among Christians in China began to trickle to the West. As news increased, Christians outside China began to take a fresh interest in what was going on. Caught up in the rising tide of prayerful awareness and challenged to think again about China's needs and how they might be met, David began to urge Chinese and other Christians to make China a focus for their concern.

At a discipleship conference he led for Chinese students in the States in 1975, David talked of China as much as he did about discipleship, insisting that since the country remained closed to Western missionaries, the Chinese carried the responsibility to take the gospel to those who had never heard it. One student present was astonished that someone should be calling so categorically for Christian workers to go to China when the country was closed to missionaries. But David was sure that God would open ways into China if there were Christians willing to use them. As this student put it, "The Holy Spirit used David Adeney to blow into life the embers of interest in China." Two years later she was working in China and has devoted her life to the country ever since.

News of China came through the gradually increasing numbers of individuals traveling in and out of China as the government slightly eased their restrictions on communication with the West. Nevertheless, it was difficult to form more than a shadowy picture of what had been going on. On the surface, Christianity seemed to have been dealt a fatal blow since the communist revolution.

By 1958, very few churches remained open in China: in Beijing, only four remained where previously sixty-four had flourished; in Shanghai only twenty-three were left out of two hundred. As Mao imposed increasingly radical measures to reinforce the revolution, the church came under greater attack. During the tragic years of the Cultural Revolution that began in 1966, authorities gave an army of young people, known as the Red Guards, a free hand to destroy everything that might impede the progress of the new regime. The church was a prime target. In an orgy of violence, the Red Guards ransacked church buildings throughout the country. Many of those buildings were confiscated and turned into factories, warehouses and offices, even schools. Bibles and other religious books were seized from believers' homes and burned. All religious activity was suspended. Christians were imprisoned, tortured, killed.

Tens of thousands of Chinese who were not Christians also suffered. No part of China's cultural heritage was spared in this relentless attack against the "four olds": old customs, old habits, old culture, and old thinking.

The first fresh news from China to reach David as the curtain lifted slightly was that Christians were continuing to meet in small groups where possible. Then he heard of individuals who had maintained their faith privately even though they were isolated from other believers. More encouraging still were indications that, far from being crushed by suffering, many Christians had emerged with an even stronger and more determined faith.

The six months he and Ruth spent in Hong Kong on their way to the States from DTC in 1976 was an opportunity to find out more. As Hong Kong was a center for "China-watchers," many of whom David knew personally, any new information about China reached him very quickly. Not only so, but he himself had many opportunities to talk with people going in and out of China.

The timing of their stay, in fact, was perfect, for 1976 turned out to be a momentous year in China. Mao died in September. David watched his funeral on television in Hong Kong wondering what the future held for China now. Then October saw the arrest of the notorious "Gang of Four," largely responsible for the excesses of the Cultural Revolution. The harsh policies carried out under Mao had seemingly created a powerful undercurrent of discontent even among China's leadership, and now a new, more moderate era was dawning in the country.

How should Western Christians respond? What new opportunities to spread the gospel might lie ahead in China? Suddenly these were questions that needed to be answered. The Evangelical Fellowship of Mission Associations, which brought together denominational missions, and the Interdenominational Foreign Mission Association, the equivalent group for interdenominational agencies such as OMF, joined forces to arrange two consultations on China. The aim was for mission board leaders to share information about the latest developments in China, and talk about strategies for responding to increasing communication between China and the West. Both consultations were to take place in the States, one on the east coast, the other on the west coast. Attendance was to be by personal invitation. David was asked not only to participate, but to help with selecting people who would benefit from such a gathering.

Helping to organize these two China consultations in 1978 kept David's finger on the pulse of change in China. He chaired both meetings, contributing what he knew as well as learning from others. So successful were these gatherings, that he and one or two others decided to continue to organize on the west coast smaller one-day China consultations, where people involved in ministry to China could meet and share information. Held annually until 1987, these events drew together people from such organizations as the Far Eastern Broadcasting Company, World Vision, the Chinese World Mission Center, and the Overseas Missionary Fellowship, providing a network of support among those working towards the common goal of assisting the Chinese church in its witness.

By the time the first consultation was underway, David was convinced that God was calling him to a new ministry: informing people about what God was doing through his church in China. Early in 1978, he wrote a short booklet called *The Church in China Today*, published by Christian Communications Ltd. in Hong Kong. In the booklet David gave as much information as he could gather about the church that had survived the communist repression, including the most exciting news yet to reach him about the resurgence of Christianity in China.

"For a couple of hours," he wrote, "I listened as a brother told me about his recent visit to his family. The story he told was one of great joy and triumphant faith. Last year in that area between four and five thousand were baptized. These baptisms took place mainly at night or in some remote place where they would be undisturbed. On one occasion a contingent of soldiers was sent to interrupt a baptismal service that was to be held up in the hills. But on the way the jeep in which the soldiers were traveling broke down, and by the time the vehicle was mended the baptismal service was over and the Christians had scattered to their work in the fields.

"Very occasionally quite large numbers in this area would meet together for a special meeting. On one occasion as many as a thousand had gathered in a very out-of-the-way place, where they felt they would not be interrupted. The meeting went on for several hours with teaching, singing, testimonies, and a great sense of the presence of God in their midst. At the end of the meeting five young men in the front got to their feet and said they had been sent to make arrests. They confessed that they had been so impressed by all that they had heard and seen that they too wanted to believe."

Meetings in such large numbers denoted a movement of the Spirit of God in China that amazed Christians outside the country. After all the church had been through, who could have predicted that such vibrant faith would be evident among so many? An indication of the suffering of Christians over the previous decade was given by the same man who told David about the huge meetings. Five Christians from his village had died during the Cultural Revolution. One of his sons was imprisoned for five years, then sent back for a further ten because of his continued Christian witness. Several members of his family were still in prison.

David by now was eager to return to China to see for himself what God was doing. For the first time since the revolution, tourists were being allowed into the country. Under the new leader, Deng Xiaoping, China was adopting a more open policy towards the West in a drive towards modernization. Foreign currency and foreign expertise were now welcome. On a visit to Hong Kong from Berkeley in 1978, David prayed that he would have an opportunity to join one of the newly organized official tours into China. His prayer was answered when he and two friends found places in a three-day tour to Canton; he was to be the first OMF missionary to return to China.

David crossed the border at the fishing village of Shenzen, walking with his luggage across the bridge which separated China from Hong Kong. Behind him were the Hong Kong and British soldiers; ahead, the green-uniformed People's Liberation Army, reminding David that China was still under communist rule no matter what changes were taking place.

Apprehension mingled with his excitement. Who could tell what might happen over the next three days?

From the moment he stepped into China he was aware that his movements were closely monitored. It was very difficult for him and his friends to get away on their own, let alone to have contact with Christians. "There was an increasing sense of tension as we knew we were being watched," he wrote afterwards, "but at the same time an amazing consciousness that God himself was leading."

The first opportunity to talk to the people milling around them came on a street corner when David managed to slip away from the tour. A crowd gathered quickly, curious to see and talk to a Westerner. Once they discovered he could speak Chinese, the people questioned him eagerly, giving him a natural opening to talk about Christianity. One young man told him that only old people in China believed in God now, although the young people were free to believe if they wanted to. Another youth was provoked by this comment to tell David privately afterwards that the last comment was not true; there was no freedom of belief in China. He spoke bitterly. He himself was not a Christian although his parents were; the family had been thrown out of their home during the Cultural Revolution. David and the young man met again later, at night so they would not be detected by the Chinese authorities, and David was introduced to the rest of his family. That night, the young man and one of his brothers became Christians.

David and his friends also managed to contact another Christian family whose address they had been given before leaving Hong Kong. Again, the visit had to be carried out with great care in case of repercussions from the communists. One of these Christians told David that the relaxation in government policy was only superficial, that in reality nothing had changed.

"I had heard of the suffering of Christians from others, but actually seeing the fear that exists made an indelible impression upon me," he reported afterwards. "There are a few country areas where restrictions seem less severe, and the communist soldiers themselves have been converted so that Christians are meeting in fairly large groups; but this is not typical of most of China. It is only too clear that in most of China Christian witness is only possible as individuals share their faith secretly with friends whom they can really trust or in small family groups."

231

The situation seemed precarious. Although Christians were gradually being released from prison and worship services were being resumed without opposition in some places, the government stopped short of official recognition of Christianity. Two churches had been reopened in Beijing for foreign visitors, but none as yet for the Chinese. In a museum in Canton, David saw evidence that Christianity was still associated with foreign imperialism; under a picture of a mission hospital, the Chinese caption stated: "Missionaries came not because they loved the people and wanted to heal the sick, but in order to manipulate the people and further their own political aims."

The tensions, the fears, the unpredictability of the future, all gave David a deep longing to muster prayer for China on a wide scale. When he came back to Berkeley, he sent his report of the trip to everyone he knew, cautioning his friends and colleagues to treat the information confidentially for the sake of the Chinese Christians; there could be trouble if it was known that they had associated with foreigners.

By early 1979 further changes gave reason to be encouraged. Several Protestant and Catholic churches had been opened under the direction of the government; Christians could meet openly together with less fear of reprisal; restrictions on correspondence with outsiders had been lifted. On a single day in February 1979, the Far Eastern Broadcasting Company in Hong Kong received 137 letters from China in response to their Christian programs. Since the communist revolution, because believers were afraid to write, they had heard almost nothing. David received his first letter from his old friend Sid Feng around the same time, after a twenty-two-year silence, and was overjoyed to discover that the scientist he had known as a student was well and could testify to God's protection through the terror of the Cultural Revolution.

As David prepared for his second trip into China in the summer of 1979, he looked forward to the possibility of meeting with old friends now that there was greater freedom for Chinese to associate with visiting Westerners. He was not disappointed. Professor Sid Feng and another old friend met him at the airport in Beijing. During the trip, which included visits to Shanghai and Canton as well as Beijing, David met half a dozen people he had known before the revolution, and talked with many other friends and contacts. A university graduate and former fellow-worker had just been released from prison after twenty years of confinement and hard labor. A former staffworker with the China IVF told how everyone associated with the Christian student movement before the revolution had been cruelly treated. David's joy at being reunited with his friends was almost turned sour by the horror of what they had suffered. He found himself asking whether he himself would have stood firm if faced with similar trials. Some had not survived the test and had given up their faith.

This second trip confirmed for David the reports he had heard about a flourishing underground church. He talked with visitors from an area where tens of thousands of Christians were meeting in what were known as "house churches"—home groups or larger gatherings that were not associated with the government churches. Among these believers were many young people. He also visited one or two of the newly opened official "Three-Self" churches, impressed by the numbers attending and the vitality of the worship.

David found a new hunger for spiritual things among the Mainland Chinese. When churches were opened or Christian preachers were released from prison, the people flocked to them. The excesses of the Cultural Revolution had left behind it a wake of disillusionment. Fox Butterfield, the first correspondent for the *New York Times* to work in Beijing since the revolution, tells in his book, *China: Alive in the Bitter Sea,* how he came across a Party member reading a Bible that had been given to her by a Christian who had spent ten years in prison for his faith. "You don't know it," she told Fox Butterfield, "but Christianity is spreading rapidly in China because people are so disillusioned with communism." The journalist could do little but treat her words with respect. "If she had been a political dissident, I would have been doubtful," he confessed. "But she was the neighborhood Party boss."

The Bible the woman had received was a Chinese-language one, printed in Hong Kong and brought into the Mainland. Apart from a few copies ingeniously preserved by determined believers, all Chinese Bibles had been destroyed during the Cultural Revolution, so there was a desperate shortage. David met three Christians at one of the newly opened churches who had traveled two days from another province to try to find a Bible. Many believers apparently had nothing but handwritten portions of Scripture, if they had any at all. Later someone showed David a complete mimeographed New Testament, one of many produced from hand-inscribed wax stencils. Some Bibles were eventually printed and distributed by the government in China, but nothing sufficient to meet the need. This was just one of the many problems David saw emerging in the growing Chinese church.

When he came back from this second trip, David wondered what more he could do besides sending out his report to praying friends. Whenever he spoke at InterVarsity conferences, or on behalf of OMF, people expressed interest in hearing more about China. Perhaps he should send them regular information so they could pray concertedly for China's needs.

David talked with colleagues of the Overseas Missionary Fellowship about what could be done and found them also wondering how to serve China effectively now that, at last, there was new opportunity to do so. The idea of a prayer fellowship emerged. And within a short time, David was producing and mailing out a monthly prayer letter from his home in Berkeley. The mailing list was built up from David's own and soon became so large that both administrative help and an office was needed. In the early days he had the help of Martha Chan, later to become director of the Education Resources and Referrals to China organization, and Jamie Taylor, now an OMF missionary in Taiwan. Within a few years, the Pray for China Fellowship grew beyond the States, and other people took responsibility for distributing the prayer letter in the different countries.

As the prayer fellowship developed, so did other areas of ministry to China in which OMF was involved—such as broadcasting, and the publishing and distribution of literature. It was emerging that Christian broadcasting had been one of the most effective means of witness in China after the revolution; many had been converted through this ministry. Now programs were badly needed to provide teaching for the fast-growing independent house churches that had so few trained leaders. Literature was also needed to replace all the material that was destroyed during the Cultural Revolution. OMF supported both the Far Eastern Broadcasting Company and Christian Communications Ltd., who were attempting to fill in the literature gaps now that there was greater freedom within China itself.

As China was welcoming tourists and also encouraging business from the outside world, new opportunities were opening for Christians to serve the people of China through visiting or working in the country. As always there was the need to muster manpower, support, and prayer for China in the West.

With all these new and growing avenues of ministry on behalf of China, the time had come for OMF to coordinate them into an organized program. David's had been one of several voices encouraging this move. In September 1979, OMF launched its China Program, with headquarters in Hong Kong and coordinators in several countries. David was appointed the coordinator in North America, with continuing responsibility for the prayer letter.

China was now indisputably back on OMF's agenda. It had taken some people in the Mission a while to concentrate again on China, involved as they were in the expanding work in other Asian countries, but now there was no question as to the importance of OMF's renewed involvement. The objective of the China Program echoed that of Hudson Taylor's: "to bring the gospel to the people of China and to stand with Christians in their witness."

As North American Coordinator, David had a finger in all the different ministries that came under the umbrella of the China Program. The prayer letter was the most time-consuming, and one of the most important. He spent a great deal of time and trouble over it, gathering information and then presenting it carefully. Because he knew the Chinese authorities were bound to see a copy, he had to present information in a balanced way and to disguise some stories without falsifying them. Always he urged prayer: "I wonder how many among the thousands of our readers are really taking time each day to join in the ministry of intercession. It is easy to regard this letter as an interesting source of news and yet fail to take the time and thought necessary to identify with believers in China, realizing that we have the privilege both of learning from them and of uniting with them in the spiritual warfare."

One of his objectives was to encourage group prayer meetings for China, working at least in part from the information in the prayer letters. He and Ruth had started a group in their own home; they met once a month.

Knowing that for many the ministry of intercession was something new, David carefully drew up guidelines as to how to go about it: "When we intercede, we first seek to be aware of God's presence so that we are conscious of his sovereign power and seek for his guidance in our prayers. Then we try to visualize the needs of those for whom we pray, asking that the love of God shed abroad in our hearts by the Holy Spirit may flow from us to them. As we think of them, we are humbled as we realize that we have never known the kind of testing through which our Chinese brothers and sisters have passed. Their situation is so different from ours; yet we belong to the same body of Christ. As we study the news from China and meditate on the needs of the church, we may find ourselves challenged regarding our own life-style and dedication to God."

Constantly David searched for ways to help China. His secretary in the China Program, Karen Lowes, remembers how he was always coming up with ideas for articles, meetings, videos, anything that would promote China's interests. Utterly caught up in the urgency of his ministry, he often made tough demands on others around him, not always realizing he was doing so.

Nonetheless David won the admiration and respect of everyone who worked with him. Dick Andrews, who eventually took over from David as the North American Coordinator of the China Program, cannot speak too highly of David's patience and devotion in training him for the job, the personal support David gave him, and the vision and self-sacrifice David had brought to the China Program. His example continues to be an inspiration to Dick.

One of the new ideas David introduced, with the help of two Chinese missionary groups, was the organization of seminars across the States about China. The emphasis in these China Awareness Seminars was again to provide information, so that Americans could appreciate how God was working in China and learn from the lessons taught to Chinese believers particularly through their suffering. The second aim was, as always, to stimulate prayer and action on behalf of China. Over a decade, David has had a part in the vast majority of the seventy or eighty seminars held so far. Says one of his colleagues: "He thrills and inspires, combining the facts of the situation with truths from Scripture, but not in a sensational way. He is absolutely honest. He challenges people from the heart. He comes across graciously, with power and yet with simplicity, with great clarity and conviction."

David returned to China seven more times, and each time met more old friends. In 1981 he and Ruth were coming out of a restaurant in Beijing, when David found himself being embraced by Chang Yu-Ming, who in July 1950 as a medical student had escorted David on a broken bicycle to Wang Ming-Dao at the student conference in Tienjin. From an exchange of letters, Dr. Chang knew David was in Beijing and had come looking for him, with orders from medical authorities to ask David to arrange a medical team to give lectures on cancer treatments in Henan province. Had he got off the bus a moment later he might have missed David and Ruth. Dr. Chang tells the amazing story in detail: After he failed to find the contact person—she was out of town on a tour—and being unsuccessful at linking up with David at the Summer Palace, Chang was standing at the bus stop wondering how he could squeeze his two hundred pounds onto the crowded bus, when the conductor said, "Why stand there? Come on! There's space for you!" "As long as I was on the bus, I prayed to the Lord, 'Where's my stop?'" Chang relates. "'Where can I see Mr. Adeney? There are twelve million people in Beijing. There are millions and millions of lanes, streets, avenues, and bus stops. There are thousands and thousands of hotels. Where is my stop to see your servant, David Adeney? For a human being like your humble servant to look for an individual of no location in the capital city of Mainland China is very much like trying to pick up a needle from the sea! But for you, nothing is impossible, heavenly Father.' At that moment the conductor shouted, 'Friendship Hotel!' Gently the Holy Spirit urged, 'Get off! This is your stop!'

"As soon as I stepped down from the crowded bus, just an arrow's throw away I saw a group of people walking out of the restaurant and making a sharp right turn along the east wall of Friendship Hotel. . . . Without thinking, I rushed up to a woman . . . and asked eagerly, 'Do you know Mr. Adeney?' Instantly her eyes were shining, and her face was full of smiles and sweetness as she rushed toward the person in front of her. Because my voice was loud enough to be heard by the front people, a white-haired man in the group turned back, stared at me, and said, 'I am he.'

"I clearly recognized him. He was really the person I was looking for—Mr. Adeney! Such a big hug we gave to each other! The sweetness of that holy hug is the fellowship of brotherhood in my Lord Jesus. It swept away all the shadows of my sufferings in the past thirty years. What a wonderful and beautiful reunion between two disciples of Jesus Christ!"

Another time, David was sitting on a plane next to a Chinese surgeon whose brother-in-law turned out to be a former fellow-worker. "It is hard to think of such meetings as just chance experiences," he wrote when recounting such incidents. "Does not God indeed answer the prayers of his servants when they seek for the direction of his Holy Spirit in all the contacts they make along the journey of life? Such experiences indeed strengthen my faith in the loving care and overruling providence of our heavenly Father."

On an April Sunday morning in 1986, David was sitting near the door in a church in southwest China. The two hundred people present looked sparse in the large building. Halfway to the front sat a group of Westerners. The pastor guessed them to be Christian missionaries from overseas; few other tourists would take time out of a crowded tour to visit his church. As always, since the church opened onto the street, there was a lot of movement towards the back of the church. In glancing toward the door, Pastor Li suddenly caught sight of David, his shock of white hair standing out in startling contrast to the surrounding dark heads. The pastor stared. The Westerner was smiling and nodding as if he understood the Mandarin being spoken.

As soon as the service was over and he had welcomed the group of missionaries—he had been right—Pastor Li moved quickly toward the white-haired Westerner now striding towards him, his tall frame adding to his distinctiveness. As the two drew close and clasped hands, the pastor found himself being greeted with a warmth and respect that surprised him. Although this was a foreigner, he did not seem like one. His Mandarin was indeed good, though spoken with an accent not learned in southwest China. As soon as it was polite, Pastor Li posed the question he had been longing to ask: "Do you happen to know an English missionary who used to work in China? He worked for a few years in the province of Henan among the villagers and then he taught students in the cities. This was before the communists took over, of course. We were both young then—" The memory seemed to distract him, and he paused for a second as if undecided about whether to go on. "I am eager for news of him," he finished simply.

David, listening with deference and attention, had a look on his face like that of a child who was being given the gift of his dreams. "I think you must be talking about me," he said, "David Adeney."

Through his friends and the many other Christians he met in China, David gained an authoritative insight into the church in China. He learned of the different attitudes among Christians to the Chinese authorities. Those who mistrusted the new open policy towards religion and felt they would be compromising their faith if they allied themselves to the official churches, worshipped in house churches or kept away from any fellowship in fear of reprisals. Others supported the open "Three-Self" churches, believing they could have an effective ministry there. The choices facing Chinese Christians were no less difficult than at the time of the communist takeover. "We cannot enter into the spiritual conflict in China today unless we can understand the agonizing decisions that Chinese Christians have to make", David observes. "We must show prayerful concern for those who believe that God has called them to work in the TSPM (official) churches, understanding their thankfulness that the government allows a measure of freedom and also their desire to have a public witness. But we must likewise appreciate the thinking of those who urge us to look beyond the great crowds in the TSPM churches and think of the dangers facing a church that conforms completely to government demands."

Despite his sympathy with some of those who defended the official church, David could not help but be cautious in his own assessment. In his speaking and writing, he presented candidly a situation that gave him no reason to have confidence in the religious policy of the Chinese government. He knew from past experience that there would always be conflict between communist philosophy and Christian truth. Marxist philosophy remained one that denounced religion as an "opiate," a by-product of capitalism and which kept people in subservience to it. Under communism, the theory was that religion would quickly become irrelevant, finally ceasing to exist, a theory which contributed to the willingness of the Chinese authorities after the death of Mao to adopt a more tolerant attitude towards Christianity.

Considered from this perspective, the so-called religious freedom in China seemed more pragmatic than genuine. Another factor that sounded a warning was the insistent governmental control of the church. The liaison body between the Party leaders and the local churches was the Religious Affairs Bureau, which in turn controlled the revived Three-Self Patriotic Movement, responsible for opening new churches and seeing that they conformed to government regulations. In October 1980, the China Christian Council was set up with responsibilities that were more pastoral, but there was no escaping the fact that it was still a government-directed body. At its head was the same man who was the leader of the TSPM, Bishop K. H. Ting.

It was of no small consequence to the Chinese government that the resurgence of Christianity gathered momentum instead of losing it, as might have been expected according to Marxist philosophy. The growth of the house churches was particularly worrying, not the least because they were not registered with the government and so could not easily be controlled. In "Document 19," produced by the government in 1982, in which the official policy towards religion is spelled out, the following statement is included about the house churches: "So far as (Protestant) Christians carrying out religious activities in house-meetings is concerned, in principle they should not be permitted, but they should not be rigidly prohibited. Through work undertaken by the patriotic religious personnel to persuade the religious masses, other suitable arrangements should be made."

That the government wanted to be in control of all religious activities in China was clear. Shortly after "Document 19" was issued, authorities ordered house churches to join with TSPM churches. Officials closed some house churches and arrested and imprisoned certain church leaders. Though the result in some areas was to drive further underground those Christians whose fears of the government were confirmed by such action, the house church movement continued to flourish.

Casual observers in the West, supportive of religious tolerance, saw every reason to be encouraged by what was happening to the church in China. The much-publicized exchanges of official church delegations suggested genuine religious freedom. In the light of this, David became a more outspoken defendant of the independent house churches. The TSPM, having won many friends in ecumenical circles in the West, was increasingly respected by Christian leaders outside China. At the same time few spokespeople balanced the picture with the testimony of Christians who refused to join the official churches. Having had the opportunity to meet and talk with independent Christians during his visits, David felt he had to put forward their point of view. His concern was twofold: to correct misconceptions about the church in China and to sound a warning about the future development of Christianity on the Mainland.

One misconception concerned the number of believers in China. Though it was difficult to ascertain this with accuracy, official reports tended not to take into account the independent house churches and so published figures that were ridiculously low. Conversely, some extreme claims cited vast numbers, all too easy for the skeptics to dismiss. David marshaled evidence to show that numbers were indeed significant, and especially in the house churches.

Another misconception concerned the relationship of the independent house churches to the government: "House church Christians and those who support them are often accused of being 'anti-China,'" David wrote. "This is not true. They are not opposed to the government. They obey government rules except when those rules come into conflict with the commands of God."

At the same time David did not minimize the very real problems in the house churches. They were not an organized entity, he admitted, and in some cases the lack of trained pastors and Bibles had allowed divisions and false teaching to creep in. Such difficulties did not mean the independent churches should be dismissed, David argued; instead, the response should be prayer for these believers and concern to provide help in the form of Christian literature and broadcasts.

As to the future of the Chinese church, the main reason for David's concern was the increasing control exerted by the TSPM. Rules limiting evangelism, governing the appointment of pastors, banning the receipt of foreign literature, preventing people listening to foreign radio broadcasts—all threatened to stifle Christian witness, the life-blood of the church. "What will be the long-term effect of the growing control of the church by the TSPM?" he asks in *China: the Church's Long March*. "Does it result in a dilution of its message and a shackling of those who are zealous to proclaim the gospel in unreached areas?" He was afraid that it might.

In an article for Fuller Theological Seminary in California, published in 1988, David summarizes his concern. "The TSPM seeks to gain support of evangelicals outside of China and justify the pressure they put on the house churches on the grounds that these churches represent only an extremist fringe of the Christian movement. While recognizing weakness and problems relating to some of the independent house churches, we must assure their leaders of the sympathy and support of evangelicals throughout the world. We need to protest the persecution of devoted servants of Christ whose only crime is that they will not accept the restrictions on the preaching of the gospel imposed by the Religious Affairs Bureau and the Three-Self Patriotic Movement. If the government religious authorities should succeed in their plan to suppress all Christian witness outside of the Three-Self Patriotic Movement and the China Christian Council, it would virtually eliminate a truly significant segment of the church in China today. Furthermore it would radically retard the training of spiritual leadership for the future. Christians in the West should not organize religious activities in China, but they should support in prayer both those who are witnessing within the China Christian Council and those who are in the independent house churches."

David's fifth journey into China in 1982 was arranged by Professor Chang, whom he had met so miraculously at the Friendship Hotel in Beijing the year before. Ruth was with him for this trip back to Henan. Invited by the Henan Medical Association, David was accompanying the team of American doctors who were to conduct a seminar on cancer treatment. As one of David's Chinese friends said, seeing David back in Henan, "It is a miracle that you are here speaking from a government platform in your old province, where you are known by the authorities as an imperialist missionary of the China Inland Mission."

Memories crowded back as David and Ruth went on a sightseeing tour to Kaifeng, one of the towns they had known well. "As we drove along the country roads of Henan with their crowds of donkeys, mule carts, bicycles, and country folk carrying heavy burdens, I was reminded of my long cycle rides during the years when Ruth and I worked in the towns and villages of Henan. Now as we watched the farmers on the threshing floors, we thought of the spiritual harvest also being reaped." It was rumored that there were hundreds of thousands of new Christians in Henan. A secret government document put the figure at one million while some Christians thought the number much higher. Other official sources admitted there were Christians in every village.

Christians had been gathering in house churches in Henan before the Cultural Revolution, a fact that had led to severe persecution during the years of repression. Now, thousands of people were being baptized across the province. David and Ruth heard that three hundred people were baptized in 1981 in Fangcheng, the town where they used to live, and over one hundred young people from another region in Henan had gone out to spread the gospel elsewhere. One village pastor, when questioned about the remarkable spiritual growth in his area, said simply that it was God who was working in China.

Henan is one of the provinces where the spread of Christianity has been the greatest. As in other provinces of China, numerical growth today can in many cases be related to the extent the area was evangelized before the revolution. Many Bible-based churches had been established in Henan before the revolution, and while David and Ruth knew this was not the only contributory factor to the tremendous growth of the church, they could rejoice nonetheless that their missionary labors had not been in vain.

In recent years, as China has encouraged more interchange with the West, Christians have had further scope to be witnesses. As David observed, "There are now hundreds of Christians from the West teaching English in scores of Chinese universities and colleges. They cannot take part in open evangelistic work, but they are able through the quality of their service and their friendship and understanding to be witnesses to the love of Christ. University officials have often stated that they would like to have Christians come as teachers because they do not introduce the unwanted elements of Western society, and also they do not complain or break their contracts. Thus there is a recognition that Christian teachers often contribute more to China than others. This gives the Christians a real opportunity to show through their lives the fact that Christianity has a real contribution to make to Chinese society."

David is always ready to respond to the latest developments in China with a comment, whether it be for praying friends, the Pray for China Fellowship, or for a wider audience through a magazine article or broadcast. Recently a television program featured his commentary on China. Several video tapes have been done with his help. He is still in close touch with the many organizations which minister in a variety of ways to the church in China, and his contribution continues to be greatly valued.

As he writes in one of his prayer letters: "Some of us received the call to China forty or fifty years ago, and our love for the Chinese church will remain until our work on earth is finished, and we join the great crowd of witnesses who will see the final triumph of our Lord in that great land." David will never cease to give himself to the Chinese church in whatever way is open to him. For him, involvement in this ministry is nothing less than a privilege, as he indicates in the same letter: "I have been realizing how wonderful it is to be allowed to see how God is working out his great purposes for China. God has indeed chosen 'the lowly things of this world and the despised things—and the things that are not—to nullify the things that are, so that no man may boast before him' (1 Corinthians 1:28)."

"As thy days, so shall thy strength be," was the promise from Deuteronomy that David took to himself before he first went to China. He is still blessed with both. Several people have described David as "truly a man of God," while another friend transposed the words and said he was "God's man," used by God because he dedicated his life to his service. David would doubtless be more comfortable with this second description, even though he would insist he could have done so much more. As far as he is concerned, there is still a long way to go. "I have often been humbled," he wrote recently in one of his many articles, "when just before going out to speak at a series of meetings, I have found myself failing in some simple test of faith which the Lord allowed to come my way. And then people come and remark: 'It is not just what you say but what you are,' and inwardly I cry out, 'Lord, make my walk to be more like my talk!'"

With the death of their daughter Rosie from cancer in 1989, leaving her husband Ken and their two children, Mark and Karen, the Adeneys have once again had to face personal loss and live with the shadow of pain. David's honesty and sensitivity have not allowed him to hide from the impact of such tragedy behind superficial Christian assurances: "There is so much 'Christian talk,'" he wrote to friends. "I sometimes wonder how much people really believe. In the face of death I feel that my faith is stripped down to the bare essentials. Death is an enemy that has been overcome, and we rejoice in the victory of our risen Lord, but I think that there is still the last battle of faith. We faced it with Rosie, and before long Ruth and I will face it ourselves." At Rosie's funeral, he expressed the hope that is no less strong in him for the questions he faces: "Rosemary's love to God, her love to Ken and the children, her love for Ruth and me, and her unflinching hope and trust in our risen Lord and Savior even now call us to remain faithful to God's purpose for our lives. Rosie has finished her race. . . . We must press forward without her until our time comes to join her in singing praise to the Lamb upon the throne."

And press forward the Adeneys have done—running straight for the goal. The thought of Rosemary's death is still painful. But love for God and love for people continue to fuel a ministry that does not stop, even when physical limitations would justify it. Just weeks after David turned eighty, for instance, he was at the December 1991 Canadian Chinese Christian Youth Winter Camp on the campus of Prairie Bible College in Three Hills, Alberta. He had given only the introduction to a five-part series of messages on the letters to the seven churches from Revelation 1–4, when he fell on the ice and fractured his pelvis. More than eight hundred campers and leaders hurt with him, but felt also their own loss.

"If you could carry me to the platform, I could finish the series," was David's first suggestion from his hospital bed.

No, the winter-camp organizers decided, that would be too painful.

"I could do a video," was David's next suggestion.

And so it was decided. David condensed the four remaining messages, and the Bible College video crew set up their equipment in the Three Hills Hospital room the next afternoon. Only one day after his fall, lying motionless and flat on his back to minimize the pain, David finished his series.

Back home, after a week in the Three Hills Hospital, and three weeks' treatment in a San Francisco hospital, David kept the letters flowing and the telephone lines humming. He wrote up details for this book (even in Calgary!). And when classtime came around for students of New College Berkeley, they came to him at home. Within weeks David was back in a local pulpit, managing with a four-pronged cane. By early spring he was carrying a full load of meetings and opportunities on the east coast.

Judged a "poor risk" as a candidate, a struggler as a language learner, a bumbler in the little things of life by colleagues, an imperialist by the communists, and imperfect by himself, David has allowed God to use him as a six-decade illustration of strength made perfect in weakness. In God's hands he has been for many people and situations the right man in the right place at the right time. And God has kept his promise to David to provide strength "as his days." Both David and Ruth Adeney can testify to the truth of these lines penned by their friend Bishop Frank Houghton:

> It is a secret joy to find
> The task assigned beyond our powers;
> For then, if aught
> Of good be wrought,
> Clearly the praise is His, not ours!

DAVID H. ADENEY was born in Bedford, England, and graduated from Cambridge University, where his interest in missions and student work developed. He served with the China Inland Mission for twelve years, joining the church planting efforts in Henan province for the first seven years. During World War II, he worked with InterVarsity Christian Fellowship in the U.S. for two years, and spent two years at the China Inland Mission headquarters in London. This was followed by five years more with the China Inter-Varsity student movement.

After a few more years on staff with IVCF in the States, he went to Hong Kong and served for twelve years as the Associate General Secretary for the Far East with the International Fellowship of Evangelical Students. He later moved to Singapore, at the invitation of Overseas Missionary Fellowship, and founded the Discipleship Training Center, working as dean and professor of Bible and church history for eight years. He then taught briefly at the China Graduate School of Theology in Hong Kong before returning to the United States.

Adeney and his wife, Ruth, now live in Berkeley, California, where up until 1992 he taught part-time at New College for Advanced Christian Studies. He continues as minister-at-large for OMF, speaking at InterVarsity conferences, China Awareness Seminars, and Chinese churches. His published works include *China: Christian Students Face the Revolution, Men of Vision, The Unchanging Commission, Christian Students in Communist Society,* and *China: The Church's Long March.*

CAROLYN ARMITAGE lives in London and is currently Editorial Director of Religious Books at Hodder & Stoughton Publishers. She has completed post-graduate studies in theology at Regent College, Vancouver, and has authored four books.